A Witch's
Book of Answers

A Witch's
Book of Answers

Eileen Holland & Cerelia

 WEISER BOOKS
Boston, MA/York Beach, ME

First published in 2003 by
Red Wheel/Weiser, LLC
York Beach, ME
With offices at:
368 Congress Street
Boston, MA 02210
www.redwheelweiser.com

Library of Congress Cataloging-in-Publication Data

Holland, Eileen.
    A witch's book of answers / Eileen Holland and Cerelia.
        p. cm.
    Includes bibliographical references and index.
    ISBN 1-57863-280-3 (pbk.)
    1. Witchcraft. I. Cerelia. II. Title.
BF1566.H647 2003
133.4'3—dc21   2003002125

Typeset in 12/15 Bembo
Printed in Canada
TCP

10 09 08 07 06 05 04 03
 8 7 6 5 4 3 2 1

With thanks to our dear friend Ryan (Ororo), Guardian of the Grove, without whom this book could never have been written.

With thanks to all of the members of the Open Sesame e-list who have made positive contributions to it over the years. This book could not have been written without them, either. Thank you for sharing your paths with us.

Blessed Be the Web, which brought us all together.

—Cerelia & Eileen

To Eileen Holland, who barely knew me and let me become such a big part of Open Sesame.

To my husband, who was always there with his love and support while I spent endless hours on the Internet with Open Sesame.

To my two sons, who always make me feel loved and very special. Their support of the book has been wonderful.

—Cerelia

With thanks to my son, for his patience with all the time I spend at the computer.

With thanks to Cerelia, for being such a pleasure to work with; and to all the Witches in my life, for friendship, laughter, and magic.

—Eileen

CONTENTS

Introduction ix

CHAPTER ONE: ABOUT WITCHES
In the Beginning 3
Types of Witches 15
Beliefs 28

CHAPTER TWO: BECOMING A WITCH
Am I a Witch? 53
Craft Names 64
New Witches 69
Young Witches 74
Learning 82
Practicing 88
Assuming the Title of Witch 91
A Year and a Day Program 94
Teachers 96
Initiation 97
The Broom Closet 103
Networking 109
Teaching 112

CHAPTER THREE: A WITCH'S LIFE
How Do Witches Live? 115
Adversity 118
Anger 125
Activism 128
Home Life 135
Life Stages 144

Human Relations 158
Life Is Magical 165

CHAPTER FOUR: A WITCH'S SKILLS
Meditation. 189
Visualization. 195
Invocation & Evocation. 199
Psychism 204
Divination 211
Healing 221
Working with the Moon 228
Other Skills 239

CHAPTER FIVE: WITCHCRAFT
The Basics 253
Magic 277
Elemental Magic. 299
Psi–Magic 320
Spellwork. 322
Ethics 332

Afterword 359
Notes 361
Selected Bibliography 363
Index 367

I no longer recall exactly when or where or how it happened, but Cerelia and I met in cyberspace. In the way of Witches, we quickly recognized each other as kindred spirits, and we became friends. Although we have never met in person, we hope our paths converge in the future. We also hope this book helps our readers with their Witchcraft and spiritual development.

A Witch's Book of Answers is an outgrowth of the Open Sesame e-list hosted by Cerelia and me, along with Ororo, since 1999. The book is based on actual questions asked on the list over the years—and our responses to them.

Cerelia and I don't have all the answers. We don't even know all the questions. No one does. Finding one's own answers to things, from the practical to the profound, is a part of each Witch's personal journey. *A Witch's Book of Answers* helps guide you toward *your* answers.

Bright Blessings,

Eileen Holland

M y zealousness to explain things, but also to protect those who ask questions, is always my first concern. As a Witch, I truly care about other Witches—especially new Witches—and what they are learning. Everyone may not always agree with my opinions, but I try to make sure that people don't just see one point of view.

There are many facts which are "real" to each individual. Each person experiences the same subject differently. I try to make sure that *consequences* (not necessarily "facts") are understood in magic. When you know what some consequences may be (whether they may happen to everyone or not), it makes for a much more intelligent Witch.

I know my attention always seems to center on the morals and spirituality of being Witch. I have heated discussions with those that do not see the importance of these things. Believe me when I say that if you want to remain on the path of light, you had better understand that the line between white and black Witchcraft is *very* thin. We are all capable of straying into the dark if we are not strong in our convictions and beliefs. Those that call being a Wiccan or White Witch a weakness or diluted Witchcraft have no idea where the real strength and power lie.

Blessings of Love and Laughter,

Cerelia

CHAPTER ONE

About Witches

What is a witch?

Witches are Pagans. We are people who recognize the inter-connection of everything in the Universe. We feel a strong connection with Nature, her cycles, and with all living things sharing this planet with us. We practice magic. We know that we are all children of the same Mother, so negative attitudes such as racism and homophobia have no place in Witchcraft.

The main thing to know about being a Witch is that this is our religion—and that it's all about the Goddess. When we speak of the Goddess with a capital "G" we mean the Great Goddess, who contains all the other gods and goddesses.

Being a Witch is a calling, an inner conviction. It is like knowing you must paint, or write, or become a missionary. Sometimes the Goddess actually calls us by name while we are asleep or coming out of sleep.

Witches know that what goes around, comes around. Many Witches recognize the Law of Three, the belief that whatever you put out will return to you tripled. We know that if you practice positive magic, you will receive blessings in return. Witches also know that those who practice negative magic ultimately destroy themselves.

—Eileen

Who were the first Witches?

Whether in Europe, Africa, Asia, the Americas, or Oceania, the first Witches were the shamans, medicine wo/men, and healers of their tribes.

—Eileen

What's the difference between a Witch and a wizard?

You may hear different answers to this question. A wizard was a term used for magicians or sorcerers throughout history. The name did at one time become synonymous with the word Witch, but it is seldom used now. A Witch can either be a man or a woman, but the word wizard is associated with males because a wizard was usually the town sorcerer, a man. Men usually held these positions back then, until the Church made it unlawful to practice divination, fortune telling, or other magical arts.

Wizards who were accused were prosecuted as Witches, although it is said that their clientele were good at protecting them.

—*Cerelia*

Do you have to be born to a family of Witches or initiated into the one true secret path or Coven to really be a Witch?

No, you do not have to be a "born" Witch. In fact, some of the most powerful Witches were *not* born as Witches. Just because someone is born into any kind of religion or belief system does not mean they fully understand or agree with their lineage or properly practice their faith. I believe that most people who find their way back to this path either were Witches in previous lives or are just finding their way here through their own spiritual journey. We are all on different levels of our spiritual journey. What you teach your children today becomes their heritage tomorrow.

—*Cerelia*

That Witchier-than-thou stuff just makes me roll my eyes. I couldn't care less about a Witch's "pedigree." Witches either feel like Witches to me, or they don't.

—Eileen

Does the Goddess make a Witch, or does another Witch do it?

The Goddess.

—Eileen

Witchcraft is a personal experience to me, a solitary journey into oneself. It can't be given away or bestowed upon anyone.

—Cerelia

Who can be a Witch?

Anyone who can find his or her way to the Goddess—and is willing to spend the necessary time reading, studying, learning, and practicing—can be a Witch. A Witch must have patience, imagination, compassion, focus, and willpower.

—Eileen

Where do Witches get their powers?

Witches credit the Goddess for our gifts.

—Eileen

What type of attitude should a Witch have?

To me, the most important thing that anyone can believe is, "I like myself." You must like yourself and respect yourself in order to like and respect others. You must be able to do this first, and then take responsibility for your actions.

—Cerelia

A big part of being a Witch is having respect for yourself. This includes never allowing anyone to mistreat you, physically or otherwise. No Witch should ever tolerate violence or abuse. Taking responsibility for yourself and accepting responsibility for your actions are keystones to being a Witch. Witches don't shirk their responsibilities. We're the ones who hang in there and somehow manage to do everything that needs to be done.

—Eileen

Do you have to practice magic in order to be a Witch?

Most Witches would answer, "yes." A person with the same beliefs as a Witch but who doesn't use magic is called a Pagan. Magic isn't everyone's cup of tea, and there is certainly nothing wrong with being a Pagan. We are each called to serve in different ways.

—Eileen

A Wiccan or Witch who does not believe in magic, to me, is a Pagan. If they do not believe in a god that physically exists and instead honor all of Nature, they are Pagan.

—Cerelia

What if you don't believe in magic?

You can be Pagan and not work with magic at all. But I think that most people who are drawn to this path and have a little understanding of what Witchcraft is, know that it involves magic. Though they may have doubts about it, they will go through a process of determining what they believe is possible and will soon realize that magic isn't evil (unless you intend it to be) and that it is very natural and powerful. So, many people change their minds after gaining some experience.

—*Cerelia*

THE WORD *WITCH*

Why do the words Witch *and* Pagan *still frighten me?*

When you first begin this path, you may be afraid to admit to yourself that you're Pagan. It's even harder to imagine admitting it to the rest of the world.

We have been instilled with fear because people told us we'd be damned if we did not believe in our families' faith. This is a very hard concept for many new to this path to let go of. It is an impossible concept for some.

—*Cerelia*

Why do some prefer to be called Wiccan, rather than Witch?

I am proud to call myself a Witch, but some Wiccans dislike that title because they feel that it stresses magic over faith. Whatever we call ourselves, we each serve the Goddess in our own way. I am happy to be called Witch, priestess, or Wiccan, but I feel strongly that reclaiming the word Witch as an honorable title is important. Read more about this topic under "Types of Witches" on page, 15.

—Eileen

Do some people just say they're Witches because they enjoy shocking others and being different?

For some "witches" it's just a game, a way to shock others with the word itself. They are not helping to reclaim the word Witch and are very detrimental to the cause of bringing honor back to the word. I for one will be glad when this fad has died down, and the Witches who really know what it is all about can talk heart to heart, sensibly.

—Cerelia

I heard that only a dozen people alive have the right to call themselves Witches. What do you think of that?

I think it's wrong. I know more Witches than that.

—Eileen

————A WITCH'S APPEARANCE————

What do Witches look like?

Witches come in all sizes, shapes, and colors. Most of us look like everyone else.

—Eileen

But I thought . . .

Looking goth does not equate with witchiness. Where does this nonsense come from? Black nail polish does not a Witch make.

—*Eileen*

Why are pointy hats associated with Witches?

"Desert Mummies" is a Discovery Channel documentary about Caucasian mummies found in the Gobi Desert region of China. These included tall blonde male mummies, female mummies with red hair, mummies with face paint indicating sun worship, mummies wearing cloaks woven in European fashion with wool from European sheep, some in tartan patterns—and priestesses buried in tall, black, pointy hats with big brims. The hats are a bit taller and narrower than the typical model, but they are clearly recognizable as Witch hats.

Fascinating. This got me thinking about the use of tall pointed hats by magical adepts in so many cultures. Tlazolteotl, the Aztec Witch goddess, wore a Witch's hat and rode a broomstick. Magicians and wizards wore tall pointed hats, but without brims (think Merlin-by-Disney). Why wear such hats? One answer that makes sense to me is that they were aids for raising the cone of power, which is the energy that builds up above a magic circle when a Witch or a group of Witches is raising magical power. The energy, or magic, is discharged from the tip of the cone at the moment the spell is cast.

—*Eileen*

Is there a uniform? Do you need a twirly skirt? Do you have to wear a pentacle all the time?

That's very funny. I don't own a single twirly skirt, and the only pentacle I own at the moment hangs on the wall over my bed. I do wear an ankh, though.

Witches are all unique individuals who dress, worship, practice, cast circles, make altars, and do everything else in whatever way suits them.

—Eileen

As Witches learn more about Witchcraft, I believe they change their outward appearance as well as their inner mentality. Some go to extremes but most of us make more subtle changes in our favorite colors, jewelry, clothing, and even home decorations. The pentacle is a symbol of protection. Though every Witch may not feel a need to wear one, many more find it and other symbols very necessary. As Witches search for a new identity, it is easier for us to find the magic within when we detach ourselves from our mundane, everyday lives. Special symbols, jewelry, and clothing can help us do this.

—Cerelia

What was the small bag I saw another Witch wearing around her neck?

That is called a mojo bag. It usually has a drawstring at the top. You can make it yourself, or buy it from a magical supply shop. The little bags that perfume samples sometimes come in also work well for this. There are many, many things you can put into a mojo bag including herbs, crystals, feathers—whatever relates to your magical intent in making the bag. You may also hear them called charm bags, conjure bags, or gris-gris.

—Eileen

Why are all the Witches in print media—for example, Witches' Bible—*thin, young, and firm-breasted?*

I can understand what you are trying to say, but see how many heavy, droopy-breasted Witches you can get to take their clothes off for any kind of publication. Usually only the young and proud of body feel an inclination to do so.

—Cerelia

Misconceptions

Do Witches have a secret agenda?

Hmm, I must have missed the memo specifying our "witchy" agenda. Free speech? Clean air? Freedom of worship for all? Witches and feminists and gays, oh my.

But seriously, it would be hard for Witches to have an agenda because we're not that organized. There's no Witch Central, no supreme leader, no one to tell us what to think or believe. We are simply people who practice the same religion.

—Eileen

Do Witches worship the devil?

No. A constant mythological theme in many cultures throughout history is a god of darkness (or evil, chaos, sterility) who stands in opposition to the god of light (or goodness, civilization, fertility). Examples of this include Satan and Jehovah/Yahweh, Shaitan and Allah, Mot and Baal, Apep and Ra, Set and Osiris, Ti'amat and Marduk, and so on.

Witches do not believe in a physical devil. But take the D off of d–e–v–i–l, and you have something Witches certainly do recognize: e–v–i–l. We don't blame an entity called Satan for evil. As Pagans, we hold each human responsible for his or her actions. Satan, "the devil," is simply a *personification* of evil. "The devil made me do it" does not exist in Wicca.

—Eileen

Evil is found in man himself. Witches take responsibility for their own actions. We blame no one else.

—Cerelia

Are there really Satanic Witches?

It upsets me whenever someone lumps Satanists and Witches together. "Satanic Witch" is an oxymoron, a contradiction in terms. Satanists choose to walk in darkness, while Witches embrace the light. Keeping as much distance as possible between ourselves and Satanists is the best thing we can do. Your basic Bible-thumping types would be very surprised if they opened their minds wide enough to learn that Witches abhor Satanists just as much as they do. I don't understand why Satanists are so desperate to identify themselves with Witches and to be accepted by us. They don't understand why Witches don't want to hang out with them.

—Eileen

Is BDSM a popular lifestyle for Witches and Pagans?

No. BDSM (bondage and discipline, domination and submission, sadomasochism) is not a Wiccan or Pagan prerequisite. Sexual lifestyles and preferences are very personal within anyone's religion or beliefs. There is no one type of sexual lifestyle or preference accepted more than another by Witches and Pagans.

—*Cerelia*

Can Witches really fly?

If Witches could fly, we wouldn't need wheelchairs. Running through a field astride a broomstick is an old fertility rite to help crops grow well. Seen from a distance, a Witch doing this in a field of grain might have appeared to be flying above it. This is where the notion of flying Witches likely got started. There are many old recipes for "flying ointments" but these were aids for astral projection, not physical flight.

—*Eileen*

I have blue eyes and blonde hair and prefer to live in the city, so I can't be a Witch, right?

Wrong. I know you don't believe that nonsense about blonde hair and blue eyes, so I won't even answer that part; and you'd surely find a bunch of angry city Witches who'd disagree with the other remark.

—*Cerelia*

Are black magic Witches more powerful than white magic Witches?

Of course not. Don't assume that those practicing white magic are less formidable than those practicing dark magic— In other words, don't mistake kindness for weakness.

—Eileen

Many people do not realize the self-discipline and downright internal power it takes to integrate the light and the dark forces that reside within us all. As Witches, we do not deny either and we learn to work with both. It takes a *very* strong, ethical, and intelligent Witch to work for the good of all. Don't ever underestimate the power of white Witches. They have learned control and are in command of every thought and action. This makes them tremendously powerful, indeed.

—Cerelia

Is it true that Witches cannot see their reflections in mirrors?

That's hilarious. Think how crooked our lipstick would be! But it's too bad they didn't use the mirror test during the Burning Times instead of the hideous things they did to "find" Witches.

—Eileen

Is it true that Witches lose their powers if they cut their hair?

Some believe this and some don't. If you believe it, you will feel less powerful whenever you get a haircut. I don't believe it, and I feel no ill effects from a haircut.

—Eileen

TYPES OF WITCHES

Are there different kinds of Witches?

Yes. An urban Witch is one who lives in the city. A psi-Witch is a Witch who works magic without props, using only his or her mind. A kitchen Witch is one whose magic mainly centers around the home and family. To call someone a traditional Witch usually means a Witch who isn't necessarily into black magic, but will use it when he or she feels it is justified. Gardnerians, Alexandrians, fam trad Witches, hedgewitches . . . these are some examples of the many types of Witches.

—Eileen

Which kind is a "real" Witch?

They are all perfectly legitimate types of Witches. Witches just come from different traditions.

—Cerelia

What kind of Witch are you?

Cerelia and I are both Wiccan priestesses, and both eclectic solitaries. I like being an eclectic and a solitary because it gives me the most freedom, the ability to explore all magical options.

—Eileen

Globally speaking, does where you live define what kind of Witch you are?

It can. Speaking very generally, Australian and American Witches tend to be looser and less tradition-bound than some Europeans Witches.

—Eileen

What are "fluffy bunny" Witches?

Witches who use black magic use the rude expression "fluffy bunny" or "fluff bunny" to denigrate Witches who practice white magic.

—*Eileen*

────────HEREDITARY WITCHES────────

What's a hereditary Witch? Do Witches inherit powers from the female or male blood line?

A hereditary Witch is one who can trace the Craft back through his or her family tree and who was taught the Craft by a living relative.

—*Cerelia*

I think that almost anyone can become a Witch, by finding their way to the Goddess, and being dedicated and patient enough to study and learn the many things we need to know. I also think, however, that some people are natural Witches and this has to do with genetics or past lives.

In Stregeria (Italian Witchcraft), hereditary Witches can be male or female. There is an ancient Egyptian magical tradition, all male, that has survived to this day. They are psi-mages who practice in secret, because of Islam. Their tradition is hereditary, through male descent.

I would love to see a massive genetic study done, one that compares DNA results for Witches and non-Witches, hereditary Witches and non-hereditary Witches. I wonder if there might be a "Witchcraft gene" that could be identified, a gene that is not present in most humans, but dormant in some people, and active in those of us who are consciously Witches.

"Opening your third eye" might turn out to be a mystical description of activating this gene! I could be completely wrong about this, of course, but I strongly suspect that I might be right.

I think my powers (along with my red hair) came from my German grandmother. She was not consciously a Witch, but she had a magical way with plants and dogs.

—*Eileen*

Rather than genetics, could Witches retain powers from past lives or genetic memory?

That's a good point. It could even be that we choose to be reborn into families with other adepts in them.

—*Eileen*

I heard that Wiccans and solitaries, by the hundreds, are making life living hell for the old hereditary Witchcraft families. Is this true?

I doubt that there are hundreds of Witches coming down on all the hereditary families. How would anyone know of them, anyway?

—*Cerelia*

Are Wiccans betraying all the secrets of hereditary Witches?

No, this is a misguided question. You speak of Wiccans as one group of people who think exactly alike, as one body with one mind. Hogwash. I couldn't care less about anything that some Witches want to keep secret. If secrets make them feel more powerful, that is fine with me and with many other Witches. I know better.

—*Cerelia*

What does it mean when someone is born with a veil over her head?

That's called a caul. In Stregherian tradition it means that she is a born Witch.

—*Eileen*

————Solitaries and Eclectics————

What's a Natural Witch?

Another name for a solitary Witch is a Natural Witch, a Witch who chooses to practice alone. Anyone can be a Natural Witch.

—*Cerelia*

Can a solitary Witch at least sometimes work with other Witches?

There is middle ground, a way of working with others while working alone: synchronized spells or rituals, with each solitary working alone at home, but all the Witches casting the same spell at the same time. You don't have to be in the same room or even in the same country to experience the collective raising of power, you just have to be in tune with the other Witches and with the working.

—*Eileen*

Why do some Covens disapprove of solitary Witches?

There are Covens that disapprove of solitary initiates, but I strongly disagree with this attitude. We are all children of this Universe and have the right from the day we are born to reclaim ourselves as Witches and Pagans.

Some Witches like to look at themselves as an elitist group. This seems very sad to me. I am not being disrespectful to any one specific Coven. I honor everyone's right to his or her beliefs, but Covens should also respect Witches who know who they are, who have the fortitude and commitment to study alone and believe and practice their whole lives.

Not all Witches are able to be in a Coven, for personal reasons, or just because they do not have access to one. Many Witches realize that Witchcraft is actually a solitary path, a path that you journey within yourself. No one else can do it for you.

—Cerelia

Are eclectic solitaries killing traditional Witchcraft?

If family trads and secretive Covens want their ways of practicing Witchcraft to continue, they have to stop whining and train new members in their traditions; even (gasp) write some books about what they do and what they believe. They have to recognize that their secrecy limits them. Everyone else is having a global Witch party, while they're in the woods doing "secret stuff" and jealously guarding their mysteries. To each his own, but I am having too much fun at this party.

—Eileen

If the art of Witchcraft is dying, some so-called hereditary Witches are killing it with hatred. It is always dismaying to me when some Witch feels the need to argue about the antiquity of Wicca. For as many books and Witches that don't respect solitaries, there are many, many more who do.

—Cerelia

—Male Witches—

Do men belong in the Craft?

Yes.

—*Eileen*

Absolutely. Though I agree that negative things have happened in the past, I don't believe every man is corrupt and evil. There are Dianic traditions that will not allow a man to even enter their Covens. There are very strict feminists. I honor their right to believe as they want, but the books and articles written by some feminist Witches are very confusing to Witches who are new to the Craft.

Witches love and cherish their husbands and their sons. They raise their sons to be good, strong, faithful men; men who should not be held responsible for something that happened ages ago. This is the job of today's Witches, in my opinion, to not alienate the men in our lives. We must instead show and teach them about the love and respect to which women are entitled. We need to show them through example, so that the excesses of patriarchy never happen again.

I believe that the beauty and the power of the Craft should be nurtured and cherished between men and women. It is very powerful, no matter what a Witch's sexual lifestyle might be.

In my opinion, we shouldn't want to exclude those we love. We should rejoice in the promise of what we can accomplish in the Craft, between men and women alike.

—*Cerelia*

My friend says that Druidism is male Witchcraft, because men can't be Witches. Is this true?

Your friend is completely wrong on both counts. Druidism is based on Celtic practice. It is somewhat the same as Wicca. It follows a more structured aspect, and it does share differences and likeness. Men can absolutely be Witches, and are.

—*Cerelia*

Is a male Witch called a warlock?

Males are called Witches, just as females are. Warlock is not really a very popular term. Men prefer to be called Witch, or wizard, or maybe sorcerer, to warlock. This is because the word warlock has a bad connotation connected to it. I would think that if a woman preferred wizard or sorcerer she could use that name as well.

—*Cerelia*

A Witch is a Witch, male or female. Warlock is in insulting word, like calling a Jewish person a shylock.

—*Eileen*

So if a male Witch is a Witch, then what's a warlock?

Warlock was a Scottish name for a male practitioner who knew how to bind people, but mainly warlocks were servants of the Inquisition. They were men who pretended to be Witches in order to penetrate and betray Covens to witch hunters during the Burning Times. Warlocks were Christian spies. That's why Witches laugh whenever some kid calls himself a warlock. If a "Christian Witch" is an oxymoron, a warlock is a moron.

—*Eileen*

Aren't men all the same (you know what I mean) and therefore shouldn't be Witches?

My problem is that "Men are this, women are that . . ." is said here. Maybe some of this is true in a general, albeit imprecise, sort of way. Stereotypes are very dangerous—not all women are good mothers, for example. Not all men only think of themselves.

—Cerelia

Are the sexual energies between a man and a woman the only sexual energy recognized by a Witch?

I am a strong believer in the forces of the female and male as the Goddess. It is the Universe. One complements the other, and re-creation wouldn't be possible without it. It is quite beautiful. It is the sexual power of the Universe among all of us.

Perhaps I think this way because I am heterosexual. Witches with other sexual preferences probably find the power and beauty in their lives, too, just as I do, with their partners. We must see the beauty in it all, in every individual, be they male or female.

—Cerelia

Do many female Witches treat men like they're disgusting just because they're male?

There may be some, but it's wrong-headed thinking. The source of this female attitude is rooted in a lifetime of having to deal with men who think their genitalia makes them superior in some way and entitles them to more rights and privileges than humans without that genitalia. We thought we got all this straightened out back in the 1970s, but I guess not. Among ourselves, let us try to celebrate our polarity.

—Eileen

A man is nothing more than a penis! Should men be allowed into the Craft?

Men are much more than their genitalia. They are husbands, fathers, brothers, and friends. Together women and men are the Yin and the Yang. If you were born into a family filled with male disrespect and violence and are attracting a similar type of man into you life, you may need to make some changes within yourself and your life. Bitterness and anger will get you nowhere. Learn to make the changes that will attract men who will fill your life with joy and magic.

—Cerelia

————URBAN WITCHES————

Do Witches need to live in the country in order to be in tune with Nature and therefore be proper Witches?

There are many urban Witches living in apartments. They aren't always in touch with as much Nature as they would like, but they make it work.

—Cerelia

Urban Witches certainly are "true Witches." Some of us have been city-dwellers for many lifetimes, so this is how we're wired. Being an urban Witch has never disturbed my connection with Mother Nature, even if I do spend most of my time indoors.

—Eileen

Do city Witches practice the Craft differently?

The toilet bowl and the trash chute are urban substitutes for the usual outdoor places to bury used spell ingredients.

—Eileen

COVENS

What is a Coven?

A Coven is a group of Witches, traditionally no more than thirteen, who worship, work magic, and celebrate the Sabbats and Esbats together. A Coven is traditionally lead by a high priestess with a high priest.

—Eileen

What do you think about Covens vs. solitary practitioners?

A good Coven is wonderful. I would never say otherwise. The power of a collective group of Witches is very powerful indeed, but it's a mistake to think that solitaries are not important or powerful enough to deem themselves real Witches. We find the power within ourselves. It is not given to us or bestowed upon us by other Witches.

—Cerelia

Are Covens expensive to join?

There should never be any money involved in initiating a Witch. No one should be charged for the right to call himself or herself a Witch.

—Cerelia

Do age differences mean a lot in a Coven?

There's a big difference between young Witches and more mature Witches when it comes to Witchcraft, and to life itself. If there isn't a varied age difference between members of a Coven, the younger Witches learn nothing.

—Cerelia

What about Covens that say you have to do rituals skyclad, and no males are allowed, and have many other discriminating types of rules?

There's a big difference between being a solitary and being in a specific Coven. Different traditions have different rules and beliefs, and Covens can even be different within each tradition. The individual must make sure that his or her beliefs coincide with the Coven's, or find another Coven.

—Cerelia

Are Witches asked to take drugs as part of a Coven ritual?

No Witch should do anything he or she doesn't feel completely comfortable with. If anyone tells you that you have to do something that feels wrong to you, leave.

This is exactly why choosing or finding a suitable Coven is so important, if joining a Coven is something that a Witch wants to do. There are too many social Witches, who are just into the sex and drugs. This is why I always warn Witches who are looking for Covens to be very careful. This is also why I choose to be solitary.

Witchcraft is a solitary journey, to me. You can only do it by yourself. You can start out by asking questions and reading, but the important journey takes place within yourself, nowhere else.

—Cerelia

Are some Covens sexist, racist, homophobic, etc.? Would you be disappointed if members of such a group called themselves Witches or Wiccan?

Yes. In fact, disappointed is too mild a word for what I would be. I would have nothing to do with a group of Witches that would show this kind of discrimination.

—*Cerelia*

───────WITCH OR WICCAN?───────

What's the difference between a Witch and a Wiccan?

If you are Wiccan, you are a Witch; but you can be a Witch and not be Wiccan. A Wiccan Witch follows the rule of harming none. Wicca is the religion of Witches.

—*Cerelia*

This is a topic you will get many different opinions on. I usually say that all Wiccans are Witches, but not all Witches are Wiccan. Wicca is a religion, while Witchcraft is more of a belief system for some Witches. Wiccans are the priests and priestesses of the Goddess. We are Witches who have decided, of our own free will, to collectively abide one rule: Harm None.

—*Eileen*

What's the difference between a Pagan, a Wiccan, and a Witch?

This is a point that confuses a lot of people. Paganism is an umbrella term that covers many religions, such as Asatru, animism, Hinduism, Native American paths, Wicca, Druidism, and so on. Broadly speaking, any religion which includes the worship of multiple deities can be considered Pagan. Some people would define the term more narrowly, but that's a whole topic unto itself.

—Eileen

Why do some people call themselves Witches and some call themselves Wiccans?

Many Witches prefer to use the word *Wiccan*, because the negative connotation of the word *Witch*. They would rather say that they practice Wicca, not Witchcraft. There are other Witches who refuse to be called anything but Witch, because they believe we need to take back the honor that the word *Witch* once held.

—Cerelia

Why do some Witches dislike the word Wicca?

The word *religion* seems to be very distasteful to most Witches who are first entering the Craft. Religion is a word they have grown to hate, but it's only a word to describe one branch of Witchcraft, the ethical side. Some Witches may say "I am a Witch, but I am not a Wiccan" because they no longer want to be affiliated with a religion.

—Cerelia

BELIEFS

Why do some people call themselves Witches or Wiccans and do terrible things in the name of it?

At this time, Wicca and Witchcraft have become fads. I hope this doesn't last much longer. Although sometimes outraged by it, we as Wiccans are not responsible for it. We cannot help it when mentally incapable or downright mean people do or say things in the name of Wicca or Witchcraft.

We are all human. As with any religion, there are always the religious zealots and crazy people who do things in the name of a religion.

—Cerelia

What's the meaning of the Witches' saying "in perfect love and perfect trust"?

Real Witches trust each other. This is what's meant by perfect love and perfect trust, not romantic love.

—Eileen

THE LAW OF THREE

What's the deal with the Law of Three?

The most important thing to know about the Law of Three is that it relates to everything we say and do (or do not do), not just casting spells. Just as what goes up must come down, what we put forth must come back to us. Witches and different magical traditions quibble about how many times the return is (threefold, tenfold, or samefold), but I don't think anyone can deny that what goes around, comes around. Put forth positive actions and energy, and you get back blessings.

—Eileen

Is there a difference between karma and the Law of Three?

They both refer to consequences—either positive or negative. Karma can be instant but it usually plays out in the next lifetime, or through several lifetimes. Threefold return can also come in another lifetime, but it is more likely to manifest in the current one.

—Eileen

Does the Law of Three mean that a murderer will be murdered, and a rapist will be raped?

The return isn't always so literal, like Jeffrey Dahmer being killed in prison. Sometimes it's a lot more subtle, or drawn out. Sometimes a cosmic sense of humor can be seen in the way things work out. Whatever the case, even if it takes several lifetimes, balance is achieved.

—Eileen

How would karmic justice apply to a murderer?

As an example, he or she could come back in his next life as a victim, instead of the murderer. He or she could even suffer the fate of a victim while in prison in this life, or he or she could suffer the loss of a loved one in the next life. The examples are really endless. It can be instant karma, or in a future life.

—Cerelia

I know whatever Witches do comes back on them three times, but sometimes, don't you think it feels like it's worth it?

You might want to think about some of the things that could really happen, and if they did happen, whether or not it would have truly been worth it. It's easy to talk about hexing before the results come back and bite you in the butt.

Remember, I don't judge anyone's magic, or anyone's decisions. They are yours, and yours alone. These are just thoughts for you to consider, to try to help you understand that your decisions shouldn't be taken lightly. Your magic shouldn't be taken lightly, but like many things in this world, many Witches have to experience the results of the Law of Three before they believe in it. Some lessons come hard.

—*Cerelia*

I don't believe in the Law of Three because I believe that as long as my intent is good, anything I do is okay. If I really believe what I am doing is for the best of someone else, my conscience is clear, and that is all that is important to me.

What does your conscience have to do with you invading anyone else's freedom of choice? Yes, everyone knows whether they are doing right or wrong (or most people do, anyway). But what is right for you, may or may not be right for someone else. You deciding what you think is best for anyone and everyone is very wrong thinking. What gives you the right to make decisions for them, or feel that in your mind, you have all the answers for everyone?

—*Cerelia*

Do people always get what's coming to them?

Yes. This is physics as well as metaphysics, in my view.

—*Eileen*

I work in a bookstore, and Eileen's book, The Wicca Handbook, *was recently stolen right off the shelf.*

What goes around, comes around. I stole hundreds of books from public libraries when I was a kid, because of anger, angst, dysfunctional family . . . all the usual reasons that kids indulge themselves in negative behaviors. I have been making up for this in my adult life, by donating books to libraries and in other ways, but I can only shake my head and laugh if my books are being stolen.

—Eileen

Why is the phrase left-hand path used? It bothers me, because I am left-handed.

I tend to dislike the phrase left-hand path. It is an oft used phrase for black magic, and goes way back to a time when being left-handed was considered very wrong and not accepted. The left hand was supposed to be used only for toilet functions. The left-handed path also became a phrase for black magic, because society at the time thought being left-handed was evil.

Though it has become something of a habit with me and many other Witches to use this term, I can understand why left-handers would find this offensive.

—Cerelia

What's the right-hand path?

Right-hand path, to me, means doing no harm.

—Eileen

Why not just say good path and bad or evil path?

I prefer to say positive/negative instead of good/evil because good and evil are such loaded, subjective words. Positive and negative can be much easier terms to use.

—Eileen

—WITCHES AND ORGANIZED RELIGION—

Can Christians be Wiccans or Witches?

Christianity forbids Witchcraft, so how can you possibly combine the two? Paganism describes a Witch. It is the complete opposite of Christianity. You can't be a little bit Pagan. That's like being a little bit pregnant.

Here's a quote from Eileen Holland's book *The Wicca Handbook*: "Witches are Pagans. We worship many gods and goddesses, but recognize all of them as aspects of the Great Goddess."[1]

Often, someone saying he or she is a Buddhist-Christian, or a Jewish-Christian, or a Christian Witch, or a Christian-Wiccan is offensive to members of those faiths. In our case, using the title of Witch is what's offensive, not the fact that the person is Christian.

—Cerelia

Why do some Wiccans and Witches seem so anti-Christian?

Witches are individuals, just like everyone else. Some have ethics and some do not, just as every individual within every religion is different. So, a Witch who acts like this has made a personal decision to be this way. Wiccans agree on a whole as to what they believe as a religion. To be a Wiccan is to say that you believe in everyone's right to believe as they wish, with no judgments. A true Wiccan believes that all paths lead to the same place. When someone says they are Wiccan, they are saying they believe in the premise of not harming or discriminating against anyone.

When talking among themselves Wiccans are not really anti-Christian, even though it may sound like that at times. Among ourselves we may talk a lot about what Christianity may have done to us in the past, or that we don't like the way Christians treat other religions. We have discussions, just like anyone else. There are many activists who fight for Pagans' right to believe as they choose, and not be discriminated against. All this talk does not mean these Witches are anti-Christian. They may still have resentment toward how they are treated by Christians, but we work hard on keeping things in perspective, and remembering that we are all on the same path.

—*Cerelia*

Why are so many Witches former atheists?

A lot of us were atheists at one time, probably because we couldn't buy into conventional organized religion and desired something that made more sense to us. Naturally, at first we thought we were atheists. But that left most of us feeling cold and out of touch with our world, ourselves, and the magic that we knew was out there. When we found Wicca, we found what we had sought all along.

—*Cerelia*

What do Witches think of Jesus?

Many Witches hold Jesus, Buddha, the Dalai Lama, and various other human teachers in great esteem for their philosophies.

—Eileen

Did a deity create us?

You can believe in human evolution as Darwin and others have explained it, or you can believe that Khnum literally shaped the human race out of clay and formed us on his potter's wheel. Creation myth, science . . . you get to decide what you believe.

—Eileen

——————PAGANISM: NATURAL RELIGION——————

Do Witches worship?

Worship is a very strong word. I don't worship a higher being. I believe in none as a god, or goddess. I worship nothing, having left Christianity a very long time ago.

Honor is a better word. I honor the male and female energies of the Universe. I honor and tap into the magic of the Earth and all of its life and energies. I honor all of Nature and its forces.

—Cerelia

The idea of divinity doesn't compute with me, so it is more correct to say that I honor or serve god/desses, rather than worship them. The only thing I worship is the Universe itself, the sum of everything. I honor, serve, or work with god/desses, with their energies. If you think about it, everything in this Universe shares atoms, so in a way we are the gods and goddesses.

—Eileen

How do you honor, serve, or work with god/desses?

I began with the Goddess, and later widened my personal belief system to include gods such as Thoth, Pan, and the Green Man. I served Aphrodite in my Maiden phase, but at this point in my life I seem to resonate more with god/desses of the mind rather than of the body: Thoth, Ma'at, Sesheta, and so on. I also like the White Goddess, the Ocean Mother, Min, Brigid, Inanna, Ishtar, Erzulie, and Ra.

I am constructing a cairn in my living room, a pile of stones with each dedicated to a different god/dess: Thoth, Marduk, Isis, Ma'at, Hathor, Oshún, Poseidon, and Kali. These deities aren't superior to others, they are just ones who resonate strongly with me. When I find the right stone, one for the Green Man will be added. I have begun inscribing them, something that will take time because I am putting a lot of thought into my relationship with each god/dess as I do it. I have already inscribed the Isis rock, a smooth brown stone from the Nile that I brought back from Egypt. It reads "Isis, The Green One, Lady of Spells, Mistress of Magic."

—Eileen

What magical energies do Witches work with?

I see the powers in the rain and the snow, in the mountains and the animals, in the oceans and the wind. This is where I draw my energy. I need nothing more. I can correspond these energies with names of deities. Giving them a name can help to focus on an energy. Other Witches use the same energies, but call them or see them differently. We are all different. We see the Lord and Lady in many things, and in many ways.

This is the magic I work with and honor, Nature in its truest form. The Universe bestows its magic on us when we are receptive enough to see it and work with it. Some Witches may say it comes in the forms of fairies, while to other Witches it is something else. Your belief, how you see these powers, is what makes them powerful for you.

—*Cerelia*

Is it possible to practice Wicca or any other form of Paganism without believing in a deity of any kind?

Absolutely. As with any tool, a deity helps you to focus, or gives a name to a certain aspect or energy. Nature is the all important aspect of Wicca and other forms of Paganism, not the belief in any existing god. Some Witches find it hard to focus their minds without something to guide them. You can use nothing, if you wish, or think of Nature itself.

—*Cerelia*

The Goddess

Do Witches believe in a deity or deities?

We believe in the Goddess.

—*Eileen*

Who is the true God, and the true Goddess?

There is no one true god/dess. The Great Goddess represents all of them. She is the Air, Earth, Fire, and Water of the Universe itself. She represents all of our feelings and emotions. Unlike Christianity, Pagans do not believe the god/desses to be physically existing gods or goddesses. That is why we are Pagan. They are the representation of many energies of the Universe. They are legends and myths created by humans, to help us focus on a certain energy that we may be working with.

That is why, when reading about the different deity names and their stories, one story may really touch you and make you feel close to that god or goddess. You may get drawn to what that deity stands for. That might then become the god or goddess you use in your rituals or spells, to help you connect with that energy. You will then find power when you use his or her name within your spells and such.

—*Cerelia*

Who is the Great Goddess?

The Great Goddess (referred to simply as the Goddess throughout this book) is a personification of the Universe itself, just as Gaia is a personification of the planet Earth. As Starhawk points out in *The Spiral Dance*, her seminal work on the importance of Goddess Religion in Witchcraft, the Goddess unifies all opposites.[2] The Universe has a consciousness, and its endlessly creative nature makes us perceive and personify it as super-female (the Great Goddess), containing both male and female energies or aspects (the god/desses). Aspects such as Aphrodite, Isis, Athene, or Brigid are easier to contemplate on the personal level.

—*Eileen*

Is the Goddess real?

"People often ask me if I believe in the Goddess. I reply, 'Do you believe in rocks?'"[3] That's one of my favorite quotes.

Discussing the reality of the Goddess is like debating about whether the Moon disappears when it's not visible from Earth. However each of us experiences the Goddess, however we define her or explain her, relate to her or deny her or ignore her, she is still the Goddess and the Universe continues to exist.

Denying the existence of the Goddess is like denying the Moon. You can disbelieve all you want, but it's still there, even when it isn't visible—or even if it is visible, but you refuse to look up.

—Eileen

Isn't overemphasizing the Goddess as sexist as Christianity overemphasizing its male god?

Most Witches honor the god/dess together, as absolute and equal powers. We may use the word Goddess, but we mean both powers. You need male and female energy in Nature— and in life itself. I would definitely not want to devalue male energies in the way Christianity historically devalued female energies. I love the balance.

—Cerelia

What do you think of some Witches only acknowledging the female aspects of the Goddess?

To me, the Goddess embodies all. She is the very heart of the Craft. She manifests the male/female polarity. The Goddess is known by many names, and each one represents a different aspect, personality, energy, and so forth. Some Witches will only acknowledge the feminine goddesses, not the male gods, but to me, not acknowledging both is to go backward on our path—back to the way most of us were brought up, taught to believe only in a male god. These are my feelings, but other Witches should do whatever feels right to them. If some Witches choose to acknowledge only the female aspects of the Goddess, that's their decision. Wicca is a very open religion.

—Cerelia

Some Witches honor the Lord and the Lady, while others only honor the female aspects of the Goddess. It's a personal choice.

—Eileen

But what about God, the one God?

This is a free planet. It's okay to believe whatever you like, but in Wicca there is no supreme god. Anyone who has a problem with this concept should not call herself or himself a Witch.

—Eileen

Would you explain some of the Goddess's many names?

As Doreen Valiente says "Listen to the words of the Great Mother; she who of old was also called among men Artemis, Astarte, Athene, Dione, Melusine, Aphrodite, Cerridwen, Cybele, Arianrhod, Isis, Dana, Bride and by many other names."[4] Mary and Sophia are her names in the Christian pantheon.

—Eileen

Why does she have all these names?

There are so many names for the Goddess because so many different cultures celebrate her.

—*Cerelia*

Would you please further explain the foundation of your pantheistic beliefs?

There is no one answer to this, because it's something that each Witch has to work out for herself or himself. My opinion is that our ancestors created the gods, as personifications of human emotions and the natural world. I think all the various gods and goddesses are thought forms, human inventions that embody concepts such as love, justice, sexuality, healing, aggression, fertility, compassion, and so on.

Humans do sometimes create things nobler and more powerful than ourselves, such as poems, symphonies, cave paintings—and deities. In creating the gods, we created something greater than ourselves. We then empowered our creations with hundreds or thousands of years of worship, supplication, invocation, and made thought forms of them.

In my view, the gods are powerful human creations that correspond to specific aspects of the Universal consciousness. In no way does this lessen the reverence and respect I feel for the god/desses I work with. This is how it all makes sense to me, but other Witches experience it differently. According to Doreen Valiente, "Dion Fortune . . . discusses the real nature of the gods as 'magical images,' made not out of stone or wood, but shaped by the thoughts of mankind out of the substance of the astral plane, which is affected by the mind; hence it is sometimes referred to as 'mind-stuff,' for want of a better name."[5]

—*Eileen*

Is there a limit to the power of the Goddess?

Ask a theological question to three different Witches and you'll get three different answers. To me, the Goddess (and all the god/desses she contains), is the Universe itself. She is therefore subject to the same laws of physics as everything else in the Universe. However, humans have only begun to understand just what those laws of physics are. It is not possible for a Witch to fly or change into an animal on Earth (except in the psychic sense), but it may be possible for Witches to do so in other solar systems.

We think we know so much, but we are really just children, still on the threshold of scientific discovery. We will have to travel into space and learn more about this Universe before we can really know the Goddess's limits.

Do the god/desses embody all that is good?

That isn't how I see it. Deities are complex. Few of them are all "good" or all "bad," just like the humans who created them. To me, the Goddess contains everything. I wouldn't use the words good and evil to describe the Universe—or the Goddess. The words positive and negative make more sense to me.

—*Eileen*

Why does the Goddess rule the night?

> Because she is the Moon,
> because she is succulence and abundance,
> because she is Venus as the morning and
>   evening stars,
> because she rules shadows and secrets and the
>   Mysteries,
> because she rules physical love and the pleas-
>   ures of the flesh.

—Eileen

I asked the Goddess to help me, and nothing happened.

That's not how energy works. The Law of Three tells us that blessings flow to us in return for our positive actions. To receive blessings we must put forth positive energy, via positive actions. When you need help, reach out to others and do whatever you can to help them. That's where you find help and healing.

Don't say "Help me, Goddess"; say "Goddess, what can I do to help others?"

—Eileen

Working with Deities

(See also Invocation on page 199)

I don't understand the concept of using deities.

Deities are a way to focus your mind. They are not physically real, but giving them a name helps some Witches to focus. The energies are more alive for them this way. Maybe a story about a certain deity really touches you—so when you speak that name in your spells, it adds power because that name means something to you. It feels real, and you physically feel the power of what your spell is about.

For some Witches, names just get in the way so they don't use them. They just speak to the god/dess as a part of Nature, as a particular energy. The magic is within your intent, not a god.

—Cerelia

What god/dess should I believe in?

Each of us make personal choices in deciding which deities to honor or work with. Many Witches work with Hecate, for example, but she gives me the shivers. Some Witches consider Lilith and Kali to be negative, but I consider them archetypes of female power and independence. Set, the Egyptian god of darkness and destructive winds from the desert, murderer of Osiris and would-be usurper of Horus, is a god I cannot imagine anyone inviting into his or her life.

We must also remember that myths are myths, told and retold over millennia; conquerors and conquered peoples tell the other culture's tales from different perspectives. For example, the high goddess Ishtar was the Whore of Babylon to the

Hebrews, whose patriarchal viewpoint prevented them from understanding sacred sexuality, or temple prostitution, as a religious order.

Jehovah makes little sense to me, since I find nothing admirable in a god who turned a woman into a pillar of salt (Lot's wife), condoned abandoning a mother and child in the desert (Hagar and her son), and tested faith by ordering children killed (Isaac and the firstborn children of the Egyptians).

This doesn't mean I am correct and others are wrong; it means we are all unique and must make choices that make sense to us. Ultimately, each Wiccan invents his or her own religion. No one can tell us what the god/desses are, because we all experience them differently. We each choose which ones we want to work with or honor; or they choose us, by making themselves known in our lives.

—*Eileen*

Who are some strong god/desses?

You'll find a wide variety of opinions about this, but I think Isis, Kwan Yin, Sekhmet, Bast, Ishtar, Kali, Freya, Hecate, Yemaya, Brigid, Venus/Aphrodite, Diana/Artemis, and The Morrigan are generally regarded as very strong goddesses. Cernunnos, Pan, Poseidon, Thor, Odin, Zeus, Marduk, Taranis, and Maximón come to mind as strong gods.

—*Eileen*

Do I have to name the God and Goddess at all?

Deciding whether to give energy a name is up to you. If you want to use Isis, Ra, Osiris, or Father Sky and Mother

Earth—or no name at all—it makes no difference. Use whatever feels powerful to you. Just focus on the energy you are trying to attract.

—Cerelia

What's meant by the terms "matron goddess" or "patron god"?

A matron or patron is the deity you feel closest to—the one who resonates most strongly with you. This is the goddess or god whom you mainly serve, and whose protection you are under. Some Witches have a matron, others have a patron, some have both, and some have neither.

—Eileen

How do I find my matron goddess or patron god?

You should honor or work with whatever god/desses feel right to you. God/desses generally come to us when we need them.

—Eileen

How can a matron goddess or patron god help us?

For many years the Lord was simply the Green Man to me, the general god of vegetation, woodlands, and wild creatures; but when my son was diagnosed as profoundly autistic, it was Thoth to whom I turned for help.

Thoth was a perfect ally, the god of magic and wisdom and communication. I still honor the Green Man and the Horned God, but Thoth is my personal god. He is a remote god, one who never gives assignments or asks for anything, but he is there when we need him and ably provides practical assistance.

My son was originally expected to spend his adult life in an institution, but Thoth and I changed that prognosis. My son has made such incredible progress that no one but an expert in autism can even detect it in him now. Love, patience, a little magic, a lot of hard work, and an ancient Egyptian god (or other god/dess) are a powerful combination, and one that I recommend to any Witch who faces a difficult task or formidable problem.

—Eileen

Two goddesses call to me. How do I choose which one to follow?

Why choose? Why limit yourself to one? Follow your heart, which tells you to follow both of them. Different god/desses speak to us at different phases of our lives. As a Maiden I served Aphrodite, and took the difficult Path of Love. As a Mother, I consider Isis my matron goddess, but I also work with Ma'at. I delight in the unfolding of my path and wonder whom I will work with when I am a Crone. Marduk? Ishtar? Oya? Not knowing is part of what keeps life so interesting.

—Eileen

A goddess came to me in a dream. Is she my personal goddess?

That is something only you can answer. It is something to meditate on.

—Eileen

Whom can I invoke to help me protect a cat?

Bast, Sekhmet, and Ra are good deities to call upon, where cats are concerned.

—Eileen

How can I learn about the goddess of the hunt?

Begin with Diana and Artemis.

—Eileen

How is the God both the son and the lover of the Goddess?

That is a difficult concept, isn't it? Goddesses often mate with their son/lover in mythology, but this isn't about incest. It's about contrasting the cyclical, dying and rising nature of the God with the eternal nature of the Goddess.

—Eileen

What is the triple aspect of a goddess?

It most often reflects the three phases of a woman's life, which mirror the phases of the Moon: Maiden (Waxing Moon), Mother (Full Moon), and Crone (Waning Moon). Triple goddesses also take other forms. The Zorya, for example, represent dusk, midnight, and dawn, and the Norns represent the past, the present, and the future.

—Eileen

Why isn't there a triple aspect for a god?

Probably because the Moon, which has three phases, is associated with the Goddess in most cultures. Read about gods such as Janus, who was depicted with two faces, and Marduk, who was sometimes depicted with four faces.

—Eileen

Different Cultures, Different Pantheons

Is it best to work with the god/desses of our ancestors?

Ethnicity is very important to some Witches in choosing their path within Wicca, but it's irrelevant to others. We were likely male and female and different races and cultures in our various lifetimes. I think we should go where our hearts lead us. If more than one culture or pantheon interest you, be an eclectic Witch and learn about all of them.

African and Middle Eastern deities interest me more than the Celtic or Teutonic ones of my ancestors. This may have more to do with my past lives than it does with this one. Never forget that we are much more than whoever we are in our present incarnation. Follow your interests and inclinations. It will be a fascinating journey. You will learn as much about yourself as you will about whatever culture and god/esses you study.

—Eileen

What's a good way to ease into the study of the Craft?

Study mythology. Learn about the Goddess, and about whatever cultures and pantheons interest you. Doing so will teach you as much about yourself as it will about deities. This kind of inner work helps you find your path in the Craft.

—Eileen

How can I ever learn Norse mythology, when there is so much to it?

Try cutting the information down to size, for example, focus only on gods, only on the Vanir, only on heads of pantheons, only on warriors, or something like that. Once you master this, you can move on to some other aspect of the subject that interests you.

—Eileen

The Asatru are angered by Witches who work with Norse deities.

How sad. Too bad. It's good to be sensitive to other belief systems, but no one faith owns the gods. Those of us who work with Egyptian deities probably annoy Orthodox Kemetics, and those who work with Tara or Kwan Yin annoy . . . . well, you get the idea. Live and let live.

—Eileen

Did Romans only worship their own gods?

The worship of several foreign deities, such as Mithras and Epona, became popular with Roman soldiers.

—Eileen

Why are Egyptian gods and goddesses so powerful?

Egyptian deities are particularly powerful because of their antiquity, and because the Egyptians built things to last for the ages. They thought about time in terms of millions of years. When they said "I make this spell to last forever," they really meant forever!

—Eileen

How can I understand the Christian deities I was raised with?

Try seeing them as types: Yahweh/Jehovah as a typical sky father, Jesus as a typical dying-and-rising vegetation god, Mary Magdalene as a typical love goddess, and Mary as a typical mother goddess.

—Eileen

Can you mix and match between cultures, e.g. Egyptian and Celtic, etc.?

That is how I work. I find it very effective so long as you have some reason, even if it's intuition, for mixing those particular deities.

—Eileen

CHAPTER TWO

Becoming a Witch

Why do I feel like I am different from other people?

Many Witches have known this, the fish-out-of-water experience. We are different from other humans, and this can make both them and us uncomfortable.

I knew from early childhood that I was different from other people, but I always thought it was because I was a poet. It's funny how you can roam the planet looking and asking questions—and then find your answers right inside yourself.

When I was a child I wrote that it seemed to me that most people are asleep, while a very few of us are awake, sitting up, looking around, and seeing one another. I didn't know it at the time, but I was describing Witches. It is my intuitive theory that the answer to why we are different will one day be found in our genes.

—*Eileen*

What do you think separates a Witch from others in this society?

People, for the most part, have been taught to put their personal responsibility into the hands of a god. He is in charge; they aren't. They have been brought up believing that they have no decision in the outcome of their lives, because he has decided their fate. They have no power in their own lives. This is the defining difference between Witches and most other people. Personal responsibility should be paramount in a Witch's life. I believe that lack of personal responsibility is why there is so much trouble in the world today.

—*Cerelia*

Are Witches superior to regular people?

We all share atoms, are all just human beings here working on our karma. Everyone is unique and precious. Everyone has something to give.

—Eileen

Why do light bulbs burn out and street lights go off when I'm near them?

That's just part of being a Witch, so don't worry about it. It's wristwatches for me. I haven't even bothered to own a watch in many years, because they always stop running after I wear them for a month or so: good watch, cheap watch, it makes no difference.

It's strange, though, that although I never wear a watch I am more punctual than most people. Perhaps it's an inner sense of time, like the psychic navigation skills that many Witches have. Witches have a different relationship with the Universe, including electricity and other forms of energy, than other people. Perhaps we vibrate at a higher frequency. It would be interesting if someone studied this.

—Eileen

I have the watch problem, too. What can I do about it?

Try a pocket watch or keeping the wristwatch in your bag or pocket instead of wearing it. I throw a small alarm clock into my bag when I really need to carry the time with me.

—Eileen

Why is it said to take a year and a day to become a Witch?

It's kind of like going to college for four years. You aren't expected to learn something completely new and foreign to your old beliefs overnight.

—*Cerelia*

How can I become a Witch? Where do I start?

Some of us do better in traditional Covens, others by studying alone (as Cerelia and I did), others in cyber-study groups, and so on.

—*Eileen*

My first suggestion would be to read. There really isn't anything more practical than starting with one good book, a book that will teach you what Witchcraft is and is not.

In my opinion, spirituality, history, and so on, should be first in a new Witch's mind; but understandably, with the resurgence of Paganism and Witchcraft, a lot of people are lured by promises of magic and higher consciousness. I hope, though, that experienced Witches will always speak up and guide newcomers toward a greater awareness of the spirituality behind Wicca. That is the main goal of the Open Sesame e-list.

—*Cerelia*

Begin with the Goddess; that is the best advice I can give you. Follow your heart and begin where you feel called to begin. Start casting spells and holding rituals when you feel ready for them. Everyone is different, so this varies greatly. Determining when you're ready is part of your inner work, part of learning to know and trust yourself.

—*Eileen*

And, remember, reading is knowledge.

—Cerelia

And knowledge is power.

—Eileen

What should I read?

Get the basics. Some good books for novices are Scott Cunningham's *Wicca: A Guide for the Solitary Practitioner* and *Earth Power*, and anything by authors such as Starhawk or Grimassi. There are also many other good books, of course. You will be buying books left and right.

—Cerelia

I think it's important to stress the mythological element of our path, so I recommend books such as *The White Goddess*, *The Golden Bough*, and the *Egyptian Book of the Dead*. To know who we are, we have to know where we came from. Our religion may have flowered in western Europe but its roots are in Sumer, Thebes, Knossos, and the Ice Age. Only reading modern Pagan authors, myself included, is not enough. We have to know our roots.

—Eileen

What kind of Witch should I be?

You can try being an eclectic Witch. This is a Witch who picks from anything that feels right. Or if you feel a strong connection to a certain tradition, you can follow that. In time, after you have chosen certain ways to cast your circles, invoke your deities, and so on, you won't even remember why you do things the way you do. It is just right for you.

A Witch may ask me why I do a certain thing one way or another, or call it this or that, and I can't remember where or when or why I started doing things a certain way. It just doesn't matter to me. That is how it will be for everyone, after a while. It just doesn't matter where it came from. Whatever works!

—Cerelia

One Witch helps Gaia with weather patterns, another heals animals, another makes wands, another is an advocate for our right to worship as we choose, another leads a Coven—there are many paths within the Craft. We each choose the one that is right for us. You may choose at some point to enter a particular tradition, such as Dianic Wicca, in which case you'd adopt those deities the tradition honors.

—Eileen

What you choose to believe is entirely your decision. There are certain traditions that anyone can follow. Whether you have to follow them to a "T" is up to you. You should learn about all the different traditions—you'll feel what fits or doesn't. Most Witches, unless in a Coven, do not follow a strict rule or tradition.

—Cerelia

I can't even imagine myself chanting or dancing around an altar— what should I do?

That's understandable. You don't have to dance and chant around anything, if you don't want to. Witches raise consciousness in many different ways. Some of them are a lot more subtle than others.

—Cerelia

I have a hard time imagining myself dancing and chanting around an altar, too. I have never done either of those things. No drum banging, no skyclad dancing, no howling at the Moon . . . we are each whatever kind of Witch we wish to be. There is no ancient book with Witch Rules that dictate what we should and should not do. The best way for us to serve the Goddess is to follow our hearts, and do no harm in the process.

If all the Witches you encounter are into wild drumming and ecstatic dancing, but you feel ridiculous drumming or dancing, don't drum or dance. If you don't feel the need for a Craft name, don't assume one. If working skyclad makes you uncomfortable, wear clothes to work and worship. There are endless ways to serve the Goddess. Finding your own way to be of service is your personal challenge.

—Eileen

What kind of Witch am I, if I am interested in more than one pantheon?

That makes you an eclectic Witch. Some Witches concentrate on a particular pantheon, but lots of us prefer working with whatever deity calls to us. We like having the freedom to use methods from many different magical traditions.

—Eileen

I hear someone calling me, whistling for me. What does this mean?

Each person has to interpret what his or her own experiences mean, but if you are new to the Craft I'd say it is the call of the Goddess. Many of us have heard it.

—Eileen

I was baptized and raised Catholic. Can I still become a Witch?

I was also baptized Catholic as an infant. It means nothing and is no impediment. I never considered myself bound to a path that was not of my own choosing. A choice made for us before we came of age does not bind us to it. Some oil and water does not decide our path for us. We always have choices. I absorbed what I found meaningful in Catholicism (incense, candles, the Lady), disregarded everything that didn't make sense to me, and moved on.

—*Eileen*

Is fifty to late to start upon this path?

It all depends on the heart and the intent of the Witch, not on age. Some people get it a lot faster than others, and some never get it at all, whether they start at a young age or not.

—*Cerelia*

Becoming a Witch in one's current lifetime is as much about remembering things as it is about learning new ones. I was past thirty before I finally figured out that I was a Witch. The Goddess had to strike me blind to get my attention, after I ignored all her gentler calls. You have a lot of time in front of you. You will use it wisely, learn much, and come into your full self.

—*Eileen*

How can I become a solitary Witch?

First, you have to be your own person—your own high priest/ess—to learn Witchcraft as a solitary. You must want it and not stop until you experience it, understand it, feel it, in every bone in your being.

It takes lots of work to become a solitary practitioner. You have to know a lot of things, so read everything you can—you may find an author who really inspires you. You will learn what some Witches consider important, and what other Witches do not. In the process, you will become your own Witch, by knowing what works for you.

—*Cerelia*

I am searching for a path that will allow me to be alone but also together with other Witches.

That's exactly how many solitary Witches would describe themselves, when they come together with other Witches on Sabbats, for rituals.

—*Eileen*

Is it possible to learn to raise power just by reading books?

I did, by reading *The Spiral Dance*. Personal training—Witch-to-Witch, female-to-male, and male-to-female—is traditional and perhaps the best way, but it's not the only way.

—*Eileen*

It must be hard to become a Witch on your own.

In some ways, it's easier. When I was new upon this path, I pointedly avoided other Witches and any situation where I might make contact with them. I was cloaking, I realized later. I avoided contact with other Witches because I wanted to preserve the purity and strength of my belief in the Goddess and in white magic. I was afraid that other Witches might not be as committed to these things as I am, and might destroy my vision of what a Witch is.

The first magical adept I met was an Egyptian sheikh, in a small village in the Nile delta. That was when I first experienced the sensation of having my energy field make contact with the energy field of another adept. The path of an Egyptian sheikh is a right-hand path, and more like ours than either they or we would have suspected. Meeting that sheikh was what taught me that we can recognize one another, and know each other for what we are, without speech or any of the normal mechanisms by which human beings interact.

I later met Witches with the same dedication to this path, and I met other sheikhs. I am still basically a solitary, but I much enjoy my contact with others of like mind. Sabbats and adversity are the things which spark a need for other Witches in me. Rituals are best performed with others, but everything else is just as meaningful to a solitary.

—Eileen

What about those of us who feel a need to be around other Witches in order to learn?

I can understand that. Some people need companionship while learning. You may be able to find a group of Witches that fits this need, but remember that in the end, you will never find in another that which you cannot find in yourself. My suggestion is to find it within yourself first.

All the power and knowledge is inside you. You have to find it on your own. You do this with a lot of reading, meditating, and studying of the Craft. When you are ready to trust yourself, you are ready to know whom to trust or not to trust out there in the world.

—*Cerelia*

Do Witches recruit?

We do not go out and look for converts. We do not have to. We do not try to discourage anyone, nor do we encourage anyone. You either come to this path on your own, or you don't. People have to find their own way to Witchcraft.

—*Cerelia*

I was involved in a spiritual group that cost me thousands of dollars before I found out it was a scam. Does it cost a lot of money to become a Witch?

The problem with any religion is that there will always be frauds out to make a quick buck. Misconceptions can excite the newcomer and the very young; excite them enough to make them think they have to spend exorbitant amounts of money to become a Witch or Wiccan. Being a solitary Witch, or a Wiccan, will cost you nothing except the price of a few good books and whatever tools you would like to collect along the way. The magic is in you, nowhere else.

We all need to help newcomers see the difference between a product or service that is fairly priced, and one existing only to make someone very wealthy—as well as recognizing those products and services they do not need at all.

We can't expect to get books free. We know that some Witches make tools, clothing, candles, and so on. Some give workshops on different topics. They are putting their own time and money into these projects and deserve a fair payment. As the consumer, you are always the ultimate judge of quality and what is fair in price.

We will never stop the thieves and fakes out there in any religion or spiritual belief. But as with anything, we need to be smart. We need to know whom we are dealing with, their background, and to get some personal references. We may be on a spiritual path and believe in harming none, but that doesn't mean we're stupid.

—Cerelia

I know that I'm Wiccan, but how can I decide which kind of Wiccan to be?

Matters of faith and belief are serious and intensely personal. Don't rush yourself. Read widely, with an open mind. Meditate on the things you read, and you will find the path that is right for you.

—Eileen

CRAFT NAMES

Why do some Witches use Craft names?

Craft names can help Witches leave the everyday world behind and aid in the transformation to the magical one. The names make us feel different. They put us in touch with something we have been taught to forget. They trick the mind, so to speak, into helping your belief in yourself and your own powers to grow. Within their rituals and spells, chosen Craft names can be as important to Witches as their special clothing and tools.

—Cerelia

What's the importance of a Craft or magical name to you?

I find a Craft name very helpful to switch my mind to a magical state. A Craft name helps me detach myself from the mundane world. It puts me in a more receptive mood for my magical works. A magical name helps my mind focus, helps me feel who I am. It helps to attract whatever energies I may be looking for.

Though I consider Cerelia my Pagan name, it is an important part of me in my magical workings, so it is also my Craft name. Cerelia is the only Craft name I have ever had. It is me, now. The name Cerelia helped me to find the magic within myself, and in the world I live in. Cerelia is as much a part of me as my given name. That is the true test of a Craft name: it empowers you.

—Cerelia

Do I need a Craft name?

Whatever works for you. Some Witches never take a magical name because their birth name speaks to them. You don't need a magical name, but if and when you do choose one, don't take it lightly. Wait until the right name comes to you.

—Cerelia

I have never felt the need for a Craft name. We're all different, and we each need to do whatever is right for us. Some Witches take magical names, and some Witches do not. Follow your own inclination in this, as in all things magical.

—Eileen

Why don't you have a Craft name, Eileen?

I have never felt the need for a new name. I've never liked my given name but it means light, so I guess it's appropriate to my path. I actually feel no ownership of any of the names that have been given to me in this lifetime. I don't feel as if my real name is lost or missing; I don't feel like I need to look for a name. I just feel nameless and rootless, and that feels right to me for this lifetime. Names are words, and words embody concepts, so when I think of myself it is with the idea of who I am, rather than with a name. That's just me, though, and all those Witches who feel affinity with magical names should seek them out (or wait for them to come).

—Eileen

Does your name have to be given to you by a teacher or a Coven?

That is true in some specific traditions, but most Witches just wait until their name finds them.

—Eileen

Should a new dedicant to a year and a day program choose a Craft name right away?

I would encourage dedicants not to worry about a Craft name and to decide not to choose one until it is toward the end of the year and a day. This way, you know more about the Craft and yourself. I have seen many Witches change their names two or three times within just a few months. This is because as they grew, they understood more: as their outlook changed, so did what they wanted to reflect in their names.

—*Cerelia*

What's renaming?

That can refer to the assumption of a Craft name or to changing that name. Witches sometimes hold a ceremony when they take a new name, change that name, or add a new name to an existing one (e.g., a Rowan becoming Rowan Ravenwood, or a Witch called Cairn becoming Oakman Cairn, and so forth). The taking or changing of names is serious business to many Witches. It is something they do to mark changes in consciousness or of life stages—or with the intention of changing themselves or their lives.

—*Eileen*

CHOOSING A NAME

When should I choose a Craft name?

There is no deadline for choosing a name. Wait for a name that describes you and fills you with power when you use it. PurpleRainBucket—that is not exactly a Craft name to me, but I guess if someone wants to be known by that name for the rest of his or her life, that's okay with me.

—*Cerelia*

How do I find my Craft name?

I take Craft names seriously. When a Witch decides to choose one, it should be done with great care and without hurry. If you read a lot, you will come across many, many suitable names, such as names of deities, and so on. Just keep reading and a name will jump out at you when the time is right.

Choose a name that will make you proud and allow you to feel the power in it. Find one that speaks to you and makes you feel its power when you use it. You should feel honored to be known by the name you choose.

—*Cerelia*

Are there any rules to choosing a Craft name?

There are no rules. I love mythological names myself, not just some pretty words thrown together. Your Craft name should speak of yourself.

—*Cerelia*

I've heard that you should reduce the numbers in your birth date to a single number, then choose a name that also has this number.

That's one way of doing it. Go with that, if it feels right to you, or just choose a name because it has resonance or meaning for you. When you find the right name, you'll know it.

—*Eileen*

But don't we have to use numerology to find the right name?

Says who? The notion that Craft names should have numerical correspondence with your birth date or name is in an opinion, not a rule. If this resonates with you, go with it. If not, choose any name that is meaningful to you.

—Eileen

It doesn't matter if you choose a Craft name or not, especially if you like your given name. But when a name calls to you, I wouldn't ignore it just because it doesn't work numerically.

—Cerelia

I think I should do my inner work and start my pathworking before I choose a Craft name.

That's sensible. There is no rush to find a new name. Some of use just keep the name we always had.

—Eileen

TITLES

Why are some Witches called Lady this or Lord that?

Lady is usually a Witch who has been in the Craft a long time, a Witch who is very knowledgeable and wise. Some Witches consider it an insult for new Witches to put Lady (or Lord or Sir) before their name. They feel that a title should not be used until a Witch has been around long enough to earn it.

—Cerelia

What should new Witches focus on?

In my opinion, spirituality, history, and so on, should be first in a new Witch's mind.

—*Cerelia*

What god/desses should a new Witch work with?

New Witches often find it easiest to begin with the general concept of Lord and Lady (or just the Lady, for Dianics). Novices can also find it preferable to work with the most powerful deities in the beginning, because it is easier to get a feel for them than for the more subtle or obscure god/desses.

—*Eileen*

What should new Witches be careful about?

Remember that there are many people out there who prey on vulnerable "newbies." Don't let yourself become one of them. Witchcraft is an individual belief system. You do not have to have an all-powerful human running the show. The show is yours.

Sure, new Witches need information and insight into what they are following; but no one is in charge of anything, except you—even within a Coven. If a group does not feel right, leave. You are your own priest/ess.

—*Cerelia*

Why does it seem to me that the more I learn, the more I don't know?

At least you know what you don't know; not many will admit that. It is the wisest of all statements, in my opinion. I agree that just when you think you know it all, someone or something will show you that you don't.

—Cerelia

This is an important lesson. As Witches, we always have more to learn. This continual birth process is what keeps us young (internally), and makes many Witches look younger than their years.

—Eileen

I am filled with doubts about whether or not I am really a Witch.

Here is a quote from Hazrat Inayat Khan that I think helps explain why our minds still try to fill us with doubts, though we try and try: "The soul brings its light from heaven; the mind acquires its knowledge from earth. Therefore, when the soul believes readily, the mind may still doubt."

—Cerelia

I'm sad because I seem to be losing friends since I became a Witch.

When magic enters your life, it has a way of pushing aside negative people, habits, and thought patterns. Magic changes us. Don't be depressed by this, give thanks for it. The relationships which will end weren't good for you in the first place. Ending negative relationships makes room for positive ones. Don't try to hang on, just go with the flow of your transformation.

—Eileen

Is it possible that I was preparing myself for the Craft, even before I knew it was my path?

That often seems to happen. I was stockpiling offbeat herbs and buying and collecting stones for years before I realized I was a Witch. I knew I needed those things, really needed them, but I hadn't a clue why.

Our inner selves often know things before our ordinary consciousness does. I made my black velvet tarot bag in high school, made it with no idea what I was making it for. Everything eventually becomes crystal clear, if we are just patient enough.

—Eileen

How do I measure my progress in the Craft?

You never understand how far you have progressed until you find yourself making a positive impact on people, without even trying. It's a good feeling.

—Eileen

Why does it seem so hard to me, to live and think like a Witch?

Living our lives as Witches isn't as hard as some seem to think. It is just a matter of switching our minds to beliefs most of us haven't been brought up with. That in itself isn't easy, but it is very possible. We have accepted and lived what we have been taught to believe in since childhood, so changing those ideas takes time.

Much love and light will come into your life as you put the effort into living as a Witch, each and every day. It may take some effort at first, but by observing the Sabbats, doing your rituals, and meditating, you will come to realize that these things are part of our lives. They are not things Witches feel they have to do physically every day, but things they do consciously and subconsciously, because they have become part of our very lives.

—*Cerelia*

I am my own priestess!

By George, I think you've got it!

—*Cerelia*

I am afraid to cast spells because I don't think that I have subdued my dark side or can control it.

That's why thorough inner work is so important when we are new to the Craft. We have to release our anger and whatever other negative baggage we have accumulated along the way. We must find balance, must truly know ourselves before we can trust ourselves with magic. When we're ready, we know it.

—*Eileen*

Is it okay for new Witches to read from copies of spells and rituals?

I think it's acceptable, especially for a beginning Witch who is very new at spells and such. But as you progress (unless you have a serious memory problem) I suggest that you speak from your heart instead of reading from a copy. You can eventually become good enough to be very inventive and spontaneous with your words.

It is hard to be looking down all the time and trying to work with your full emotions while reading and doing other things within your ritual. It does take practice, but if you absolutely can't remember what you want to say, you must do what works best for you.

—*Cerelia*

What should I do, now that something amazing has happened?

You had your first magical experience. Savor it. Give thanks for it. Meditate on what it means for you. Have a plan for what to do with the energy next time: heal someone, make wishes, give it back to Gaia as healing energy, or whatever.

—*Eileen*

What will become of me if I determine that Witchcraft isn't the right path for me?

Witchcraft isn't a cult that tries to prevent you from leaving. This is a free planet, and only you can make your spiritual choices. It's okay if you come to the decision that Wicca is not the right path for you. There are many roads leading to the top of the mountain. All that matters is walking in the light and finding the path that is right for you.

—*Eileen*

YOUNG
WITCHES

What do you think of young Witches?

Many young "Witches" seem to take delight in just using the word *Witch* to shock people. There is no depth to them. They understand very little about what it means to be a Witch or about what a great responsibility it is. All young Witches aren't like this, but many are. Perhaps this is because most of them haven't had the advantage of working with other Witches. They have had no one to teach them how to find their own power, or how to find the spirituality within themselves. For them, Witchcraft is just a party.

—*Cerelia*

My friend says . . .

Kids learning about magic from their friends is usually a major problem. Lots of strange magical rumors get started because one teen tells another something outrageous, swears that it's true, and the story flies as fact through cyberspace.

I want to stress to all teen Witches how important it is to do your own research, to read serious books, and to learn about the Goddess and the wheel of the year, as well as about casting spells.

Serious kids get offended when I say these things because they think other teens are like them, but there are hundreds of young people out there who think they can't cast spells until they find the fourth Witch for their circle.

—*Eileen*

Another kid told me I was full of it and didn't know what I was talking about because I said I practiced Wicca. What did I say wrong?

Oh, to be in school again. Of course I'd like to say that this kind of thing doesn't happen after high school, but I can't. It's just rough being young and in school with these kinds of people. They can make you feel like you are always under their scrutiny. You said nothing wrong, but there are always people who will try to steal your energy, try to flatten you like a pancake. Don't let anyone do that to you.

You owe no one explanations, especially if they are not smart enough or kind enough to ask nicely for information. Be ready to give correct information when someone asks out of sincerity, but you owe them nothing when they act as that person did.

—*Cerelia*

Do you think that some Witchcraft books are just written to make money, rather than to promote spirituality?

I think that a few works by a few authors look very suspiciously like a way to cash in on the teen crowd, mostly on the very young teens of thirteen or so. The authors defend themselves by saying that someone is going to do it, so it should be done by someone ethical, but it doesn't look that way to me in all cases.

Kids tend to look for a quick fix. Most of them don't want to hear about spirituality and harming none. They need time to grow, need very insightful and caring information, before magic and spells are even mentioned. Someone needs to get back to the ethics of Witchcraft for teens.

It is no wonder there are so many misconceptions about Witchcraft. Some of our very own are letting themselves fall into the hype and easy money that the subject of Witchcraft is bringing these days.

—Cerelia

Witch kids are different from other kids. This makes for a hard time at school, doesn't it?

Of course we were always different—we're Witches. A lot of us were proud to be different. We enjoyed dancing to the beat of music that only we could hear. We had plenty of friends and normal relationships, despite being different. Please don't assume that all Witches had a bad time in school.

—Eileen

What should young Witches watch out for?

No young person should go to meet anyone from the Web unless they have an adult, preferably a parent, with them.

—Eileen

Remember, in your search for knowledge, that there are terrible people out there: in your own town, on the Internet, etc. Be careful whom you put your trust in.

—Cerelia

I have long feared that some creep would lure young people with pseudo-Gardnerian hogwash in order to gratify himself sexually. The best way we can protect our Pagan young, and all the wannabe witches out there, is to get the word out: such "initiations" are totally bogus.

—Eileen

I am still very young and unsure where I'm going, spiritually speaking. I'm in a hurry to find my spiritual path. How can I help myself?

Take your time. There is no hurry. You still have to decide what path you are on and where you will go with it. You are very young and have lots and lots of decisions to make in the coming years. Making yourself stable and self-sufficient is always first in a young person's life; then come the other decisions. Get through the toughest one first: becoming your own person.

—*Cerelia*

What's a twitch*?*

Twitch is my word for the kind of teen witches who learned everything they know about Witchcraft from ridiculous films like *The Craft*, from Dungeons & Dragons, or who otherwise blur fantasy with reality. Twitch-topics include how to cast circles without four witches, shooting fireballs from the palms of your hands, and magical interference in high school relationships.

—*Eileen*

PARENTS

When should I tell my parents that I am a Witch?

You will know when the time is right, whether it is in the near future or when you move out on your own. Sadly, some Witches are never able to tell their parents or family—even though they're grown, have children of their own, and make their own choices about what they believe.

—*Cerelia*

Where should I hide my Wicca stuff from my parents?

It is not our practice to come between kids and their parents. Trying to sneak things past them is unlikely to give them a favorable impression of your religion. When parents seriously oppose Wicca (especially parents who are paying for the food, shelter, clothes, education, and so on), kids should consider saving practice until they come of age and live in households of their own.

—Eileen

My parents are completely against me choosing to be a Witch. What can I do?

Some kids are able to talk to their parents about Witchcraft, but for most it is a very volatile subject. Parents usually don't understand. They are afraid because of what they think they know about Witchcraft and Wicca. They fear for their children, and that is perfectly understandable.

You may not like to hear this, but you should wait until you're older, when you won't have to hide your religion. Young people should respect their parents. It's a rough wait for many.

—Cerelia

Is there anything else I can do, besides wait until I'm old enough to move out?

Read and study subjects that will be an asset to you as a Witch: history, mythology, herbalism, physics, chemistry, languages, astrology, psychology, and so on.

—Eileen

My mom won't let me be a Witch, or even a Pagan. How can I learn anything, with her completely against it?

Out of respect for your mother, you should do as she asks. When you are older, you will be able to make the decision for yourself and follow your own path. You can still follow a Pagan path in your heart, though, even if you are making your mom happy by observing her religious beliefs for now. All paths lead to the same place, the place of the heart.

Wicca is lived every day, by loving and revering nature, all of the animals, plants, and humans on Earth. Start there. That is definitely something you can do in your heart.

—*Cerelia*

My parents won't let me burn candles in my room. They just don't understand!

Unless you're paying for the fire insurance, it's hard to argue about candles. The way to show parents that you are mature enough to choose your own religion, and responsible enough to burn candles in your room, is to impress them with your integrity and trustworthiness. Doing well in school, keeping your room clean, having a good attitude, getting rid of negative friends, being helpful around the house, respecting deadline and curfews . . . all these things help.

—*Eileen*

Why does my mom hate what I have chosen to believe in?

Why argue and hurt your mom now? A good parent should be honored and respected. The Pagan path, and especially the Witchcraft one, is a beautiful path that most people do not understand. They are afraid of it, especially a parent who fears for his or her child. The word Witch brings enormous fear to the hearts of parents, with good reason, after the Christian church made it such a horrendous word of horribly evil practitioners.

Try to understand her fears. Know that as a child you will not be able to talk to her about this, but as you grow and you're more able to talk with her about such things, she will realize that you are following a wonderful path of light. She will see this by your example.

Always let your mom know what is going on in your life, even if you know she will be angry. Usually the anger fades, and parents are just happy that their child can come to them when they are in doubt.

—*Cerelia*

Will family conflict about my religion end after I leave home?

Who is to say that your own children won't dislike your path? To me it is unlikely, but still possible. Unlike other religions, we wish our children well with whatever path they choose. All paths lead to the same place.

—*Cerelia*

My family doesn't understand about Witchcraft. I can't wait to move out!

You sound like a typical teenager. Unless you have serious family problems, this is a basic teenager/parent problem. Everyone's in such a hurry to move out. Be patient. Are you able to do some spells quietly, without upsetting everyone, until you feel you can talk to your parents?

Yes, some kids will never be able to talk about it until they do move out. There are also adult Witches who feel they will never tell their parents. It doesn't really matter, though. Everyone is on the same path, they just don't know it yet, and things are changing. Maybe not fast enough, but people are starting to become more aware. The public understands the words Witchcraft and Wicca more and more each day.

Wonderful strides have been made by Witches who are able to be spokespersons, Witches who are trying to stop the stereotypes and teach what Witchcraft and Wicca really are. If you truly care about your parents you can wait to grow up. Understand that you are the person whom they care the most about in this world. You have to be as patient with them as they are (or try to be) with you. It's not an easy job for either side. Time goes by fast, so don't waste it by wishing it away.

—Cerelia

LEARNING

Why does almost every Witchcraft author say something different about the same subjects?

Wicca is a faith with guidelines, not rules. Consider all the books you read to be providers of ideas and methods that you can adopt or reject. Don't be intimidated and do things that don't make sense to you, just because some other Witch says you should. Do, however, listen to the wisdom that other Witches have accrued through experience (trial and error). Doing so can prevent you from making dangerous mistakes, such as summoning things you don't know how to get rid of.

—*Eileen*

Witches find out what works for us as individuals. You may read how to do something one way, and the next author says, "Absolutely not." You'll begin to learn what works for you, and it doesn't matter what any single author may say.

—*Cerelia*

Why does there seem to be a disagreement about what we call this path we are all on and where we are at on this spiritual journey?

It doesn't really matter if we want to call it a journey, a road, or call it beginning right where you are at. We may say, philosophically, that we have already arrived, but in our own minds, we don't really comprehend it as such. Many Witches need to re-learn and re-think, in order to realize they have known the answers all along.

—*Cerelia*

It confuses me that so many Witches do things differently, and they don't always agree.

The differences are minor, or inconsequential. They usually make no difference at all. One Witch does a ritual or spell one way, but the next Witch does it slightly differently. For example, one Witch uses deities, and the next Witch doesn't. The first Witch's candle color or correspondence is not the same as the second Witch's. It's okay. You use what works for you. The magic is in the intent, not in the ritual or tools used.

To learn and to share is what we are all here for. Every Witch may not agree totally on certain subjects, but as long as a Witch is following the path of his or her heart, and respects others, whether we agree or not is not the most important part.

—Cerelia

It bothers me that other Witches seem more knowledgeable and more powerful than I feel.

We each have a special gift of one sort or another. Keep searching. Don't allow envy of other Witches' gifts to prevent you from discovering what yours are.

—Eileen

What if my library doesn't have the books I need?

Librarians can be extremely helpful about ordering books. Try asking a librarian to help you with specific titles or utilize many library systems online catalogs.

—Eileen

It bothers me that I have no one to turn to for answers.

You are having the same problem most newcomers have, that is, letting go of their old beliefs and religion. You still feel the need for a church or some kind of structured religion, but that isn't Wicca, nor is it Witchcraft. We have no dogma. This is a personal religion, and you are the most important person in it. You have to look within yourself, not outside, for all your answers. It's not easy. In Witchcraft, you are on your own. Take responsibility for yourself, instead of leaving it to a god or goddess.

I wish you the best in your search for answers. Learn that you are what is most important, not a church, nor dogma, nor a congregation.

—Cerelia

I feel naive when I ask other Witches questions.

Please don't feel that way. We all remember starting, and we are all always learning. I learn new things from novices all the time.

—Eileen

I'm very impatient. What should I do if I can't stand to wait for what I need to know?

Don't think of it as waiting, but as a time for learning. Witchcraft is a life-long learning process. There is no need to be in a hurry. Patience is the hardest part of becoming a new Witch. There is a lot of reading and experiencing that has to be done. It doesn't happen overnight. To do it right takes a lifetime of living and learning.

—Cerelia

Study, meditate, and your answers will come in time. This is your personal journey. It is perhaps the most important thing you will do in this lifetime, so take your time and enjoy it. Be patient with yourself.

—Eileen

I have been reading every day and visiting tons of Web sites, but I still feel lost on a lot of subjects about Witchcraft. I am so stressed.

It just takes time. You are trying to change your whole world, your upbringing and whole way of thinking, in a very short time. That causes stress. There will be less confusion if you read some good books, instead of relying on Internet sites that may be filled with a lot of misinformation and contradictions.

The absorption of all of this new knowledge is one of the hardest problems for new Witches. You will only be comfortable with your new path after you have practiced it. We take our former religions, such as Christianity, for granted. We were raised on them. We know our old religion very well. Most Witches haven't grown up Pagan, so changing your thoughts and whole belief system is very difficult. It takes time, so don't hurry yourself. You don't have to learn everything at once.

—Cerelia

Sometimes I feel overwhelmed, like I can never possibly know it all.

Science, the environment, spirituality, Nature, mythology, tarot, divination, deities, Craft history, and so forth . . . the list goes on and on. If you find yourself getting overwhelmed, try to concentrate on one aspect at a time. I always suggest reading about the spiritual side of Wicca first, and also reading some Craft history. You might find it helpful to focus on just a couple of things at a time. You won't feel so overwhelmed then.

—Cerelia

You have information overload, so you need to put all your books aside for a while. Meditate. Think about what things and experiences have been most meaningful to you since you began practicing. Remember what gave you joy. Incorporate those things which resonate with you, and jettison the rest.

None of us will ever know everything, because there is always something more to learn. This is what makes life so interesting. We are all always learning, no matter how long we have been Witches, or how adept we are at magic.

—Eileen

Is it okay to take a break for a while?

Absolutely. Always take a break when you need it. Once you learn enough, and you are comfortable with what you've learned, you can slowly incorporate the Craft into your everyday life. In this way, it won't feel so stressful.

You have to pace yourself, so that you do not get overwhelmed, or you will just end up confused. Relax. You have a whole lifetime to learn and explore.

—Cerelia

That's perfectly normal. Some days I don't even turn the computer on, to give myself a rest from everything.

—*Eileen*

Since I began in the Craft I have had more dreams than ever before, dreams which are more vivid and intense than my dreams used to be. Does this make sense?

It makes perfect sense and is something that other Witches probably experienced when they first began. Studying Witchcraft is unlike studying ordinary things. It opens your third eye. It raises your consciousness. It makes you aware of your connection to everything else in the Universe. It activates the process of remembering, if you have been here before—especially if you have practiced magic in a previous life. Try keeping a dream journal during this phase. Perhaps your dreams have things to teach you.

—*Eileen*

The more I learn, the more convinced I am that this is the right path for me.

Most of us know exactly how you feel.

—*Eileen*

I read, I study, I subscribe to e-lists, and I am making a Book of Shadows. What else should I be doing to become a Witch?

You are learning, just as you said. You have a BoS, you read, watch, and listen. What could be better? Now just give yourself time. You have the rest of your life.

—*Cerelia*

PRACTICING   *What do I do, after I feel like I have read enough?*

Start doing things. Do whatever calls to you, whatever interests you:

> set up an altar
>
> start meditating
>
> pray
>
> burn incense
>
> begin making or collecting tools
>
> practice rituals, from books or of your own devising
>
> plant a garden (even if it's actually a window box)
>
> start your Book of Shadows
>
> get a cat
>
> start casting spells

The choices are endless. Follow your bliss, as Joseph
Campbell wisely taught. Do whatever feels right for you, in
whatever order feels right.

—Eileen

Am I deserving of being able to practice magic?

We were conditioned by our former religions for years. We
were told that we were not worthy enough, or spiritual
enough, and that someone else is always more worthy than
we. Our priests and ministers were worthy, anyone who had
a religious title bestowed on them, but we, personally, were
not good enough to have everything we want in this life.
Hogwash.

Remember that you are your own priestess or priest in the
Craft. You are entitled to everything lovely and wonderful in

this world. It isn't that we don't have to work for things, but that we have every right to live a wonderful, fruitful life. As we learn our lessons, we attain more and more. There is no more waiting for a god to let you know when you are worthy. You were born worthy.

—*Cerelia*

Yes, you are worthy. We all are.

—*Eileen*

When can I begin practicing magic?

There are no rules for when or where. Begin after you have read and studied a bit. Begin when you feel comfortable in the knowledge you have attained. You will know when the time is right. It is different for everybody.

—*Cerelia*

There really isn't any one answer to when a new Witch should begin with spells and rituals, because we are all so different. Only that person can determine when he or she is ready for spells, I think.

Most Witches will tell you it is a good idea to have a good grounding in the Goddess and spirituality first, before starting magic. Magic is one of the blessings the Goddess gives us. This knowledge leads to respect for magic, to ethical usage, and keeps us from going astray with it.

—*Eileen*

I've never done magic before. How do I begin?

Many of us cast spells without meaning to, before we realized we were Witches.

—*Eileen*

People do magic every day and do not even realize it. Magic can be as simple as a prayer or a request, sent from your heart, even if you do not know where it is going. This is pure intent. The same thing is true with negative thoughts. That is why it is important to learn how important words and thoughts are.

—Cerelia

How will I know if I am doing things the right way?

I want to emphasize the lack of rules. You will, sooner or later, read books and articles whose authors instruct you on the "right" way to do something, be it worship, casting a spell, dressing a candle, celebrating a Sabbat, invoking a deity, or something else. There is no right way to do these things; there is only the way that is meaningful and works for you.

—Eileen

Can I count on other Witches to help me, if I screw up a spell?

If other Witches come in and clean up your magical messes for you, you will never learn not to make them in the first place. Prevent magical mistakes by listening to the advice you get from other Witches and heeding their warnings before you do magic. Consider the ethics of any spell before you cast it and don't work magic if you're angry. The one who casts a spell is usually the only one who can something about it if it goes wrong, so focus on preventing mistakes rather than rectifying them.

—Eileen

When can I call myself a Witch?

You can call yourself a Witch whenever you feel you are ready. Witchcraft is a lifetime of learning and living. There is never any hurry or feeling that you can't call yourself a Witch until you have learned everything. We learn every day until the day we die. You are entitled to call yourself a Witch from the time you feel it is right for you.

—Cerelia

In traditional Wicca, a person was called a Witch as soon as he or she was accepted into a Coven. Their year and a day studies began shortly thereafter, within the Coven structure.

Most of us are solitaries and don't really follow the traditional rules, though. I think people are entitled to call themselves Witches whenever they feel entitled to do so. It isn't a title anyone assumes lightly, and we each know ourselves best. So start calling yourself a Witch whenever you feel comfortable with that.

—Eileen

I felt empowered when I finally accepted the title of Witch.

"I am a Witch!" Those four words contain all the power we will ever need: liberation, exhilaration, self-realization, freedom, and empowerment.

—Eileen

I agree, it is very empowering.

—Cerelia

ASSUMING THE TITLE OF WITCH

Can I call myself a Witch before I am initiated?

As soon as you can say the words, "I am a Witch," without any hesitation or feelings of shame or damnation, you have that right. But I also suggest that you self-initiate yourself, by learning the Craft and participating in it for the usual year and a day. You can do this yourself. Take it seriously and know as much as you can before you take on this title.

—*Cerelia*

Why does the title make me nervous?

Some people, I think, feel that they are not sure or know enough about the path they are on. They haven't consciously made the decision that this is the path they are looking for. They should never feel unworthy. I would hope they just weren't sure yet.

—*Cerelia*

I am a man just starting out on this path, and I find it hard to use the word Witch. Is there another description I can use for myself?

Even though there's no real reason to feel this way, I can understand why Witch is hard for a man to call himself. You can call yourself a Wiccan, which is the same as calling yourself a Witch.

The majority of people killed during the Burning Times were women, so the term Witch automatically makes one think of women. Hopefully sometime in the future, the word will be comfortable for men as well. Then all of us will be working together, as the Goddess has meant it to be.

—*Cerelia*

I am over fifty and feel like I am running out of time. How long does it take to call yourself a Witch?

Remember that some twenty-year-olds never really "get it" until they are in their fifties. Becoming a Witch depends on the experiences and knowledge that we have accumulated in our lives, not on age. Some Witches may start at earlier ages, but the wisdom and knowledge that is gained by the time we are fifty is something that younger Witches do not yet have. You can call yourself a Witch as soon as you accept yourself as such.

—*Cerelia*

A Year and a Day Program

What is a Year and a Day Program?

The typical time for a Coven and our Year and a Day Program is just that, a year and a day. You learn new ideas within that time. You follow each Esbat and Sabbat until it becomes as comfortable to you as Easter and Christmas were. You are learning your spirituality and beliefs all over again. There is no hurry, but focusing yourself is something only you can do.

—*Cerelia*

What should I know before I apply for a program?

A Year and a Day Program is something you need to be certain is right for you before you commit yourself to it. It would be a shame to waste your time and the time of others on a program that isn't right for you, so if you have any doubts, don't sign up.

—*Eileen*

Isn't it true that an initiate must maintain absolute secrecy during their year and a day?

Says who? Go with what feels right for you. There are those who will disagree with this, but I am a great believer in "Guard the mysteries—reveal them." That's why my Web site is called Open Sesame.

—*Eileen*

Why does a year and a day usually begin with a dedication?

You dedicate yourself to the service of the Goddess because you are becoming a priest or priestess. This is a beautiful and appropriate first step upon your new path.

—*Eileen*

Can I dedicate myself to the God as well as to the Goddess?

The Goddess, to me, embodies the female and male energies. When I speak of the Goddess, I am also speaking of the God. Some Witches only worship the female aspects of the Goddess, but to me that goes back to the god of Christians, who only see the male aspect.

—*Cerelia*

TEACHERS

I am searching for a teacher. What should I do until I find one?

Every teacher appreciates students who have prepared by learning the basics on their own.

—Eileen

I would like to find a teacher, or other Witches to teach me, but I am afraid.

Then be a solitary. Exchange thoughts and ideas with other Witches through the Web, but make up your own mind about things. No one can prey on you through e-mail, not unless you allow them to.

—Eileen

I want to take classes in the Craft, but they charge a fee for the lectures. Should I be suspicious?

It's okay, if the fee is a modest one, meant to pay for time and cover expenses. But if the Witch who gives the lecture arrives in a new Lexus or Jaguar, listen to whatever your little voice tells you about this.

—Eileen

What is initiation?

INITIATION

Initiation is a personal transformation of crossing over into the Craft both psychologically and symbolically. When one is initiated either into a Coven or as a Solitaire, one experiences three stages: suffering, death, and rebirth. A new Witch symbolically dies and is reborn into the Craft. He or she begins a journey into him- or herself and becomes a new individual, possessing new knowledge and wisdom.

—Cerelia

What should I know about initiation?

While historically initiation was considered dark and forbidding and a promise of service to the Devil, in today's Witchcraft, being initiated usually revolves around the symbolic experience of suffering-death-rebirth. Rites vary according to tradition and can entail elaborate rituals within a Coven.

—Cerelia

Do I have to be initiated before I can start practicing?

Nope. Just enjoy being a Witch and do your thing.

—Eileen

Coven Initiation

Does a Witch have to be initiated into a Coven?

Traditionally speaking, a Witch must be formally initiated into the Craft or have a family member initiate them. He or she must be in training for a year and a day and a women must be initiated by a high priest and a man be a high priestess. By now, however, many Witches are practicing Solitaires who either feel no need for a Coven or believe there is no Coven available to them.

—*Cerelia*

Self-Initiation

Does the solitary Witch go through the three initiation levels?

The solitary Witch decides when he or she has reached each level, according to personal experiences and practices. Whether as a Witch in a Coven, a Wiccan, or a solitary practitioner, dedicating yourself for a year and a day is taken very seriously.

Solitary Witches can attain the stages of initiation in alternate ways that can be elaborate or very simple. For example, a Witch can do an initiate bath or experience the outdoors in order to make contact with the Goddess or he or she can simply make a verbal pledge to the Goddess. Initiation can come all at once, such as in a dream or while meditating. Native Americans and shamanistic practitioners have their own versions of suffering, death, and rebirth. Solitary Witches choose how they will define their own initiation into the Craft.

—*Cerelia*

I had an intense dream where I was initiated into a Coven. Is it possible to actually be initiated this way?

Dreams are very personal, and can mean many things to each individual. In my opinion, you could self-initiate yourself through a dream. That is really quite an exciting way to do it, and if I were going to guess, I would say that you self-initiated yourself. You have decided this is the path for you, and have accepted the Goddess into your heart.

—*Cerelia*

Dreams are sometimes just dreams, even when very vivid.

—*Eileen*

Some Witches tell me that only those who are born Witches and initiated into Covens are "true" Witches.

These Witches are trying to belittle you or belittle the powers of other Witches. These Witches have no more powers than you have inside yourself. Though they may have been taught how to bring these powers out and use them, anyone who truly understands magic and how it works can do the same.

Everyone has a right to the powers that lie within themselves, whether they are born into the Craft or not. The powers are there, and it's your choice to use them.

—*Cerelia*

Scott Cunningham wrote, "Never feel inferior because you're not working under the guidance of a teacher or an established coven. Don't worry that you won't be recognized as a true Wiccan. Such recognition is important only in the eyes of those giving or withholding it, otherwise it is meaningless."[6]

—*Eileen*

What about the Witches who say, "It takes a Witch to make a Witch"?

Yes, some Witches need help finding power within themselves, but this is not the rule. Witchcraft is a solitary path, a path that you journey within yourself. No other human can tell you that you cannot take this journey, or that you are not worthy because another human being did not say it was okay for you to be a Witch.

—Cerelia

I absolutely reject the notion that it takes a Witch to make a Witch, or that only hereditaries are "real" Witches. There are Witches, particularly Gardnerians, who strongly believe this. I strongly disagree, however, because I believe that it is the Goddess who makes Witches. I was never initiated by anyone. Gardnerians would probably say that I am not a "real" Witch because of this, but I just laugh. This is between me and the Goddess. She called my name, and reached out to me. She helped me to remember who I am, and who I have been. Being in her service is the greatest honor of my life. It is the reason I chose to be reborn at this time, in this place, and in this body.

The fact that a Witch does not belong to a Coven, or was not initiated by another Witch, does not make her or him any less a Witch than anyone else. Some of us have been Witches or other magical adepts for several lifetimes, so we simply do what comes naturally to us in this lifetime. Many, many Witches are being reborn at this time. The Goddess needs her Witches, because this is the cusp of an evolutionary leap for humans. Who are we to deny her?

—Eileen

What is the Gardnerian Tradition?

Gerald Gardner holds the distinction of bringing contemporary Witchcraft to the modern world, and he will always be remembered and acknowledged for his contribution. However, there is a lot of controversy surrounding Gardner's practices and the truth may never be known for sure. While many Gardnerians will disagree, I am one who believes he used many of his personal likes and fantasies—especially his love of sexual adventures—in his practice and called it the religion of Witchcraft. For example, being skyclad (in the nude) while doing Witchcraft was said to be mandatory for a Witch. An idea probably constructed by Gardner.

—Cerelia

How are Gardnerian initiations conducted?

In the Gardnerian tradition, an initiation is very formal and held within a magic circle. There are three degress to go through and they can be quite frightening to a totally unaware novice.

The first degree requires dedicants to be blindfolded and tied with cords. In the nude. The initiates must then proclaim that they are ready to be cleansed, "in perfect love and perfect trust." After, they are placed inside the circle and whipped with cords. They then give an oath to guard and protect the Craft and all of its secrets as well as the brothers and sisters of the Craft. Initiates are anointed and the title of Witch is bestowed upon them. They also take a Craft name and are given a set of magical tools.

In the second degree, the Witch is bound and blindfolded again and an affirmation of the original oath is recited. A ritual whipping follows and the Witch chooses a new Craft name.

The third degree concerns the understanding of the Mysteries. This is when the Great Rite (a sex ritual) is done, either symbolically or in actuality.

—*Cerelia*

What do you think about the idea that only Gardnerian initiates are legitimate?

If all Witches had to wait to be Witches until they were initiated by a Witch who had been initiated in an unbroken line of Witches stretching back to Gerald Gardner, there would be very few Witches indeed on this planet.

—*Eileen*

THE BROOM CLOSET

Do I have to tell everyone that I'm a Witch?

It doesn't matter—whether you want to keep it to yourself or shout it from the rooftops, it's your choice. If you feel comfortable, you can tell anyone you want to. All of our circumstances and situations in life are different. Some Witches can come out, and some cannot. It is an individual choice.

—Cerelia

When is the right time to come out of the broom closet?

There are many factors to take into consideration. The number one fear is usually for our children, our jobs, and so on. Times are changing. Though Wicca is becoming more known, it will take time before everyone feels safe enough to say they are a Witch or Wiccan. Some Witches have the freedom to do just that, but some don't.

There are Witches out there who are able to put their lives in the light and speak and teach others about Witchcraft and Paganism. We should be very grateful to them, but we also have to honor the decisions of those who cannot do so.

—Cerelia

I have to be very careful about who I tell, but this doesn't mean I am ashamed of being a Pagan and Witch.

Absolutely! That is how you will be for a while, cautious and, yes, even paranoid. I wish society would change right now, but that will take time and intelligent, caring people. To me, it doesn't matter if I go around shouting, "I'm Wiccan! I'm a Witch!" So many people do that just to get attention. The important part is how I live my life, how I treat others and the world I live in.

What is going on in the background of every Witch and Pagan will play a big role in the future of all of our Pagan families. That is important! Every Witch has a part to play in this life. No Witch is any more or less important than any other Witch, whether he or she can play an active role at this time or not. The Witches who come out often come out slowly, with care. They are our spiritual brothers and sisters of the future.

New Witches and Pagans should not be scared silly thinking they have to tell everyone in the world that they are Witches. Otherwise no one would join us, and learn this beautiful path of the heart. Everyone is on his or her own level, and this is as it should be.

—Cerelia

If all the closet Wiccans came out of the closet, would we get the recognition we need?

Some Witches are meant to be political Wiccans, on the front lines, but some Witches are not able to do this. I know a very outspoken Wiccan who lost his job, three times, because of being "proud." He is protecting his fourth job, because he has to take care of his kids. I wish times were different, but each Wiccan has to do what is right for himself or herself.

—Cerelia

Is it wrong for a Witch to lie about being a Witch?

Coming out of the broom closet is a very personal decision, something only that Witch can decide. It's easy for me to be out because New York is such a diverse, open-minded place. I was afraid to be out of the broom closet in Egypt, though, where Muslim intolerance comes armed with machine guns, so I have a lot of respect for Witches living in the Bible Belt and places like that who bravely come out and be themselves.

—Eileen

These are personal choices, made by different individual Witches with different experiences. Everyone's opinion is appreciated, but always keep in mind that they are opinions. We have seen Witches lose good jobs (and bad ones), but it was the only job they had, so it was very devastating for them.

Most Witches who have to lie, do it in order to keep a very good job or because they need to protect their family. Due to the world we live in, Witchcraft, Paganism, sexual orientation, and so on, can cause many people to do and say things they are not proud of. Witches who are forced to lie about being Witches are not harming anyone. Self-preservation is human, and necessary. We aren't going to hell.

—Cerelia

I live in a small town, and it looks like I might have to move because I have been open about being a Witch.

You are learning why so many Witches live in the broom closet. If you decide it will make your life easier to pretend you have lost your interest in Wicca, there is no harm in that. If you decide to remain out, you had better develop a thick skin and learn not to give a damn what anyone thinks of you. Life can be very hard out of the broom closet. As Old Dorothy said, "Witchcraft doesn't pay for broken windows."[7]

—Eileen

I am so sorry for your situation. It still isn't a perfect world where every Pagan can feel free to expose their beliefs. It is a personal choice, based on the situation of our own lives. But you never know, maybe there is some higher power at work with some outcome you have yet to discover. Maybe you will be able to enlighten some small-minded people with facts. Things could blow over after a while, but small towns are very hard to deal with. It doesn't sound like it is going to be very easy. These are decisions only you can make, by what is going on around you.

—*Cerelia*

Why should a Witch ever bother to come out, if there is such a downside to it?

For me, a big part of being Wiccan is reclaiming the right to live openly as a Witch in the world. We cannot change minds about who and what we are unless we reveal ourselves. This is, in many places, a very dangerous thing to do.

—*Eileen*

What can I do when someone asks me directly what my religion is?

When I lived in Egypt I would answer, "My family is Christian." Muslims would assume that I also was, and I would avoid having to explain things to people who could simply never understand them.

—*Eileen*

How can I ask someone who I suspect is a fellow Wiccan if he or she practices, in a way that won't draw attention in public?

Try mentioning the Goddess, or working Blessed Be or Merry Meet into the conversation. If someone didn't know, they probably wouldn't get it.

—*Eileen*

How do I go about explaining my new path to my spouse and family?

Involving your mate and family in your beliefs does feel strange at first, especially if you all started out with the same old beliefs that most of us grew up with. The way it worked for me was to just take it slowly.

Whenever you have a chance to throw in some bit of information on the history of Witchcraft, spells, candle magic, or whatever may come up, just start talking about it. Don't push it. Don't make long speeches, just a fact or two thrown in now and then. You'll be amazed at how much your husband and kids will absorb. This way they learn slowly not to be afraid or worried.

I have dished out so much information over the years that my family knows and understands what I am, and why. After a while, they discovered that they believe the same. Like most people, at first they had a hard time with the stereotypes (cauldrons, pentacles, athames, and so on), but I took every chance I got to talk about these things, and they grew to understand.

—*Cerelia*

I am hesitant to discuss my religion with people who seem very Christian. What if I have to explain my beliefs?

First of all, there are a lot of open-minded people out there, even Christians. You will know what kind of person you are dealing with as time goes on. There is no need, unless you feel it extremely necessary, to even bring up your religion or talk about your own spiritual choices. It is nobody's business, unless you feel the need to tell someone.

A lot of people mistake my altar for a sign that I am Catholic. It doesn't bother me in the least to have them think that. I have never had anyone even ask. They just assume.

Also read, read, read. Know as much as you can about being Wiccan before you are put in the position of having to explain it. Knowledge is power. Be confident about the subject before discussing it with anyone.

—*Cerelia*

I admit that I have been hard to get along with lately, but a family member had the gall to tell me that Wicca was making me bitchy.

There is a lesson here for all of us: when we are out of the broom closet, Wiccans (and Witches in general) are judged by everything we are and everything we do. We must lead exemplary lives when we come out of the broom closet, must be poster children for the new image of Witches that we hope will replace the old stereotypes. This is a heavy burden indeed, and something we must prepare ourselves for before we come out to the people in our lives.

—*Eileen*

I feel a need to meet some "real" Witches, but I can't seem to find any.

I think they will come your way when the time is right.

—Cerelia

How do Witches know each other?

We recognize one another by our energy patterns, not by what we wear or the color of our hair or skin. I feel another Witch, rather than see his or her exterior.

—Eileen

How can I meet other Witches?

I believe that as you read, read more, and expose yourself to the energies, like-minded people are attracted to you. They will find you in the least expected places.

—Cerelia

Luckily the Goddess blessed us with the Web, and we can now easily find our own kind, others of like mind. There is such relief in spending time with other Witches, in being free to say what you really think without anyone looking at you like you're crazy.

—Eileen

I am afraid to meet Witches on the Web, because they might not be ethical practitioners.

I have often felt that way as well, but the few real connections you make with wonderful Witches are well worth wading through the other nonsense on the Web.

—Eileen

I can't find Witches or Wiccans in my area.

Sadly, many wonderful people are too afraid for their jobs and their families to list themselves on the Internet as Pagans and Witches. I can't blame them. I believe there is a vast amount of us out there, but many are not able to come out at this time. I look forward for a day when it is not this way.

—*Cerelia*

I finally found a group of Witches, but they use drugs as part of their practice. Am I a prude, for disapproving of this? My family comes first.

This is exactly the reason why I push spirituality so much. If someone doesn't have the spiritual ethics to become a Witch or Wiccan, they end up in groups like the one you just mentioned. It sounds to me like you know your priorities and what kind of life you want. Your family and livelihood come first, which is as it should be. This is something to be very proud of.

A Witch takes responsibility for himself or herself. That isn't accomplished with drugs and disrespecting your own life. Be proud of being a prude! It just means you have ethics and pride in yourself and your family. You will be a much more powerful Witch than those who have no pride, or respect, or understanding of the true mysteries of the Craft. I think you are much better off being a solitary, but that is just my opinion.

If you could look for some Pagan gatherings, so you can celebrate with others and not worry about a Coven right now,
you would feel a connection with others, without the pressure of Witches who don't sound to me like they have it all
together as Witches. Or know what it means to be one.

Don't get me wrong. Covens are great, when you find a wonderful group of Witches to work with——not party with.
With the right Witches, it does feel like a celebration every
time you get together. I wish this for you. Be patient, and it
will happen.

—Cerelia

TEACHING

There have been a lot of wonderful changes in my life since I began accepting students.

That is why I always say, "Blessed be those who share knowledge." The more we give, the more we get; especially when we give without any thought of what we will get in return.

—Eileen

Why don't you take students?

I don't take students because I haven't got enough time or energy for it. I'm disabled, function best at home, and have a lot of obligations that keep me tied to the computer, so I seldom leave the house. There are lots of good people who do take students, though. Keep up with your own studies as well, and ask your teacher (when you find one) to clarify anything you have trouble understanding.

—Eileen

CHAPTER THREE

A Witch's Life

Should our aim, as Witches, be to live apart from the reality of this world?

As Witches, we know that we live in this world. We are a magical part of it. To try to exclude ourselves from the world is not what being a Witch is all about.

—*Cerelia*

What's a Witch's life like?

I think that a lot of Witches find themselves in the role of caretakers. It seems like a natural way of life for us, always being there for someone else. This is very hard. We have to remember to take care of ourselves, too, or we are not able to take care of others.

—*Cerelia*

What kind of jobs do Witches have?

It's no accident that we see so many Witches who are nurses and teachers. There are no statistics on this, so far as I know, but if there were I'd bet that nursing would be the most common profession among Wiccans: nursing, midwifery, every kind of hands-on healing and care giving. Teaching and computer jobs would probably follow right behind nursing.

—*Eileen*

Is it possible to connect the spiritual side of myself with the everyday reality of my life?

Yes, we as Witches can and do connect the two, but this takes time. We are human. We are learning many lessons every day. We connect the two, but we never deny either one. Witches still have to deal with the daily nonsense, but with time we learn to laugh a bit more, back off a little more, lighten up, and try to figure out what lesson we are learning, or what energies we may be attracting by reacting a certain way.

—*Cerelia*

Should we try to achieve perfection?

Perfection is usually out of human reach, but I would agree that we should always try to do our best. This is about having pride in oneself and one's work, not about trying to avoid negative consequences from the god/desses.

—*Eileen*

How do I change myself and my life? Can I use magic for this?

Find out who you really are, and learn to love and respect yourself. There is much to it, including lots of changing yourself from the inside out. Yes, you can do this with spells and rituals, and a deep belief in yourself and the Goddess.

It's not an easy journey, but it is worthwhile one. No one can solve all your problems, because it is only you who can do that. You have to believe in yourself and your own powers. You have to read and study all about Witchcraft, and know what every author is talking about. It's magic alright, but you have to understand how it works before you can start to help yourself.

—*Cerelia*

Our thoughts have strength and force, have magical power. We can manifest results and transform our lives and ourselves with the power of positive thinking.

—Eileen

Why do so many Witches seem to have martial arts backgrounds?

The mental discipline is a big reason why so many Witches are or have been involved with martial arts.

—Eileen

Where can I find a metaphysical fitness program, something for the mind, body, and spirit?

Look to the East: yoga, Tai Chi, Shaolin kung fu, and so on.

—Eileen

ADVERSITY

How do Witches deal with problems?

We find strength within the Craft. A lot of Witches have very stressful lives, for one reason or another. Maybe this is the way it is supposed to be. Our lives are full of turmoil and problems so that we learn to deal with them, and change for the better. If we didn't have the challenges, perhaps we wouldn't have looked for a spiritual path. Witches look for ways to overcome our problems, and make whatever changes we need to make in our lives. We are being led back to the Craft.

Some of our greatest problems and most devastating challenges in life are also blessings. They are gifts, without which we wouldn't learn all the many lessons we have yet to experience.

—Cerelia

There is great truth in these wise words. The Goddess tempers her priest/esses. She gives us challenges to make us strong enough for her service. How we react to the things we face is what determines who we are: how much backbone we've got, and how deep our spirituality runs.

Witchcraft definitely isn't for wimps and whiners. Finding the blessing in a tragedy is a sacred task, as is finding meaning in difficult circumstances.

—Eileen

Why do I have so many problems?

Most Witches seem to face a lot of serious adversity, to have more troubles than other people do. Almost every Witch I know is ill in some way, or faces a particular challenge in his or her life. Gay Witches have the hardest time of all. I can think of two reasons for this: the Universe doesn't give us more than we can handle, and Witches can take more than most people could bear. I think this is how the Goddess makes us strong enough to become what we are meant to become, and to do the work we are meant to do. One of my favorite quotes is, "Whatever does not destroy me makes me stronger."[8]

Adversity strengthens us, challenge builds character, and illness teaches us important lessons, such as compassion. The Goddess tempers her Witches in the forge of life. Believing this is a source of strength for me. It helps me to make sense of my life.

—Eileen

Is there any disease which is peculiar to Witches?

There hasn't been a study of this, so far as I know, but it seems to me that there is an amazingly high number of Witches with fibromyalgia.

—Eileen

My whole family seems to have been sick all winter. Am I cursed?

Things mostly just happen. If your household is usually very healthy, it was just your turn of the wheel to have a cycle with illness. Changing weather patterns, such as those caused by global warming, are affecting many life cycles, including those of plants, animals, and viruses. Everything is connected. There is a lot of illness every winter, in many places on the planet.

I know some magical practitioners, mostly non-Witches, who are extremely paranoid. Whenever something bad happens, they assume someone hexed them. They spend a lot of time practicing defensive magic, and even aggressive magic, because of this. They spend lots of time, energy, and money on charms and spells to protect themselves and send back whatever they think is being cast on them. Our lives are what we make of them. That's a sad way to live, in my opinion, but to each his or her own.

—*Eileen*

When I'm having a really bad day, I find that it helps to laugh.

That's a good insight. It is a Native American teaching that we may not be able to control most of the things which happen to us, but we are completely in charge of how we react to them. There are many things in life that will either make us laugh or cry. Choosing laughter is positive and life-affirming. Spirituality isn't austere, as some may think, it is filled with merriment.

—*Eileen*

I try to be positive, even when bad things happen, but I don't always succeed. Can this create bad karma?

We are only human. We don't always have perfect positive thoughts. We get depressed, angry, hurt, and sad, just as anyone else does. The trick is realizing when these thoughts invade, and quickly exchange them for more positive ones. It then gets easier to think positively, rather than negatively.

Usually, after much practice, as soon as that negative thought creeps in, a better solution is quickly provided, as quickly as the negative thought came. I believe that thoughts, good or bad, affect us personally, as to what energies we attract or repel. Our thoughts are magic. As long as we acknowledge them, and do not act on the bad impulses, I don't believe our karma is affected.

In fact, the realization that we are working through our darker side is very important to us as Witches. We don't deny our darker side. It is part of us, but we are learning to balance all thoughts and actions in our lives. That is very good karma.

—*Cerelia*

If you aren't blind or crippled or something, you have no right to be depressed or to feel sorry for yourself.

As a disabled person I feel obliged to point out here that blind and crippled people aren't necessarily depressed, sad, or miserable. I am crippled, going both blind and deaf, and have a small child with special needs to take care of, but I am never depressed.

Life is whatever we make of it. If I got up every morning and thought about all my problems, I guess I might be depressed, but I don't do that. Instead, I count my blessings. Life is magical, unless we screw it up.

—*Eileen*

I have health problems, no money, and can't seem to get ahead without help from my parent. What can anyone do to help me?

The power of a Witch is based on first taking responsibility for yourself. Though I understand you have health problems, you must look at your situation realistically. If your health problems are bad enough to keep you from working, you should file for any kind of help you can get, such as disability benefits, to take some burden off of your parent.

If you are able to do some type of job, you should look extensively into what you are able to do, even if it seems beneath you at this time. If you get a job, you will not only boost your own self-esteem and sense of self-worth, you will be helping your parent out by getting some help. Magic will not help you if you do not believe in yourself, and help yourself first. All the power is within you, nowhere else.

—*Cerelia*

I was abused, and cannot seem to get over it and get on with my life. What kind of help should I seek?

Being Pagan means being personally responsible for ourselves. This means taking personal charge of our own recoveries and overcomings; it means not expecting that we can take our troubles to other people and they will solve them for us. Life doesn't work that way, no matter how much we may wish that it did.

If you were abused or mistreated or taken outrageous advantage of in some way during your life, take action and do something about it: get therapy, activate the legal system on your behalf, let it go, start a support group, or try to help others suffering the same pain you endured. The answer is always different for each of us, and only each of us can individually determine what our own answers are.

Try asking Mother Kali to set you free. Ask her to help you slay your demons. You still have to do the work, but she can be a powerfully supportive goddess in such matters. So can Isis, or any strong Mother Goddess.

—*Eileen*

I had a miscarriage, and I can't seem to get over it and get on with my life. Why did this happen to me? Is it my karma?

Miscarriages don't happen because you are a bad person, or don't deserve a baby; they just happen. Nature usually knows what is best. It's not always something we have done in another life. Even if we feel it is, it is not a punishment, it is just another lesson. There are many lessons to be learned. They are not always easy, but they must be learned nonetheless.

—*Cerelia*

This definitely isn't what you want to hear, but the best advice I can give you is this: get over it. Mourn, grieve, then heal. We are all much stronger than we know. Bad things happen; that's part of life. Dealing with them and overcoming them is part of the karmic work that we are here to do.

—*Eileen*

How can someone deal with the loss of physical function, especially at a relatively young age?

I know how that feels. Multiple sclerosis means "many scars" and is so-called because of the scars it leaves on your brain and spinal cord. The part of my brain that deals with numbers is affected. I can still do basic math (thank the Goddess for calculators), but my ability to do anything complicated with numbers is gone, along with my peripheral vision, and lots of other things. One thing I have learned, though, is that life gives to us with one hand even while it takes back with the other. For every loss, there is a compensating gift.

—Eileen

ANGER

Can anger affect magic?

Yes. Anger tends to color everything it touches, so it can make your spells go wrong.

—*Eileen*

I know that anger and magic don't mix, but I'm always angry. Where do I start?

Where else would you start, but with yourself? Find out what you are so angry about. Work on getting through the anger, and taking responsibility for yourself.

—*Cerelia*

How do I get rid of all the anger I feel?

Anger is a basic human emotion, but what we choose to do with our anger is part of what makes us Wiccan. Nursing grudges is toxic, and expressing anger physically usually involves doing harm. Venting anger or channeling it in a constructive way are good choices.

Exercise: Find a reasonable way to vent your anger. Yelling is my method of choice. Whenever something aggravates me, I yell (preferably when I'm alone, so I don't upset anyone else). I yell, slam things, immediately feel better, and promptly forget why I was angry. Try this. It's a great way to release life's little frustrations instead of allowing them to build up inside you. I wasn't always like this, but having a chronic illness taught me the need to vent. Yelling and slamming aren't for everyone, so it's a good thing that laughter also works.

Exercise: Literally writing anger out of your body is another good method, one that won't upset the people around you. Whenever you feel angry, stop and write down why you're angry. Get a piece of paper and start writing down every black thought and negative emotion that you're feeling. Pour all the venom onto the paper, swear words included. Write small, or use the back of the paper as well, if you're very angry.

You'll probably be laughing at yourself by the time you get to the bottom of the page, and can then burn the paper to totally release the anger. You could also save these papers, and read them every week, or month, or whatever. Don't be surprised if you find yourself laughing at most of the things you got all worked up about. As the months pass, you should find yourself having less and less anger to vent, and can then make a little ceremony out of burning or flushing or burying the papers.

When anger is very deep, or rooted in fear, constructive action is the best way to channel it. I think of my father as I write this, and something he did when I was a child. Crime was rising in New York City at the time, and many homes in our neighborhood had been burglarized. The neighbors, mostly men, went down to the police station to complain about the situation.

When my father came home, he was no longer angry. He had signed up as a volunteer for the Auxiliary Police. He did something concrete, and took back some control of a situation that had seemed out of control to him. Several people signed up that night, but he was one of the few who stuck with it. That was 25 or 30 years ago, and he's still an auxiliary cop, the old sergeant who does the paperwork now instead of going out on patrol. He still gets angry about crime, but he has a positive outlet for his anger.

Channeling negative emotions, such as grief and anger, can result in things that have a wide reaching positive impact. Think about how John Walsh, the host of *America's Most Wanted*, channeled his feelings about his son's murder; or the mother who lost her child in an accident and started MADD, Mothers Against Drunk Driving. They aren't Wiccans, but those were "Wiccan ways" of coping with tragedy.

—*Eileen*

What do I do about the anger I feel toward evangelical Christians?

Though we may come to Wicca full of anger toward the religion we were brought up in, the anger will subside after a while. Most of us have been there. You have to open your heart and remember why you chose Wicca: mostly because it doesn't judge, not like the god you left behind in your old religion.

—*Cerelia*

Carrying anger is very toxic. Try to ignore them, or turn your magical attention to wishing for their enlightenment. If that doesn't work for you, at least find an outlet for the anger and vent it.

—*Eileen*

ACTIVISM

Though I am generally shy, I find that my voice is strong when it comes to protecting our animals.

It is nice when you learn how important it is, as a Witch, to work within your own community whether it is for animals, the environment, or for people in general. If we could all find one way in which to help someone or something, what a difference we Witches could make.

—*Cerelia*

How can we change public perceptions of us?

The best way to change society's attitude toward Witches in particular, and Pagans in general, is to be the best people we can be, the finest and most honorable people. We who are out of the broom closet need to think of ourselves as ambassadors who represent all Witches.

It is up to us to make the truth about us known, up to us to debunk all the ridiculous myths and stereotypes. It's important to let no media slur or factual error pass without notice. Writing letters is one of the ways we can encourage enlightenment, and help things to change. Anything we can do to help, from organizing petitions to casting spells, is an excellent use of our time and special abilities. Most people, whatever their religion, come to respect Wiccans once they get to know us.

—*Eileen*

I get so angry when . . .

I'm a big believer in "don't just get steamed—write letters." Don't rant. Be polite, and be specific. Make your point as clearly and succinctly as you can. It is very important, I think, for all of us to make our voices heard as Wiccans whenever something offends or outrages us. I think that when enough people write enough letters, positive changes take place.

—*Eileen*

I do not think Pagan activism is a big deal. Others will take care of it.

If it is not a big deal to someone, then no matter what the cause, they will wait around for someone else to fix everything.

Just being on this list with Eileen and others sharing lots of information, such as this topic, opens a Pagan's mind to what is going on in the world, and what could possibly happen, not just to Pagans, but to people of any other religion and their rights as well. It may help some Pagans make up their minds when it comes to voting, and that is a big deal.

—*Cerelia*

I lost my job because I am a Witch, but the support I got from other Pagans turned this terrible ordeal into a positive experience.

That's what the whole global Pagan community is for. Remember this as the years pass and be of assistance whenever you see another Witch attacked in person or in print.

—*Eileen*

Our government and political structure are too corrupt to ever properly recognize Wicca as a religion.

If you're talking about the U.S.A., try living in some other countries before you condemn the system here. We have it a lot better than most people on the planet do. America has plenty of problems but it's still a country that people line up to get into, not get out of. We just need to keep reminding Christian fundamentalists that this is a democracy, not a theocracy. If we are unhappy with the way things are here, it's up to us to work to change them.

A good way to begin is by registering to vote and taking the time to vote in every election for the candidates who come closest to sharing our viewpoints. Finding out where candidates stand on questions such as freedom of religion and tolerance of diversity is something we need to learn to do, in order to make informed decisions. We need to use a Witch's point of view in deciding whom to vote for.

—Eileen

I don't care to get involved in Pagan activism because it's such a waste of time.

If no one did anything to make our government accountable, women would still not be able to vote, slavery would still be going on, and so forth. Our rights would be their rights. They would decide as to how they see fit to bestow on us what they think we are entitled to. Very scary. I respect your opinion, that you don't like to get involved with what is unimportant to you, but I would hope you would highly respect all the people through history who fought for their rights and the rights of so many others, whether Pagan or Christian.

—Cerelia

When I look the word Witch *up in dictionaries, the definitions I find really upset me.*

What most dictionaries say about Witches is offensive. This sounds like a project that needs doing, a letter-writing campaign to dictionary publishers. I'd like to believe that hundreds of letters about this from all over the planet crossing an editor's desk would bring about a positive change. It would be very helpful if we could get publishers to include the religious aspect of Witchcraft, to at least say that it is a Pagan belief system, or a Goddess religion, or something like that.

If you have read *Ivanhoe*, or *The Merchant of Venice*, you will recall how offensive the descriptions of Jews are in those otherwise great literary works. The notion that it is acceptable to describe Jewish people in such terms is long gone, so it's up to us to make sure that Pagan faiths and practices are treated with the same respect and sensitivity.

—*Eileen*

Don't you think that Pagans and Witches should be more informed before supporting fellow Pagans when they do not have the whole story themselves?

That is a good reminder to everyone, that just because someone says something, it doesn't always mean it's factual; especially when we are dealing with personal opinions and stories that are spread on the Internet. Don't repeat them, unless you are absolutely sure you know the whole story, which is almost impossible when we are dealing with the Internet.

I am not saying that any opinion is true or untrue, but when we as Pagans and Witches want to get involved in something, we should at least make sure we know all the facts. There are organizations that fight for the rights of Witches and Wiccans, that go out and investigate these kinds of stories. These are the ones that we usually consider to be true, and then consider whether we want to get involved and help out.

Please don't ever assume that Witches considered any story absolutely true just because someone put it in print. We're a little smarter than that.

—*Cerelia*

It offends me when shops and Web sites sell black magic supplies as well as the things I need.

If all Wiccans were to refuse to patronize suppliers who also carry dark side merchandise, we would see the marketplace change.

—*Eileen*

Most Witches can make little difference for the Pagan movement. Those who are very active are usually that way because they are so anti-Christian.

Every American Witch, if eighteen, can vote; so they most certainly can make a difference. Many Witches are into human rights, animal rights, environmentalism, and so on. They do a lot of good about different things, every day. Don't underestimate Witches. We have doctors, teachers, lawyers, nurses, moms, dads, and others who may have mundane everyday jobs but who make a difference in this world, one way or another. They do this because they care a lot.

It's offensive to say that we only care about ourselves and just talk about our religious rights because we dislike Christians. We respect all the other religions that need to have their rights upheld and respected, just as much as Christianity. Every

Witch knows that to be a Wiccan, is to respect all other religions. Those new to the path may struggle with this at first, but I hear very little Christian bashing from Witches, except from new Witches, who need to let it out at first. Then they learn more, understand more, and learn to ignore the one-sidedness of Christianity. They learn to accept their beliefs as theirs.

We are not hating or bashing Christianity when we actively pursue our own religious rights. That's ridiculous. We are demanding the same rights as any other religion. This will not happen by taking the attitude that it is wrong to do so, or to just let someone else do it.

—*Cerelia*

Having to swear on the Bible *in court bothers me.*

It doesn't really bother me. I'd tell the truth whether I was swearing by Odin, Jove, Isis, Thoth, or Brigid. It's just a custom.

—*Eileen*

My school has restricted the computers so that we cannot use them to search the Web for information on things like Wicca, Witchcraft, and Paganism. What can I do about this?

If they do allow students to search for information about other religions, and you live in the States, that's actionable. Contact the American Civil Liberties Union if you want to make a big fuss about this. If not, look for information on related topics they cannot possibly object to: mythology, astrology, herbs, Pagan cultures, history, and so forth.

—*Eileen*

I love books and bookstores, but the way that some shops deal with books about Witchcraft makes me angry.

I agree. Something which really annoys me is finding books about Wicca in the New Age (or Witchcraft or Metaphysics) section, instead of the Theology section.

—*Eileen*

I was so angry when a major bookstore chain dropped all their Pagan, Wicca, and Witchcraft books, that I had to write to them.

—*Cerelia*

I was deeply offended when my local government proclaimed a "Jesus Day." Why couldn't they have made it "Practice Your Faith Day" or something like that, instead?

That would have been less offensive than Jesus Day, but still offensive to atheists. For those in other countries who may not know this, American democracy is based on the idea that religion and government are separate. When Christians try to push their religion in official ways (prayer or Ten Commandments in school, Jesus Day, nativity scenes outside municipal buildings at Christmas, and so on) they are violating the Constitution. When it is elected officials who do this, it is extremely alarming to citizens who value democracy. It's treason, in my view.

—*Eileen*

THE FAMILY — HOME LIFE

I feel like I have been neglecting my religion, because I have been so busy taking care of a family member.

Witchcraft is very much about service to others. In helping your relative, you are indeed serving the Goddess.

—Eileen

MIXED FAMILIES

I have explained everything that I could to my mom about Paganism and Witchcraft, and she does not look down upon me or my path.

It's great that you two can talk, and that you have the fortunate circumstances of her actually listening and trying to understand. Many Witches do not have this. Be patient and respect her beliefs, as she is trying to understand yours.

—Cerelia

I am Wiccan, but my spouse is Christian. We're constantly running into issues. Holidays are a major one.

Many of us live in families in which we are the only Wiccan, or the only Witch, or the only Pagan. Working through religious difference to achieve mutual respect and tolerance isn't easy, but it is a worthwhile journey.

My husband was Muslim before he became Kemetic. Some years, it was both Yule and Ramadan at our house. (Ramadan is a moveable feast, so it doesn't always fall in December.) The best course in mixed families is to just merrily celebrate everyone's holidays, I find.

—*Eileen*

My spouse is of a different religion. Someone accused me of recruiting, by telling him about Witchcraft, but I think all I'm doing is trying to explain things to him.

It is nice when you have someone to share and discuss your beliefs with, whether they want to undertake everything you have undertaken or not. It does cause problems when one of our partners is of a different faith. We would like it if it did not matter, but in many cases it does.

You are not recruiting anyone. I see it as a wonderful chance to share your path with someone you love. Sharing your path with a partner makes studying and exploring that much more exciting. I am glad you can share things with your husband, because some Witches absolutely can't.

Just recently, someone I know gave up Witchcraft because her new husband was a devout Catholic. She was told it was either him, or Witchcraft. To some people, it is a very big deal when they are faced with this situation.

—*Cerelia*

My husband thinks Witchcraft is Satanism. How can I reassure him that it is not?

That's a very hard situation for both of you. It is perfectly understandable why he is reacting this way, after so many years of misinformation. You cannot force someone to understand, but by your actions, thoughts, and deeds, he will surely see there is nothing to fear. Patience is definitely a virtue.

Learn all you can in the way of answers beforehand, because he will start asking questions before you know it. Be prepared, so that you can answer with knowledge and heart. Maybe start by just lighting some candles, especially on the Sabbats; candles that correspond to something. He will start to ask, "Why are you burning that today? Why are you burning that color?" This is a very easy way to help someone understand the beauty of Witchcraft.

Then maybe, slowly, questions will arise that you can answer and you both can talk about it together. It's a slow process (as I know), but it usually has very happy results. Even if he doesn't understand the magic part, and never does, that's not important.

Just getting an understanding of the spirituality will ease his mind immensely. Be patient, and hopefully he will be patient and understanding with you, too.

—Cerelia

My family are not Witches and they really get on my nerves, with their dress code and dietary rules.

Living with a Witch isn't the easiest thing in this world, either: billowing incense, getting yelled at for having negative vibes, not being allowed to touch certain things, and so on. We have to be patient with the people we live with.

—Eileen

Pagans who allow their Christian families to push them around and make them deny their faith, have no right to call themselves Witches.

I never go as far as to tell people that they cannot be Witches. They may have a terrible struggle trying to keep their sanity in terrible family situations, but it is their decision to be part of their families, or not. This is not my decision, nor do I have the right to say that because someone made a decision I don't like, that he or she does not have the right to call herself or himself a Witch.

They are walking down a very hard path, trying to keep everyone happy; but I trust that they will make the best decisions for themselves. They will either deal with it as best they can, as Witches, which is possible; or if the constant harassment is a very serious problem, they have to decide whether or not to sever all ties with their families. There are lots of Witches whose families don't like it, but they still remain Witches.

—*Cerelia*

THE KITCHEN

Studying herbs, since I became interested in the Craft, has made me into a good cook.

Most witches are good cooks, no surprise there. When I think of Witch food (food prepared by other Witches or myself, for Witches) I think of dishes with lots of herbs in them. I often make herb butter for gatherings where each Witch is bringing something. Herb butter and baguettes go with just about anything.

—*Eileen*

I am the rare Witch who cannot cook at all.

For all you Witches who think you can't cook—give it a try sometime. Start with easy things, such as cold foods (salads, raw vegetable platters, drinks made in blenders, and so on). It isn't as hard as you probably think it is.

I barely knew how to boil water when I left home at eighteen. Friends taught me how to make Tunisian Stew in Paris, and that was the only thing I knew how to cook for a long time. When I finally settled into my own apartment the next year, it was cook or starve. I learned quickly, needless to say. I got some cookbooks and learned from them. I also used to try to recreate things I ate and liked in restaurants.

Don't be afraid to experiment in the kitchen. Even if you have to throw some of your first meals away, you learn. Witch knowledge kicks in quickly, and the next thing you know you're a gourmet chef.

—Eileen

What advice do you have for kitchen Witches?

Kitchen Witches should remember to keep their magical implements separate from those used for cooking. I like wooden shish kebab sticks for stirring magical things, since you can just throw them away afterward. Chopsticks work, too. I use an electric coffee grinder as a spice mill for magical recipes, but never use it for anything that anyone will be eating.

—Eileen

—NEW HOME—

I feel lonely and out of place in my new home. What can I do about this?

Congratulations on your new home. Although I know that being on your own can be an exciting time, being alone is often also lonely. With time, I think that you will find solitude and the ability to make decisions on your own to be very satisfying. If you like your own company, then you are halfway there.

Exercise: Bless your home. Smudge your home. Setting up an altar in a special place will make it feel protected, and part of you. An altar is a personal expression of what you believe in, so use statues of deities, flowers and herbs, candles, stones and gems, or whatever appeals to you. You can also pick up many ideas by reading from different books and authors about their suggestions for your altar.

Have you thought about any pets yet? A pet is a wonderful way to share your home, with what may become a beloved familiar.

—Cerelia

When breaking ground for a new home, should I cast a spell to assure harmony with Mother Earth?

If you feel the need for a spell or ritual, you should do one. Some sort of Spirit of Place working might appeal to you.

—Eileen

If I do a house blessing, should I do it on the earth, on the house before it's completed, or when we move in?

All of them, none of them, or whatever feels right to you.

—*Eileen*

Something sad happened on the land where I will be building my home. Is there something I should do, because of this?

Again, cast a spell or have a ritual if you feel the need. I expect you do feel the need, or you wouldn't have asked about it. Some sort of ritual of Peaceful Passage for those who died, or a healing ritual for the spirit of the place might be appropriate. (Spirit of Place doesn't mean an entity, it means the energy signature of the location.)

—*Eileen*

If people who owned the house that we're buying got divorced, will this have a negative impact on our marriage?

At least half the homes in America were probably occupied at some time or another by people who divorced, so I wouldn't allow that to bother you too much. Do some sort of cleansing of the house, such as smudging it with incense or sprinkling it with a magical powder.

—*Eileen*

——————————————————NEIGHBORS——————————————————

What can I do about a very creepy neighbor?

Exercise: Four Thieves Vinegar is the standard potion to use when dealing with negative neighbors. You pour it around your property, especially across the dividing line between your property and theirs. (In an apartment building this would be the hallway, the elevator, the wall that divides your apartments, or any place where your paths cross.) You must be sure to state your specific objective as you pour it (leave me alone, move out, be quiet, or whatever), and to add a phrase such as "for the good of all, and with harm to none."

Four Thieves Vinegar is something that different Witches make differently. To me, based on my research in herbs, it must have garlic and rue in a red wine vinegar base in order to be called Four Thieves Vinegar. Some American folk magic traditions make it with four ingredients.

—Eileen

What can I do about seriously bad neighbors? Everything seems to be going wrong since they moved into the building.

Some suggestions:

Mundane: Report them for anything reportable, such as vandalism and drug dealing. If possible, buy or borrow one of those "nanny cams" and set it up to film anything illegal they may be doing, such as entering your space.

Magical: Get Four Thieves Vinegar, or a Go Away Powder, and sprinkle it where they will walk or otherwise come in contact with it. If you fear doing harm by this because of your understandable anger, get someone else to sprinkle it for you.

Put the sign of the pentacle upon your door. Do this with water, so that it will dry and be invisible, but its energy will still be there. Put the sign of the pentacle on anything that seems to be acting as a portal. Seal any openings that exist between their apartment and yours. Nothing magical is needed, as plain old duct tape will work just fine.

Perform a strong, general cleansing of your space to neutralize any negative vibes they may have given off. Smudging, asperging, sweeping . . . do whatever you usually do. Cast some heavy protection around you and your loved ones. These people may also be casting some form of chaos magic, consciously or unconsciously. Do whatever you can to make them see the wisdom of moving out and moving on.

—*Eileen*

House Guests

Everything has gone wrong since this person came to stay. Could he be a demon?

He's not a demon, just a houseguest from hell. Your home is your sacred space. There is no obligation in Wicca to house people who annoy us, or overstay their welcome. Get him out as soon as you can, and don't allow him to guilt you into extending his stay. We are each responsible for ourselves, so he has to figure out how to put a roof over his own head.

Wish him well if you use a Go Away oil or powder, and ask the Goddess to make the magic work in a way that harms none.

—*Eileen*

LIFE STAGES

————MAIDEN, MOTHER, CRONE————

Don't we best understand whichever phase of life we happen to be in?

Yes, I think all people tend to understand whatever station in life they happen to be in at the time. As young adults, we female Witches know what it is to be a Maiden. We also know the excitement of wanting to experience the Mother aspect. Younger Witches may have trouble believing this, but after we have gone through the Mother phase, we welcome the Crone into our lives. It is just as exciting a time in our lives as Maiden or Mother. We pretty well know what we are by then, and how we believe. We are more relaxed with ourselves. We've been there . . . done that. . . . So it becomes a time to share our wisdom with others.

Enjoy each aspect of the Goddess. You learn so much with each phase of your life. You may believe that all your beliefs and expectations and feelings about things could never change, as Maiden or Mother, but with age, you will be surprised . . . they do, many times, and you begin to wonder how you ever came to some of the conclusions you made, when you were younger.

—*Cerelia*

Can you experience the Mother phase without having children, or do you skip it, and go straight from Maiden to Crone?

I think the Mother phase can be experienced without personally having a child. It may be as a teacher and her class, or with neighborhood children, or with your sister's or brother's kids. It could also be experienced by working for different causes that affect children.

There are lots of different ways of looking at this, as far as how the mothering phase might be experienced. Just because you may not have children, it does not mean you will not still learn many of the lessons of the Mother phase. Don't be in a hurry to get to the Crone. Getting there is half the fun, whether you have children or not.

—*Cerelia*

The Mother phase can be about more than parenting, nurturing, or mentoring. You can give birth to a book, or a business, or a Coven . . . to many things. Lives are so much longer now. Someone has wisely suggested a new ordering of life stages for women: Maiden, Nomad, Mother, Crone. Others would replace Nomad or Mother with Warrior, but I like the addition of a Nomad phase because that mirrors my own life experience.

—*Eileen*

At what age does a female Witch become a Crone?

I think you Crone whenever you feel the time is right. Age is relative. Some women have babies in their 40s, so they're still in the Mother stage in their 50s. Others are busy teaching, or being mentors to young people, or raising their grandchildren . . . you're not a Crone unless you feel like a Crone. I'm very much looking forward to it, myself. The Crone stage means freedom from excessive responsibilities and the chance to finally live a little for oneself. Those of us in the Mother phase look toward it longingly sometimes.

—*Eileen*

————Male Life Stages————

Do males also have life stages?

I have heard several names proposed for the male stages, such as Warrior, Nomad, Mentor, Elder, and so on. Female life stages are biology-based: menarche, childbirth (or mentoring), menopause. In primitive cultures males had an initiation rite that corresponded to menarche, the time at or before puberty when a boy left the women's huts and went to live with the males of the tribe.

If you've read anthropology books about it, you know that these initiation rites were usually arduous and sometimes even abusive. The basic Native American ritual is one example: the youth was separated from the tribe and sent alone into the wilderness for a period of fasting, during which he was expected not only to survive but to find his spirit guide or totem animal, and learn what his path was. When the boy rejoined the tribe he was considered a man—a hunter, a warrior, or a shaman. Male initiation rites enacted death and rebirth, so physical change such as circumcision or scarification, or assuming a new name, was often part of the rites.

The equivalent ceremony in Goddess cultures was sexual, the initiation of a young man into the mysteries of sexuality by an older woman. Gilgamesh bringing a harlot to tame Enkidu in the wilderness is a mythological example of this practice.

Mentoring is the male equivalent of the Mother phase, a time when men help younger males to find their way in the community, the army, or the business world. The third phase of male life is (or should be) that of Elder, of statesman or yogi or sage. This is a time for wisdom and for leading by example, whether it be through active engagement or retirement from the world into spirituality. The god Odin hanging himself from the world tree to gain enlightenment is a good (if extreme) example of this transition to the third phase of male life. Retirement at sixty-five is pretty much the modern equivalent.

—Eileen

───────Pagan Parenting───────

If you don't feel that you can tell your kids about your religion, isn't it dishonest to lie to them about it?

This may sound very dishonest to some Witches, but I don't think it is. Our kids are our first priority. We have to live in this world, even while hoping that someday we will not have to deceive anyone about our religion. If we teach them well, our kids will be open-minded, loving adults who will accept anyone, no matter what their religion. That is what is most important. The future is where everything you have taught them will show.

I know there are Witches who bring their kids up Pagan, and who may not have any prejudicial, or threatening situations to worry about with their children, but this isn't the case for every Witch. Good mothers and fathers always think of their children first. Things are slightly better in our society and schools now, but not a lot better, from what we see and hear. As Witches, I think we know that true religious tolerance is still a very long way off.

So if your question is, "Should I feel guilty for not telling my children of my path, now?" I would say, "Of course not." Do what you feel is best for your family at this time.

Continue on your path, but make sure that you talk to your kids about all the issues and questions that other religions will raise for them. Don't be afraid to ask them. Don't be afraid to let them know how you feel about aspects of certain religions. Hopefully, there will come a day when Witchcraft will no longer be an issue, a day when we can speak aloud with pride about who we are, and never feel any persecution or fear from others. Be open about your religion as well as all others. Then they will be able to make their own decisions.

—Cerelia

Secrets are toxic, especially to children.

—Eileen

How can we teach our children?

Kids are essentially Pagan. That's our natural state, unless a patriarchal culture or religion represses it and imposes a single Sky Father with an all-male priesthood to tell us how to think, feel, believe, act, be. One of the things I most treasure about Wicca is that it is the only faith I have ever heard of that does not try to compel children to any spiritual path. We are always teaching our children, both by word and by deed. I teach my son about ethics, character, and Mother Nature in simple lessons suited for his age. I teach him to have respect for himself and others, reverence for the Earth and the seasons, and kindness to animals.

In our old apartment, there was a lesson about vandalism. We came outside to wait for his school bus and discovered that a graffiti tag had been spray painted on the wall of the post office, so we discussed how bad boys write on walls while good boys would never do such a thing.

Mother Nature was a recent issue, when his friend accidentally shot his new rocket onto the roof, where it got stuck. He wanted me to get a ladder and climb up to get it, but I told him not to worry because Mother Nature would send the wind and return the rocket. It hadn't blown down the next morning, so he was angry with Mother Nature (he said she must be in bed with the flu), and his father got him a new rocket. But the next morning, there was his rocket on the lawn. He was suitable impressed with Mother Nature, and with me.

The next day, he asked me if there is a Father Nature. I said yes, and showed him the Green Man image over my altar. He was quite content with that answer, but insisted on calling him Father Nature instead of the Green Man.

When I light a candle for someone who has asked for help, I call my son over to the altar and explain what we're doing, and why. We hold hands for a moment, and send positive energy (making a wish) for the person. This teaches compassion and charity, as well as magic. If I get feedback about how the person is doing, I tell him. My son will choose whatever religion calls to him when he is old enough to make this choice, but these are lessons which will serve him all of his life, no matter what religion he practices.

—Eileen

How can we teach our children to protect themselves?

Some kids instinctively ward off personal space and put out "don't mess with me" vibes, but other kids need to be taught how to do this. Think about your own childhood: one fat kid was teased, while another wasn't; one low income or skinny child was called names, but another such child wasn't. Some children get picked on, but others don't. Why? This has to do with the way we project ourselves, with how we feel about ourselves, and how we expect others to treat us.

Exercise: Talk to your kids, in age-appropriate language, about their personal space, an imaginary sphere of about an arm's length that surrounds them. Tell them that no one (except mom or dad) has the right to violate this space by entering it without their permission. Teach them to visualize it, imagining it like a force field around them. Kids have great imaginations, and usually take right to creative visualization.

Tell them to look anyone who is threatening or frightening them straight in the eye and stare them down. Have them practice this with the cat, if you have a cat. Tell them to imagine the person being zapped backward by the force field if he or she violates it. This is warding, setting your boundaries and guarding them magically.

Try to respect their personal space yourself, as much as possible, so they begin to believe in it. This will work, but only if the kids also have self-respect and good self-esteem. Enroll them in martial arts, and encourage them with sports or any other activity that makes them feel good about themselves. Use affirmations with them, simple ones they can understand according to age: I am someone, I matter, I am important, I respect myself and others, or whatever. Monitor your own language and that of other adults whom they interact with, to be sure that no one is sending them negative messages without meaning to.

—Eileen

How can we teach our children the Pagan code of personal responsibility?

My son is four as I write this. I am trying to teach him this now, in terms he is able to understand: the television or computer gets turned off whenever you do something you know you shouldn't do. I tell him the same thing every time, "For every action, there is an equal and opposite reaction." He understands this in the most basic way now, but in time he'll really grasp the concept. This will also help his Witchcraft, understanding the laws of physics and how energy works.

—Eileen

Can children appreciate magic?

When I was a child I grew up by a little rock road, next to an enormous farmer's field. Every year it was full of gladioli, in every color imaginable. It was glorious. I, of course, love glads! They make me very happy and peaceful when I see them. Gladioli always take me back to the magic of being a child.

—Cerelia

Magic comes naturally to children. Being a Witch means never losing touch with the magical part of childhood.

—Eileen

What can you do if your kids keep interrupting your drum circle?

Doing anything with kids in the house can be difficult. Try getting them drums of their own. They might really enjoy participating.

—Eileen

How can we encourage psychic abilities in our children?

Acknowledge their abilities. Encourage them. Validate them. Take them seriously. Don't let anyone else teach them that psychic gifts are nonsense. Ask them what they can remember about the life before this one.

—Eileen

How can I prevent miscarriage?

Good nutrition, positive thoughts, a loving partner, prenatal care with a doctor you like and trust, prayers to the Goddess, and love for the baby are all you need. (If you smoke, drink alcohol, or do drugs, cease immediately.) The psychic connection between mother and child is strongest while the baby is in the womb.

Exercise: Speak to the baby with your heart and mind. Tell her or him how wanted and welcome he or she is. Surround both of you with a softly vibrating magic circle of love, and trust that all will be well.

—Eileen

What if you did everything you could, and still lost the baby?

If a pregnancy ends in miscarriage despite all precautions and the best of care, we have to trust that there was a good reason for it. Not making it through was part of that soul's karmic journey. As hard as such a loss is to take, it should be about the baby, not about our heartbreak. Many Wiccans believe that we are reunited with our miscarried and stillborn children in the Summerlands. That is where we will get our answers about our pregnancies.

—Eileen

My family wants to baptize my child, even though I am a Witch.

All religions are on the same path, so to me it depends on the situation. If you are going to let your child be baptized just so that your parents feel their grandchild isn't going to hell, it may not matter. Are they going to continually interfere in your life, though, if you decide to let them have their way in this? Will they badger you about church, and things like that?

You are no less of a Witch if you decide to let your child be baptized. Just be aware of how much more involvement or trouble may be caused by future interference into you and your child's spiritual life. Only you can judge this.

—Cerelia

Is there anything wrong with letting my husband have his way about sending our children to a Catholic school? It's the best school in the area.

My mother was Catholic, but she was not a strict Catholic. She believed in letting us choose our own paths when we got older. My father didn't care what religion we were brought up in, just that we be brought up in one; so of course, Catholicism was what we were raised in.

I understand why a parochial school for your children is a choice that you and your husband are considering. I went to Catholic grade school and high school. They were both excellent schools. I must admit, though, that I would have a very hard time sending my kids into a Christian school now. This is not because there was anything wrong with any of the schools I went to. Academically, they were terrific.

Be very up front and discuss issues with your kids as they grow up in this religious environment. Bring your thoughts and beliefs to your kids, to counteract some of the dogma, guilt, and outright bigotry toward others of different beliefs and lifestyles that is mandated by the Church. Be very instrumental in correcting what they are hearing and being told is fact, then you might be able to handle it.

You can see how other Witches have such a hard time with things they were made to believe as children. Changing lifelong convictions, things that were drummed into you as a child, such as fear of hell and damnation and a vengeful male god, are very hard things to let go of. Don't allow your children to be raised to believe that all these things are true. The choice is always yours. Think it out carefully.

—*Cerelia*

I am afraid that the Catholic school my kids will be attending will find out I am Pagan and come down very hard on them.

Remember that your children don't have to really know the name of your path. Paganism is so natural and beautiful that you can teach it to them without ever giving it a name, until they are older and understand more, and are in a less scrutinized and judgmental environment. You will, however, have to be very concerned about certain things that they will be told in school. You have to be very vigilant about discussing with them what they are learning in all the religious classes.

—*Cerelia*

What can we do about the possibility of violence at school?

We have seen a lot of death and violence in American schools. The Secret Service studied surviving perpetrators of these incidents, and found that a history of teasing and bullying was almost always the cause. We all need to learn from this that allowing kids to be mean to other kids breeds violence, be it suicide or mass murder.

We haven't seen any Pagan kids go to school with guns and hurt others. Teaching our kids about the Law of Three, making them aware that everything they do is eventually returned to them, is obviously a positive thing. Every time there is another horrible school shooting I think about two things:

1. No Pagan kids have shot at classmates.

2. Part of my responsibility as a mother is to keep my son as far away from guns as possible.

Boys and guns; it's a fatal attraction. This is a liberal East Coast attitude, but I cannot understand how anyone with young children, especially sons, could allow a gun in the home. I also think parents should be supervising their kids a lot more closely. If I fail to notice pipe bombs and shell casings in my son's room, I'm definitely not doing my job as a parent. I don't mean we should police our children, I mean we should be interested and involved in their lives, and in their development as human beings. We give up our right to be self-absorbed when we decide to have children. Love means loving our children enough to set limits and say "No" when that is called for.

—Eileen

I am upset because my twelve-year-old daughter says she wants to be a Catholic.

Don't worry too much. I was also very Catholic when I was twelve.

—*Eileen*

Many young Wiccans have adopted the gothic look. My son is one of them, and there is much about this fad that worries me. I have talked to him and feel better, but what do you think about this fad?

Even though we try to understand what our youth is going through with appearance, rebellion, and so on, we must, like you, not forget our role as parents. You talked with your son. You asked questions.

Whether they can see it themselves or not, the very young can and do get caught up in things which at first seem perfectly innocent, so "butting in" is definitely our job. We don't know, most of the time, the extent to which their beliefs or friends take them. One group may be perfectly innocent, while another is deadly. Although I understand what many of the young people are saying about the goth look just being a fad, we parents have to make sure, so that we can help them in case they get too deeply into something negative.

Any fad may have started out very innocently, but these days kids can easily be exposed to things that are ultimately frightening and dangerous. No matter how angry they get, we as parents should never be afraid to ask questions, and demand some answers. You have to be a parent first.

—*Cerelia*

I am troubled about the suicide of a high school girl.

There is an old adage that girls act inwardly, while boys act outwardly; meaning that troubled females are more likely to hurt themselves, while males with the same troubles are more likely to hurt others. A young person's suicide is always a tragedy, but it is less of a tragedy than taking a gun to school and blowing classmates away before turning the gun on yourself.

—*Eileen*

It bothers me that my children are nearly grown and won't be needing me much longer.

Ah, but there are so many needy children in this world. Perhaps you are meant to help others.

—*Eileen*

HUMAN RELATIONS

———————THE WORKPLACE———————

How can I deal with malicious coworkers?

Putting a big bulb of garlic in your desk drawer wouldn't hurt. Garlic is extremely protective, and anyone who comes across it will likely think twice about messing with you.

—Eileen

I know the pain and torment of the back-stabbing of so-called friends at work. Some people steal your energy intentionally, while others do it without knowing they can. Get back your own power, and don't let others steal it from you.

Exercise: One of the best things you can do is to visualize a protective shield around you at all times. Strengthen it every few days. Imagine every mental or physical harm that anyone is directing at you being unable to get through that protective shield. The shield can be white for the Goddess, blue, or purple. Pick a color that means strong protection to you.

If done correctly and strongly, you will be amazed at how much better you will feel. Everyone will wonder why you are feeling so good, when they are trying to send you such harm; especially when things at work are going your way and not theirs.

Also, don't forget the reality we live in. If you are comfortable talking with your supervisor or boss, discuss this with her or him.

Do the same protection visualization with your home. This may help with any negativity that you may be bringing home with you. A shield is something I use continually, like a prayer, before I go to sleep. I protect those I love, myself, and my home this way.

—Cerelia

It bothers me when my coworkers play Christian music tapes.

Turnabout is fair play. Bring in some music that you find spiritual, such as Enya or drumming or whatever.

—Eileen

PAGAN HEARTS

Do Witches believe in soul mates?

Some do, and some don't. I believe in soul mates, but not in the way a lot of others might perceive the idea. Most people who believe in soul mates think this is something that sounds so romantic. They think it means never having any problems, just joy and bliss with this particular person. However, it is the opposite to me.

Yes, you are extremely attracted and do love each other deeply, but you both have a lot of lessons in this life to share and experience. This is the reason you keep coming back and finding each other. Some of these lessons are not much fun. You either choose to learn from each other, or do not. Sometimes soul mates can't get along, because they refuse to learn from each other. That is when the relationship, soul mates or not, will not work.

—Cerelia

I'm the wrong Witch to ask about this. I'm the bah humbug type who doesn't believe in twin souls, soul mates, true love, or any of that. Physical love makes more sense to me, as a Taurus, than romantic love does.

What I do know is that we humans are very complex, each with many aspects. I believe it's very possible to find someone who strongly resonates with a particular aspect of your self. This usually makes for a very intense, very meaningful connection or relationship, but not necessarily for a lasting one. That's just my view of things, though.

If I were a Native American goddess, I'd be Moving On Woman.

I think it's a blessing when you find someone who makes your body sing. It's a greater blessing if that person can also make you laugh. It is the greatest blessing if you can still enjoy that person's company, can stand to have her or him around, after the passionate stage of the relationship evolves.

—Eileen

What do you do if you cannot decide between two potential husbands?

Polyandry is an option for us, as Pagan women. I have always thought that would be an ideal situation, one woman with two husbands, but it would probably work no better than multiple wives do in Islam. Instead of an incredible love life and more security for your children, you'd probably just get more mess in the bathroom and endless sports on the television.

—Eileen

What's the right way to approach a woman?

Honesty and sincerity usually work. There are books devoted to pick-up lines, but that's unnecessary. All a male has to do when he wants to meet a female is go up to her and say, "Hi, I noticed you and I thought you were really interesting/beautiful/attractive/nice/whatever, so I wanted to meet you. My name is _____."

Accompany this with a firm handshake, direct eye contact, and no invasion of personal space. An honest, sincere approach like that will work with most women. It might result in a friendship rather than a romantic or sexual relationship, but a connection will be made.

—Eileen

I am in love with my roommate, who does not return my feelings.

That's an emotionally volatile situation, one that is sure to do harm to one or both of you. You need to move out, as soon as possible.

—Eileen

Someone whom I love has to live with an alcoholic, so I ask the Goddess to watch over her.

She doesn't have to live with him. Coming to that realization might be what helps her to apply tough love, or save herself. We always have choices, even if they are usually difficult ones.

—Eileen

My friend is afraid to do anything she thinks her boyfriend won't like.

That's very sad. Tell her to read *The Feminine Mystique* by Betty Friedan. It's an old book, but your friend has a very old-fashioned attitude.

—Eileen

———————FRIENDS———————

I am sad about my friend, because her religion prevents her from doing things she enjoys.

Our lives are whatever we make of them. I hope your friend can find some awakening soon. This is a beautiful life, in a magical world, and to be restricted in her growth is a shame for her. The same can be said for humans in every abusive situation, not just religious ones.

—Eileen

Several of my friends turned their backs on me after I told them I had become a Witch.

No one needs people like that in their life. Religious conversion is not the only issue that can make you see who your real friends are. My first husband was African-American, and he was shocked by the racist attitude of some of his black friends after he married me. Several of his long term friendships ended because of our marriage, but he saw it as no loss. I had no racists in my life, so it was not an issue for me.

—Eileen

I need a spell to help someone who is being abused by his friends.

Forget the spells. He needs new friends or therapy to help him understand why he considers people who mistreat him to be his friends. I don't know if this applies here, but keep in mind that casting spells for people who have not requested magical assistance usually comes under the heading of magical meddling. It is most often kids who get caught up in this issue, judging from my mail. That makes sense, because youth is the stage of life when one is preoccupied with friends, friendship issues, and social relationships in general.

—Eileen

————PEOPLE OF OTHER RELIGIONS————

The behavior of some Christians makes it hard for me to release my bitterness toward them.

We can't judge any group by its lunatic fringe, nor all American Christians by those in the Bible Belt.

—Eileen

Why do some people fear and hate us?

When my mother died, there was a Catholic mass for her. There were friends and relatives who would not enter the church, but instead waited outside for the burial. I was very hurt that they could not get beyond their own ignorance and acted as if Satan himself was inside that church. If they would have known I was a Witch, they would not have even attended the burial, I am sure.

The hatred stems from ignorance and centuries of brain-washing. These people usually can't help how they feel. Witchcraft and Wicca have been synonymous with the Christian devil, as the Christian church intended. They have succeeded. No matter how long and hard you talk, some people will hear nothing but what they have been taught to hear and believe. They talk about cults and brainwashing, without realizing that the very same thing has been done to them, in the name of a Christian god that seeks vengeance and damnation for anyone who doesn't believe as they do.

—Cerelia

How can I get through to less open-minded Christians about the truth and beauty of Witchcraft and Wicca?

Sadly, the people that we want to listen rarely do. We can choose, by our examples and the way we live our lives and treat others, to show those who are filled with hatred what truly wonderful people Witches or Wiccans can be.

—Cerelia

What's a good comeback line, for people who refuse to stop trying to convert you to their religion?

My own favorite on that topic is from the *Koran*: "You shall have your religion and I shall have my religion."[9]

—Eileen

Does a collective consciousness exist in the universe?

To me, yes. Every living thing in the Universe is contributing to this consciousness (whether they know it or not). It is a consciousness that we can all tap into.

—*Cerelia*

LIFE IS MAGICAL

What do you mean when you say that life is magical? Can you give me an example?

For me, being a Witch means living a magical life. I had an experience this week that is a good illustration of what I mean—that how we experience reality can transform the mundane into the magical.

I went for an MRI of my brain, the third one that I have had in recent years, since it was a part of my participation in a drug trial. It turned out that I was on the placebo, but I really enjoyed the MRIs. For anyone who has never had an MRI, your body is slid into a machine and electromagnetic energy is directed to the part of your body being scanned.

The way that I react to having an MRI is shocking to the technicians who run them, so I assume from this that they have never seen another human being react as I do. Most people hate MRIs. They feel claustrophobic, because of the tight space and the fact that you are immobilized so they can get a good image. I love this, though, because it makes me feel like a mummy. I imagine Nut stretched protectively over me, as I sleep the sleep of a million years. The machine makes a lot of noise, so you are offered earplugs, or they can pipe in music to cover the sound. I decline these things, though, because I love the thumping and humming of the machine.

When they turn the electromagnetic energy on, it is an intensely magical experience for me. I instantly fall into a trance state and get better rest from fifteen minutes in the machine than I do from a whole night's sleep. If I could remain in an MRI machine long enough, say an hour or two, I am sure that I could cast some major spells from in there. Magic is simply the manipulation of energy, and the energy of an MRI machine makes it unnecessary to raise power.

—*Eileen*

——————Sleep and Dreams——————

Is it true that humans cannot dream in color?

Both spectrums are available to humans. Everyone is different. I can't recall ever having a dream that wasn't in full Technicolor.

—*Eileen*

Is it normal to dream in color and to remember each detail vividly?

It's normal for me.

—*Eileen*

Dream work can play a big part in being a Witch, not unlike meditation and visualization. My dreams are very vivid, and very detailed. It is normal for many Witches to dream in color. Remembering small details may just take more concentration and practice, for some Witches. Remembering dreams and working with them can be accomplished, even for those who are not prone to it.

—*Cerelia*

If you have an upsetting dream about someone, should you consider it a premonition?

When I have a disturbing dream about someone, I get in touch with them and check on how they're doing.

—*Eileen*

When I am angry, I sometimes dream that I do horribly violent things. Does this mean I might be a sociopath?

I often wake up horrified that my subconscious is capable of coming up with the things I dream about. Look at it from the other way round, though, and be glad your mind has a coping mechanism that prevents you from running amok.

—*Eileen*

Dream Interpretation

What does my dream mean?

I very seldom try to interpret dreams for anyone, because dreams are so personal. What means something to one person, can mean something entirely different to the next. Developing your talents for deciphering your own dreams is very important for a Witch.

—*Cerelia*

As Cerelia pointed out, dreams are very personal, and very subjective. It is especially hard to know what someone's dream means when you don't know the person. Your dream means whatever your gut tells you it meant. The tarot can be helpful with figuring out what our dreams mean. Runes and the *I Ching* would also help, I imagine.

—*Eileen*

I had a very intense dream, and different people have given me several possible interpretations for it. Which one is the right one?

Every interpretation could be possible. Then again, as Freud pointed out, "Sometimes a cigar, is just a cigar." Dreams have to be analyzed mainly by you. Certain things and places are special symbols, that may mean one thing to one person, but entirely something else to another. Sometimes they are just dreams.

—*Cerelia*

What does it mean to dream of your own death?

Dreaming of your death is like drawing the Death card in tarot. It doesn't mean you will die any time soon. It usually means that a big change is coming into your life.

—*Eileen*

Sometimes I have dreams where I can make things happen in them.

That's called lucid dreaming, the ability to control dreams. Astral projection is a kind of lucid dreaming, so lucid dreaming is a good skill to master if you want to do astral work.

—*Eileen*

A week before my brother committed suicide, he came to me in a dream and said that he was sorry. The dream was very real. What does it mean?

My brother and I are very close psychically. I will have a dream about him knocking on the door, and the next day he will be there just as I dreamed . . . even though he lives out of state. Or I'll dream I get a phone call from him, when he is in trouble or needs help. My mother, who is dead, will let me know somehow, or his wife (who is also deceased) will let me know he is having problems.

I get the feeling that your brother was telling you good-bye. This was because subconsciously he knew what he was about to do.

He may have been astral traveling and visited you, to see if you were okay, to say his good-byes, and to let you know that he was truly sorry for what he was about to do. This was because at some level, he knew. I am very sorry for your loss.

—*Cerelia*

A dog growled at me in my dream. What does this mean?

It sounds like a warning, but you're the only one who can figure out what it might be. Meditate on it, or ask the cards what it means, or ask for another dream to clarify the first one.

—*Eileen*

When I dream about goddesses and ancient cultures, am I just having Wiccan dreams, or is there some meaning in this?

Such dreams might be past life memories, surfacing. Write them down, if you can.

—*Eileen*

What does it mean if you have recurring dreams of a tornado?

The tornado could be a metaphor for approaching disaster. Try keeping a journal that correlates the dream with events in your life, to see if it's any sort of omen.

—*Eileen*

—————————— *Nightmares* ——————————

What can you do to recover from a nightmare?

Here is a beautiful custom from Japan: you tell your nightmare to a tree. They use heavenly bamboo, but we can use any tree or plant that is special to us. In telling the dream you release it, and suffer no harmful aftereffects from the nightmare.

—Eileen

I have been having dreams where I am attacked. Do you have any thoughts on this?

In the books by Carlos Castenada, who was taught by the shaman Don Juan, he wrote that being able to fight off your attackers in a dream is very powerful. You can get rid of nightmares like this, by defeating your enemies. You can become a stronger and more powerful person, by learning to stand up to your enemies in dreams. You can actually practice this in your dreams.

—Cerelia

I am afraid to sleep, because I have weird dreams that make me wake up screaming. Why does this happen to me?

Sometimes we have strange dreams for no reason at all. I have weird dreams, too. Last night I dreamt that Dionysus had just died and some of his grief-stricken lunatic followers crowded into my kitchen, where they tried to immolate themselves. I was throwing water into the kitchen, but it was too late and I had to just get my son out of the house. It was a creepy dream, but we all have them from time to time. When I went back to sleep I dreamt that Saddam Hussein was asking me for help.

Dreamscapes can definitely be very weird sometimes, but we can also drive ourselves crazy by obsessing over dreams. Sometimes dreams are just dreams, and we should just laugh, or cry, and forget them. The sun rises, the dream ends, and life goes on.

—*Eileen*

I am nine months pregnant and I had a nightmare where I put my baby down for a moment, and someone stole her. Does this mean it will happen?

Don't be upset by your dream, because it's just typical mother's anxiety surfacing in your sleeping mind. A baby is a tremendous responsibility because it is so tiny, so precious, so vulnerable. There are so many dangers and so much that can go wrong, so of course we (especially first-time mothers) worry ourselves sick.

"What if . . ." This anxiety is part of our job, trying to antic-ipate threats. We start doing it even before the child is born. A mother hears her baby cry no matter how deeply asleep she is. We keep one part of our minds attuned to the baby, even in sleep, so no wonder we have dreams like that.

I had some horrible dreams about terrible things happening to my son, before and just after he was born, but he's four and a half now and none of them ever came true. Don't worry.

—*Eileen*

I keep having the same dream, night after night. I take sleeping pills, but still the dream comes.

When you keep having the same dream, get a pen and note-book and put them beside your bed. Write this dream down as soon as you wake up, every time you have it. Noting any-thing new or different in the dreams may help you to figure out what your sleeping mind is trying to tell your waking self. If you'd rather not have such dreams at all, replace the sleeping pills with chamomile tea at bedtime. Chamomile will not harm your body, as sleeping pills sometimes can. It is also a sure-fire remedy for nightmares, the best potion I know for this sort of thing.

—Eileen

What about a recurring nightmare?

Avoid melatonin to aid sleep, as it intensifies dreams. If there is any chance the bad dreams are rooted in some kind of psy-chological issue, see a doctor to explore this. Work on getting to the bottom of whatever might be bothering you.

—Eileen

Sleep and Dream Disorders

Are there other explanations for strange experiences during sleep besides astral travel or lucid dreaming?

They can be caused by sleep paralysis, rather than astral trav-eling or lucid dreaming. You get caught in between the wak-ing and sleeping state, and it can be quite frightening. I get it from time to time. Your mind is awake, but your body is asleep. With practice, I am able to calm myself, tell myself to let go, wake my body up, and come out of it.

I have also found that if I keep myself awake a bit after I've had one, they don't come back. If I go right back to sleep, I go back into the same state. It does seem very real. You feel you are screaming your lungs out for someone to help you, but they usually don't hear, unless you get really frantic and they hear you mumbling and thrashing about.

This is not the same as astral travel or lucid dreaming. This is not a state you are striving for. If you have these very often, you might look into a book on sleep paralysis or visit some Web sites. They will have some suggestions to help you with this.

I don't believe they can be a positive experience. They are completely different from AP and lucid dreaming. I don't have them often enough to call them a problem. I can now, usually, talk myself out of them. They are very disturbing and scary, but learning about anything always helps with being afraid and worried. Just knowing what it is helps. Then you can take it from there. Some people who have had these experiences all their lives are just now finding out what they are.

—Cerelia

I never dream. What can I do about this?

Dreaming is a physical necessity for humans. You dream every night, as all humans do; you just don't remember your dreams. Dreams are important to everyone, but even more so for Witches. Drinking chamomile tea just before bedtime works for some people, as does keeping a dream notebook.

Exercise: Buy a notebook, write "Dream Journal" on its cover, and place it beside your bed with a pen. This is a powerful magical act that reaches your subconscious as well as your unconscious mind, with positive thinking. Knowing the pen and notebook are there, waiting, trains your subconscious mind to recall the dreams.

Write dreams down as soon as you wake up, before you get out of bed. The first full blown dream you do remember will probably be a significant one, so be sure to record it. This method can take time and patience (give it at least six months), but it's worth it.

—*Eileen*

What can I do about insomnia?

Try melatonin or valerian, both available in health food stores and vitamin shops. Even regular pharmacies are starting to carry things like this. If you are certain that a medical problem is not a factor, try the herbs. Moving your bed sometimes also helps.

—*Eileen*

──Entities──

Do Witches believe in supernatural beings, like spirits and elementals?

A lot of Witches do not believe in fairies or dragons, and so on, just as all Witches do not astral travel or have lucid dreams. The energies can have different names or different ways to recognize them. We are all different, and each work with the gifts we have.

—Cerelia

Not all of us. I am one of those people who doesn't believe in anything unless I see it with my own eyes, or personally experience it in some other way, so I do not believe in fairies, dragons, or angels because I have never seen them. I do believe in ghosts, but only because I have seen one. I wouldn't call elementals supernatural. If they do exist, they are natural entities who are simply different from humans.

I'm not very visual, and I tend to sense things more than see or hear them. I am certain, however, that there is far more to this world than what meets the eye. We are privileged when we have encounters with non-human entities, even if it can take us years to make sense of what we saw or felt. In Wicca we each believe whatever we believe. Rely on your senses, to determine what you believe in.

—Eileen

Elementals

What are elementals?

They are believed to be a group of beings without souls. They are active as a group, but are not able to do much individually. I tend to think of them as very mischievous beings who can be downright mean, so I find no thrill in dealing with them.

The term *elemental* is also applied to nature spirits, which exist in all things in nature: animals, insects, birds, rocks, and so on. Depending on what traditions someone may be speaking of, or belong to, elementals correspond to the four elements of Earth, Air, Fire, and Water. Elementals live and dwell on Earth, just as we do. The names given them are:

> salamander: fire
>
> undines: water
>
> sylphs: air
>
> gnomes: earth

—*Cerelia*

Can we use them in our magic?

I have a definite opinion about working with elementals: it's too dangerous. Why even bother, when you're a Witch and can raise your own power without them? That's my opinion. I wouldn't own a dangerous pet either, wouldn't give house room to a creature that might maim or kill a member of my household. Other Witches feel differently and that's fine. They can try to make pets of tigers or black mambas or tarantulas, but I would never invite something dangerous into my sacred space.

—*Eileen*

There are those Witches who feel that some elementals have the capacity of one day being able to achieve a soul, when there are humans who work with them. If Witches would make conscious choices to work with elementals, they need to realize that the elementals will be around a very long time, and that it is very hard to make them leave if you suddenly decide you are not interested in their development any more.

—Cerelia

You should not tell people that elementals should be feared. There is nothing to fear.

Though I totally disagree with you, it is very much your right to have this opinion. I say opinion, because that is what it is, as with what I have said about elementals. There are many other books out there which say that elementals are something to be very careful with, that they can cause danger and even death.

This is also an opinion based on my experiences, and the experiences of Witches I know. I would never tell someone they have absolutely nothing to be afraid of, as you have done.

Remember we may be talking to Witches who have absolutely no magical skills yet. To say they shouldn't be afraid, or cautious, is not good advice. As I mentioned in one of my posts, I did say that some Witches work with elementals. That's okay, because they usually know what they are doing. They do get positive results. I gave both sides, and the Wiccan must make her or his decision about elementals.

Dion Fortune wrote, "Elementals have got a one-way intelligence, and it is not well that they should be senior partners in any alliance with human beings."[10]

—Cerelia

Elementals are more often harmful than helpful to humans.

—Eileen

There is a presence in my home. It doesn't make me feel threatened, but I am wondering what, if anything, I should do about it.

Why don't you try smudging your house, every inch of it, with the intention of ridding your home of any entities? Even if you do not feel threatened by them, entities can develop. They can begin making more and more occurrences, and that may not be welcomed. Though some Witches enjoy these types of visitors, I believe they need to be told to move on. They have their home, you have yours, and both should be respected.

—Cerelia

Is it possible to summon an entity?

If you are going to try to make contact with spirits, elementals, fairies, or any other entities, make sure that you know this: they are easier to invite than they are to banish. A great deal of my e-mail has come, over the years, from people who held seances, tried their hand at dragon magic, invited fairies into their gardens, or in some other way failed to live and let live. They write to me for help when they are unable to get rid of what turned out to be a malevolent being. I can tell them about smudging, Ghost Powder, or banishing rituals, but I can't run right over and physically help them to banish it. These are frightened people, very freaked out people (and not just new Witches), who were sure they could handle whatever magical operation they undertook—but who learned otherwise, and learned it the hard way.

I have gotten hundreds of letter like that, so I am making a very informed statement when I say that working with entities of any kind is seriously dangerous unless you know what you're doing before you begin. Such knowledge is usually gained through years of apprenticeship in a shamanic tradition. Read *The Teachings of Don Juan*, by Carlos Castaneda, for an idea of what such training can entail. Very few Witches have been fortunate enough to have had benefit of such training.

—Eileen

There is a strange presence in my house, and I have disturbing dreams. Should I try to channel it, try to communicate with it?

If I were feeling negative vibes about the place I lived, and especially about the place I slept, I'd perform some sort of clearing and then place heavy protection around myself and my space. I would seal any entities out of it, and disperse any negative energies. I definitely would not try to communicate with anything that was invading my sacred space (my home). I would simply banish it, and clear my sacred space.

You, however, should do whatever feels right to you. You might want to ask for a dream message that tells you what it is, and what you should do about it. Right before bed, ask the Goddess to send you a dream that makes things clear with respect to this presence.

—Eileen

I sense things in my house. Could they be elementals?

They could be. They also might be thought forms, if someone in the household has a drinking problem, or is very emotional or upset.

—Eileen

How do you banish or clear entities?

Exercise: One method to clear entities is to sweep out the
area with a besom, burn incense, open a window, and order
everything out. Order them to leave your home in no uncer-
tain terms, but wish them well. Smudging can be helpful with
this, as can spraying or sprinkling potions like Four Thieves
Vinegar, or Santerian staples such as Florida Water or Kananga
Water, and so on. Cologne, or even air freshener, will also
work. Your intent and your intensity are what matter.

—Eileen

*I fear that my powers will go with it, if I clear the entity from my
home. What should I do?*

This is something only you can decide, but your powers are
your own, not contingent on any other entity. Personally, I
cannot bear entities in my space. I would definitely clear it
out, but that's me. You will have to find the answer that is
right for you.

—Eileen

Demons

Are demons real?

I don't believe in the so-called word *demon*, but I do believe that an evil entity or spirit can exist. This is why I caution about ouija boards.

—*Cerelia*

Get past the notion that demons are malevolent entities. They're not. Demons are things such as addictions, depression, bad habits, compulsive behaviors, and negative patterns. You could, however, make a pretty good argument that serial killers, serial rapists, wife beaters, and child molesters are demons of a kind.

We fear demons because we fear we cannot control them, but in fact we can. That's what Twelve Step Programs are about, facing demons and controlling them. There are no quick fixes, just lots of hard work and the pride and self-esteem that come from overcoming a personal demon.

—*Eileen*

Fairies

Do the fairies accept my offerings, or do animals eat them?

My vote would be for animals, birds, or insects . . . but a lot of people do believe in fairies.

—*Eileen*

Vampires

Are vampires real?

I do not believe in vampires. I have, however, gotten creepy letters from people who say they are vampires. They claim to actually drink each other's blood (yuck). Lots of people say lots of things, but none of it convinces me that immortal preternatural creatures walk undead among us. Vlad the Impaler was a serial killer, not a vampire.

—Eileen

Incubi and Succubi

A presence entered my room, and pressed down on me in my bed. I became paralyzed, could not move or speak. What was this?

It may have been an incubus, a male entity who embraces sleeping females. They sometimes seem to attach themselves to a particular person and make repeated visitations. Eye of Satan is specific against them, so get some of the seeds if you can. Placing them in the corners of your room, and near the bed, should prevent it from returning.

—Eileen

What's the deal with succubi?

Succubi (like Lilith) were blamed for men's nocturnal emissions. In the Middle East, any sex that takes place outside marriage is often considered to be the woman's fault—even if she is an invisible entity who visits at night.

—Eileen

Ghosts and Spirits

Do ghosts really visit us?

I prefer the word *spirit*. Yes, I believe they interact with us. I have had too many experiences to believe otherwise; to the point where I work consciously to not attract spirits.

—*Cerelia*

How do you feel about having a ghost or spirit in your home?

Some Witches like to have them around, or even seek to commune with them, but I cannot stand them in my space or anywhere near me. I use garlic, sea salt, and rosemary when a spirit is around. It makes a barrier they cannot cross, so it is useful for keeping them out of places you don't want them in.

—*Eileen*

How can I channel or otherwise communicate with the spirit I feel in my home? It is tormenting me.

One of you has to go, and since you're in the correct realm and it isn't, the spirit must go. Clear it right out of the house. I don't mean to harm the spirit in any way, merely to send it to the light, where it belongs. It's the right thing to do. You may want to get someone else to do this for you, though, since the experience may have sapped your strength.

—*Eileen*

I heard a music box playing and smelled cigarette smoke when I was alone.

That sounds like a spirit was visiting, someone who was a smoker in his or her lifetime and had some connection with that song, or with music boxes.

—Eileen

How do I use an ouija board to communicate with spirits?

This is something I have said many times, but it bears repeating. If I had a dollar for every letter I have ever received from a freaked out person who had used a ouija board, or held a seance, and was now unable to get rid of the troublesome or malicious spirit he or she attracted, I would have enough money to take my son to Disneyland, first class. Spirits are easy to call, but difficult to banish. Be warned. Beware.

—Eileen

Is there a safe way to use ouija boards?

I don't have any safety nets, because I am one of those Witches who believes that ouija boards are dangerous. I don't believe there are any so called safety nets. Ouija boards deal with entities of the lowest kind. To me, using a ouija board is like issuing an invitation to them to join you in your home. This is something I have had bad dealings with.

I would not allow my kids to bring a ouija board into the house for this reason. But people are always curious, and it is hard to listen when someone says don't. Sometimes only experience can teach.

—Cerelia

Why do you guys get so bent out of shape about ouija boards?

We take it very seriously because we have seen great harm done by or visited upon people who fooled around with things they didn't understand, things they took lightly and embarked upon without study or consideration.

—*Eileen*

CHAPTER FOUR

A Witch's Skills

What is meditation?

We have to learn to look within ourselves, to learn to not always be looking outside for everything. That is what meditation is: looking within and listening to the truths that lie buried within us. Meditation comes in many different forms. If you do not do it the way an authority on the subject does it but it works for you, it doesn't matter.

Meditation is relaxing the body and mind. Because your thoughts seem to get in the way, it takes practice to calm them down.

—Cerelia

If you can hush your thoughts, find your way to a spiritual silence, and listen with your whole self, you can hear the Universe singing. You hear it with your mind, rather than your ears. I think of that music as the lullaby of the Goddess. It's as comforting as womb music.

—Eileen

Why do Witches meditate?

Not only does meditation relax, it teaches the art of concentration and focus. It is a true way to "know yourself," your real self. Meditation is an art. It is a spiritual journey in itself, not just something to relax by . . . although if that is all you want out of it, that is fine.

Meditation can, when done properly, alter your state of consciousness and bring about changing your consciousness, which is exactly what magic and being a Witch is all about. Meditation comes easily for some Witches, while others have to practice it faithfully. It just takes practice, and patience.

—Cerelia

One of the reasons that so many Witches meditate is because of the mental discipline that meditation teaches. Another reason is because we can get answers to our questions through meditation. It can be helpful with making decisions.

Many Witches also find meditation helpful when they face a crossed condition in their lives. Others prefer turning to the Goddess, or taking action and casting an uncrossing spell. Adversity helps us to grow in our path, and learn what we are meant to learn in this lifetime. Meditation helps us to discover the meaning in our suffering. That sounds grim, but it is actually a joyous process.

Try meditation and divination when you seek an answer to a question. Remember that answers often seem to come when you stop consciously thinking about something, and allow your higher mind to handle it.

—*Eileen*

How does one meditate?

Meditation can be quite simple. Many books have been written which can help you through the problems that may arise. There are different theories about meditation, and different ways to get to the same place. A lot of us meditate in our own ways all the time, and don't even realize it. The amount of books out there on the subject make many people feel that meditation is something that is very hard to attain, but it isn't.

To become one completely within yourself isn't easy, but we don't have to be meditative gurus to have success with meditation. Meditation is called by many other names now. This is helping it to become more acceptable, or less intimidating, to Westerners. We do not have to devote our whole lives to meditation, as some have done. We can integrate meditation into our everyday lives.

Exercise: Don't fight the thoughts that come when you try to meditate. Go with them, and see where they lead you. Learn to find your higher self, which will show itself with practice. Start simply, such as while taking a warm bath. Let your thoughts come and go. To be good at meditation takes practice, if it doesn't come naturally.

Exercise: Find a quiet place that you are very comfortable in. Take deep breaths, clear your head, and relax as much as you can. Find a mantra or chant or phrase that hold special meaning to you . . . anything, such as, "in perfect love and perfect trust." Whatever you feel connected to.

Start breathing through your nose and repeat this phrase over and over. You don't have to shout it, just whisper it, or repeat it in your mind. Follow your breath as it goes through your nose and out. Being aware of your breath is a good way to distract your thoughts. You don't have to do this, but it is a good way to help calm the thoughts zipping through your head, because you are concentrating on your breathing.

Get a couple of simple books to teach yourself about breath control. Meditation is not as hard as many feel it is. It can be done quite simply. Those who feel a passion for meditation can go on, can study and perfect it for years. The choice is yours.

—*Cerelia*

There isn't any one correct way to meditate; there's whatever works for you. Everyone meditates differently, in whatever way works best for them. Generally, meditation means getting comfortable in a quiet place where you will not be interrupted, and freeing your mind to go where it will. It's important to be relaxed and uninterrupted, so meditation is best done in solitude, wearing something comfortable.

Some Witches like to use a candle, scent, music, an image or other focal point, to help them concentrate. Other Witches like to burn incense while they meditate, while others prefer soft music, or candlelight, or even to be outdoors surrounded by Mother Nature's sounds and scents. We're all different. Experiment until you find what works for you. The bathtub and your own bed, just before you sleep, are good starting places if you don't have a natural setting you can be alone in.

—*Eileen*

If I can't meditate, am I still a Witch?

I wouldn't say you can't be a Witch if you can't meditate. Meditation sometimes is a word that frightens people because it sounds so unattainable or hard to do. You may actually be meditating at times, without realizing it. We don't have to feel that we cannot be Witches because we don't have exemplary meditation skills.

—*Cerelia*

What can you do if you have trouble meditating?

The state between sleep and waking is a very magical time, great for meditation and astral projection, for psychic and creative work of all kinds. Try meditating late at night, when your house and the neighborhood are quiet. Try meditating in bed, just before you drift off to sleep. That's a great time for anything which requires concentration.

Finding stillness, within or without, is a challenge for most of us in the modern world. Here are some things which work for me:

Exercise: Still the noise. Take a two-day vacation from modern life. Turn off the computers, televisions, and radios (as much as possible). Turn off telephone ringers. Turn on the answering machine, but turn down its volume. Don't read the newspaper. Spend time with yourself, and with Nature. Water the plants. Go for a walk. Hang out with animals. Go barefoot. Go to bed early. Take naps. Cut out nicotine and caffeine, if you use those chemicals. Eat healthy food. Buy yourself flowers. Take long, luxurious baths. Read a book that you have been meaning to read for a long time. Get a massage. Wear loose clothing. Go to a museum. Go alone. Take some vitamins. Do stretching exercises, or yoga. Burn incense. Still all the noise, and reconnect with yourself.

Few of us have lives where we can do all of these things at once, but you get the idea. Try meditating at the end of the two days, and you should find it easier. Be patient with yourself. If you keep at it, you'll get there. It helps to make some small ritual of meditation: sit in the same place, wear the same outfit, burn the same incense, and so on. Whatever you use (sound, posture, scent, or something else), your brain will log it and it will become a trigger—a shortcut to get you to a magical or meditative state of mind.

—Eileen

A couple of books on different types of meditation that you might want to look into are: *The Wisdom of No Escape*, by Pema Chodron; and *Kundalini Awakening: A Gentle Guide to Chakra Activation and Spiritual Growth*, by John Selby.

Otherwise, try the simple things that we have suggested.

—Cerelia

I usually fall asleep when I try to meditate. Is this bad?

There is nothing wrong with falling asleep while meditating. Our brains are still working while we're sleeping. This is why we often wake up with answers, or inspirations, that were unavailable to us the previous day.

—Eileen

Something odd happened . . .

Don't be frightened by it, you've just learned to reach a deeper level of meditation.

—Eileen

What's visualization?

VISUALIZATION

Visualization is the next step in imagination. It's being able to accurately picture something in your mind's eye. A really good visualization includes sounds, smells, emotions, and so on. This is a skill that comes easily to some Witches, but other Witches have to work at it to develop it in themselves.

—Eileen

How can one learn to practice it?

You use mental exercises for this.

Exercise: Remember someone whom you haven't seen in years, such as a good childhood friend. Begin by seeing his or her face, then add details: what this person's voice or laugh sounded like, how he or she walked, personal habits and speech patterns, eye color, an article of clothing he or she often wore, how you felt when you were with this person, the place you usually met this person, and so on. You work at it gradually over a period of days, and build the memory layer by layer until it is so real that you find yourself recalling things which surprise you.

Other good subjects for this kind of exercise are the room you slept in as a child, a favorite childhood toy, something which frightened you when you were little, the first school you attended or birthday party you went to, and so forth.

Exercise: If it appeals to you, read poetry. As you read a poem, images suggested by the words form in your mind. This is a good technique for jump-starting your imagination.

If poetry isn't your thing, try a novel with a lot of visually descriptive passages. (*The Prince of Tides* by Pat Conroy comes to mind.)

—Eileen

How does visualization relate to magic?

Visualization is one of the most powerful tools of a Witch. Visualization is the ability to focus attention on your intent. It is the power with which you spark that intent which makes magic. Visualization is a great aid to a Witch. You should visualize what you intend, as if it has already been accomplished.

Visualization usually takes practice, but some Witches have a natural tendency toward it. Working on your visualization skills is a good place to start. Visualization is very powerful. It takes lots of practice and focus to be done correctly, but many Witches use this instead of rituals and circles.

—Cerelia

Meditation and visualization are important because they are the building blocks of psi-magic. Witches tend to get hung up on the whole circle casting thing in the beginning, but there can come a time when you seldom need or want to cast circles.

—Eileen

Creative visualization can be very powerful, when you become skilled at it. Imagine your result as already accomplished. This doesn't mean to just wish anything off the top of your head, with no thought or care whatsoever. Everyone wants a million dollars! Be sincere about your visualization, and be realistic.

You have to work at visualization over time. Not all of our spells can be accomplished quickly. Some take time. Some visualization spells are not answered because they were not completely thought out, and their negative results would not be to our benefit.

—*Cerelia*

Could I be visualizing, without realizing that I'm doing it?

You may not realize what visualization is, and therefore think you are not doing it. I call it your mind's eye. You are forming mental images, but not by closing your eyes and seeing them in your field of vision. It's kind of like thinking about your grandmother and seeing her face in your mind. You know exactly what she looks like. You can do this without closing your eyes, so you won't be distracted by colors and such. This is what you can practice doing.

You can see something in detail, not physically, but mentally. Seeing things when you close your eyes and try to visualize them into the darkness is much harder. You may see a scene or a face or something that may mean something to you, or get sudden flashes of intuition, or visions.

—*Cerelia*

How can I use visualization in magic?

Exercise: Start on a New Moon. As with your candle magic, find a quiet place to visualize. Get yourself very comfortable, but always keep your spine straight. Begin your visualization of your need.

Don't wait until late in the night to do this, because you will tend to fall asleep. Close your eyes and visualize. Know that whatever you want is yours. Know it . . . see it . . . feel it. . . . Be absolutely positive about the results you want. Do this for about ten minutes. Repeat it for several months, if necessary.

It's hard work staying focused, but keep trying. You can't sit lazily by and expect the energies of the Universe to just throw everything in your lap. You must always be working to bring about these changes. Working. We don't like the word work, but it is still a necessary exchange of energies.

Exercise: Imagine your whole home, yard included, surrounded by a protective sphere of light. Some Witches visualize white light, some visualize purple, some blue. Use whatever color speaks of protection to you. The sphere must be huge, of course, and visualized as going underground as much as it goes above your home. Hold this image and speak words of protection for your home and all who enter. You can also do this with yourself, and with those you love and want to protect.

—Cerelia

INVOCATION & EVOCATION

What is invocation?

Invoking the Goddess is simply requesting her presence. The magic is in your head and heart, and in your firm belief that whatever you truly need is already here.

—Cerelia

Is invocation something to be nervous about?

Invoking the Goddess is nothing to be worried about. You can use invocation with any spellwork, whether you use the name of a specific deity, or just the word *Goddess*. Having a good talk with her any time, whether in ritual or not, is nothing to be nervous about.

—Cerelia

Why do Witches use invocation?

Here's something Scott Cunningham wrote that I thought was great: "Wiccans invoke the Goddess and God to bless their magic with power. During ritual they may direct personal power to the deities, asking that a specific need be met. This is truly religious magic."[11]

—Eileen

How do I invoke the Goddess?

You can invoke the Goddess by simply talking to her, and letting her know of your need.

—Cerelia

Invoke the gods in whatever way feels natural to you.

—Eileen

How do I ask the gods for help? What if I am not worthy?

If you don't believe you deserve help, you cannot receive it. The Goddess isn't like a Christian god that you ask for help because you've been good, or feel he is damning you because you are not worthy. You must really get over this type of conditioning quickly. Whether it is was caused by your past religious beliefs, or how you were raised, these are very detrimental ideas to your well being and to your very life.

With Witchcraft, you are tapping into the energies that everyone is deserving of. We are all children of the Universe. We are all deserving. We each have different lessons to be learned and dealt with. We are all on different stages of our spiritual journey. It is realizing that we must help ourselves and take responsibility for ourselves, that makes us truly powerful Witches.

You aren't really asking for help, or asking for a better life. You are working with the energies to attain what you want. You work toward it mentally and physically every day, because you know that you are as deserving as the next person.

—Cerelia

You are worthy. Don't be surprised if, as your relationship with the Goddess develops, you one day find yourself talking to her as naturally as you would to any person you have great respect and esteem for.

—Eileen

If I just pray to the Goddess, is that okay?

A prayer and a spell can be the same thing. Talking to the Goddess from your heart is what is important, no matter how you do it.

—Cerelia

May I invoke the Goddess in my native language?

Absolutely! The Goddess speaks all languages, and our communication with her is actually psychic, anyway. We should all pray and cast spells in whatever language we are most comfortable using.

—*Eileen*

When I invoke a Lord and a Lady, do they have to be a divine couple, or even from the same pantheon? Could I invoke Thoth and Eos, for example?

We can call upon whoever feels right to us. Isis and Osiris are the divine couple, but he's too spineless for me. To me, Isis is the Lady and Thoth is the Lord. I don't invoke them as a couple, but as individuals. Ma'at and Thoth are a divine couple. I also work with Ma'at a lot, but I do not invoke her and Thoth as a couple either. This might not make sense to other Witches, but it makes perfect sense to me.

Thoth and Eos . . . why not? He is night and the Moon, she is dawn and the Sun. In the Middle East the Sun is usually female, and the Moon is usually male.

—*Eileen*

Can I invoke gods from different pantheons in the same working?

Again, whatever makes sense to you.

—*Eileen*

Does it offend the gods if I invoke more than one of them at a time?

I think not. Deities have been addressed together since very ancient times.

—Eileen

How do we work magically with the gods?

Each deity sort of vibrates at his or her own frequency, and we feel their energy when we work with them. We access the particular quality of their energy in accord with how it corresponds to us, or to our magical working: Venus for a love spell, Freya for trance magic, Poseidon for sea power, and so forth.

When we invoke a god/dess we experience his or her particular energy. As you work with different deities, you become aware of how different their various energies feel. This is a subjective thing, though, since we are all different. I might sense Kali as female energy, a strongly positive transforming force, while another Witch might feel her as horrifying darkness.

—Eileen

What else should I know about invocation?

The Goddess often gives us what we need, instead of what we think we want. Remember to give thanks for your blessings.

—Eileen

What is evocation?

(See also Entities on page 175.)

Evoking a spirit or elemental is different. This is something that a Witch can look into if he or she is interested, when he or she becomes more adept. It is best to have worked with another Witch before doing it alone. I myself see no point in evocation. Entities and spirits should not be bothered, just so I can have fun, or bid them to do what I want. I also do not care to have them around my home.

Perhaps some Witches need the experience. Just as we try to teach our kids from our own mistakes, we also know that they have to learn life's lessons on their own. It's good to know about the possible consequences, though, things that some Witches have experienced, so that you have all the facts.

I have seen and heard enough to know it serves no productive purpose to evoke elementals. This is just my personal experience. I try to give both points of view, so that other Witches can make these decisions for themselves. I am glad that I could at least separate the two terms, and let other Witches decide when and if they care to delve into such things.

—Cerelia

PSYCHISM

How does one develop psychic ability?

The first step is opening the third eye and learning to perceive the flow of energy around us; to see the unseen. The next step (an on-going process) is learning to integrate this information, and discover what it all means.

—*Eileen*

How can we break communications blocks, to make us more receptive to psychism?

Poetry is a good tool for breaking that blockage. A great poem can paint pictures in your mind's eye that cannot seem to be found in the words of the poem.

—*Eileen*

How do you know when someone is trying to harm you? And what should you do?

I get a deep foreboding, or maybe a very dark feeling that doesn't go away, and then I know someone is either talking about me in a not so friendly way, or wishing ill will toward me. I really can't say if I sense it at the exact same time that it starts to happen, but as soon as I feel it I will do a protection spell for myself, my family, and my home. When this feeling lightens, then I know it is working.

—*Cerelia*

What does it mean if I think of something, and then it happens?

Don't be alarmed, that's very common—especially with Witches. Don't be frightened or surprised if you dream something and then it comes true. This also happens to many Witches. All humans are psychic to one degree or another, but some people are just more gifted than others, or more in tune with their psychic selves.

—Eileen

What does it mean if you think of someone, and suddenly they show up?

That's a psychic gift, one shared by more humans than you would expect. It is the reason Witches are always cautioning people to be very careful about what they summon, intentionally or accidentally. There are a lot of books and Web sites about developing psychic potential that you can turn to, if you want to develop or better understand your gift.

—Eileen

What should I do if I have a premonition?

It's always worthwhile listening to your little voice.

—Eileen

What should I do if I have the feeling that someone is going to be in an auto accident?

With car crash premonitions, my friends and I usually scatter some Eye of Satan seeds in the trunk of the car the person most often drives or rides in.

—Eileen

Why do I always seem to know it when something is happening with my relatives?

Psychic connections between family members are often very intense. I had a strong psychic connection with my brother all our lives, until he went so wrong that the connection broke under the weight of all the darkness surrounding him.

—Eileen

Is being empathic a blessing or a curse?

It is a gift, a blessing. It is meant to be used to help others.

—Eileen

Words or dialogue seem to come into my head, and I am compelled to write them down. Is this strange, or is there a name for it?

What you are talking about sounds like automatic writing. Some authors have written very popular books and attributed this phenomenon to how their books were written. I believe it happens. When my mother died (and I didn't know yet that she had passed away), I was completely compelled to write a letter on her behalf to a family member. In my mind, she was telling me what to write, and was very insistent about it.

This was how I knew that something was wrong. She lived in another state, so I called. When I got no answer, I sent the police out there to find out what was wrong. She had died in her home. The letter was definitely written and sent.

—Cerelia

How do we interpret signs, omens, and visions?

Exercise: Keep a journal of them, and things which happen that confirm or deny them. In time, patterns, clues, and signals will emerge. You will learn what to look for, what to listen to, and how to interpret them. Be patient with the process, though, because this isn't something that you learn quickly.

—Eileen

What did a certain omen mean?

It means whatever you think it means. Signs and omens are personal, like dreams. They have to be interpreted by the person who receives them.

—Eileen

What do you do about someone who causes others psychic pain?

I banish, cut people like that right out of my life. Binding is another option, as is erecting a psychic force field to protect you from whatever darkness is leaking from that person.

—Eileen

Is consulting psychics, mediums, and other readers a good idea?

In the end, it is a matter of taking responsibility for yourself. Which means that if you give someone $300 for a reading, you will probably be among the many who have made this person very wealthy, while your family could have used that money for something much more important. If you have $300 to blow, then go for it, if it makes you happy. Better yet, just do the reading yourself.

—Cerelia

It's generally a good idea to be wary of anyone who separates you from your money over things which cannot be verified.

—Eileen

What do you call someone who is the opposite of a psychic vampire?

Different faiths have different names for such people: mahatmas, world souls, sheikhs, and so on. In Wicca we call them priests and priestesses.

—Eileen

————Astral Projection————

What's the difference between astral travel and lucid dreaming?

Astral travel and lucid dreaming are two different things, but they are both very hard to explain to those who have never done them. Astral travel is being able to leave your body, move, and go to different places. Lucid dreaming is like being in your own movie (for lack of a better analogy), and making it up as you go along. You are completely aware of everything, and know that you can change anything within your dream. It is your fantasy, and you are in complete control of it.

I love to lucid dream. It is a dream state, whereas astral projection is not; although I reach the astral by going to sleep first. Some Witches do, and some don't.

—Cerelia

Do I have to be able to astral travel or dream lucidly to be a Witch?

No Witch needs to feel that he or she isn't as adept as someone else, just because he or she does not have these skills. I don't think it is something everyone has to experience. I know astral projection sounds intriguing for those who have never done it, but we all have our strong points in whatever aspect of spirituality or gifts we may have. We don't all have to experience the same things. That's what makes us all unique.

—*Cerelia*

How do I get onto the astral plane?

Astral traveling and lucid dreaming come to me naturally. I don't have to think about it to do them, so I cannot really tell anyone how they are done. It is something that comes too naturally for me. I just let it come when it does.

—*Cerelia*

What's it like, when you astral project yourself?

Like magic, different people experience AP differently.

—*Eileen*

What if your body starts jumping when you relax and try to astral project?

Twitching and vibrating are the first steps. Keep at it.

—*Eileen*

Is it dangerous?

Safety is an issue whenever one is attempting anything that does not come naturally.

—Cerelia

What if I can't get back into my body?

Dion Fortune recommended thinking of your feet as a fast way to return to your body. It works.

—Eileen

Could something I did cause problems on the astral plane?

Chaos on the astral concerns all of us, but that's highly unlikely. Don't worry about it.

—Eileen

I need some good advice on scrying.

DIVINATION

Scrying, which is gazing into a bowl of water, a crystal ball, or mirror, just takes time and patience. For water gazing, I use a cauldron because it is dark. I drop a silver coin (a dime) into the bottom. This helps with focusing.

—Cerelia

What are some of the different forms of divination?

A couple of ways are water scrying and mirror magic. By gazing and meditating into one or the other, you can see if your face changes into something else that you can recognize as another part of yourself, or see past lives. This takes a lot of practice. Don't force it: if it doesn't work, quit and try it again later.

The *I Ching, Book of Changes* is an ancient Chinese system of divination. There is a coin method, and a more complicated set of fifty yarrow sticks. As with the tarot, it does not give you answers. You must be able to see the patterns of the forces that are shown to you. You really need the book and its explanations to understand the *I Ching*. It can get quite involved, but I think you might enjoy this type of divination. The library usually has this book, so if you can't buy one, try there.

I also have a quartz pendulum. If you are a dreamer, pay attention to your dreams.

—Cerelia

Medicine cards, rune cards, past life cards, dragon cards . . . many card systems are available. Choose the one which resonates with you.

—Eileen

TAROT

Why is the tarot called the Royal Road?

Tarot is called the Royal Road for good reason, because working with the cards is an endless voyage of discovery.

—Eileen

Is it true that tarot cards are dangerous?

Who told you that? I have been working with the tarot since I was eleven or twelve years old, and have found it to be nothing but positive.

—Eileen

How can I learn to read the cards?

You just think of the most logical progression of questions, in an order that would make sense to you, or has the highest priority in your mind. Here is how Nancy Garen explains it, in *Tarot Made Easy*:

> I wrote each question down, then searched the categories to find the ones that answered them most thoroughly. I continued the process until I had categories to answer all my questions. The order of the particular layout wasn't important. In the Category Spread, I wanted an in-depth reading, and the best way to go about it was to read all thirty-two categories from thirty-two different cards.[12]

She also gives some examples of spreads in her book. Remember that "just one card" can answer an important question, and that you can also use a clarification card to help with the interpretation. So experiment, and see what you come up with.

—*Cerelia*

I love Nancy Garen's book, *Tarot Made Easy*. It is easy, so easy that you can start reading the cards immediately with it. Like runes, you develop a relationship with the cards over time. You'll read other books, too, and come to understand the cards in different ways, but that's a great book to get started with.

Read the cards in any way that makes sense for you. (Didn't you just know I'd say that?) Experiment with the cards, work with them daily, and you will find the spreads or methods that work best for you. Keep at it, always using the same deck until you master it. Listen to your little voice, even if it tells you something different than whatever book you're using. Try different things until you find what works for you.

—*Eileen*

How do you read the cards?

I use a medicine wheel spread, which I really like. It is quite simple, and to the point.

—*Cerelia*

I'm as untraditional with the cards as I am with everything else, so my own method for the cards is extremely unorthodox. I never use the Celtic Cross or any of the usual spreads. I ask my question (usually "What's going on?" or "What's coming down?" or "Tell me what I need to know"), then I shuffle the deck in an upright position. I always do this over the black cloth I keep the cards wrapped in, and atop Nancy Garen's book. I shuffle them until a card falls out or sticks up, and there's my answer. Sometimes two or three cards pop out together, when the answer is complicated. Weird? Yes, this is definitely a very strange way to read the cards, but it is the one I have used for many years and it works well for me.

Years of practice with the cards leads to a personal relationship with each of them, so I get a basic message from the cards themselves, but I like to also use Nancy's book for additional information. The *Motherpeace* book by Vicki Noble is also good, especially for complicated questions and answers. My tarot method is eccentric, but it works for me.

—Eileen

Can I do my own tarot card reading?

I think that all divination is very powerful when done for yourself and by yourself. You are tapping into your own psyche, so who is better qualified? Sometimes you are so close to a problem that it can make the reading hard, but I don't know how anyone can say you absolutely cannot do readings for yourself.

Get a good friend to do a reading for you if you feel you aren't being objective. Some Witches are more gifted in certain areas, but with practice I think you can be objective. Only your experience or inexperience will affect your readings.

—Cerelia

I think divination is a way for the Universe to communicate with us. I only read the cards for myself, never for others, but I also appreciate it when another Witch reads for me. Sometimes another person can see the whole forest, while we are just looking at trees.

—Eileen

I have trouble remembering the meanings of the cards.

The meaning of the cards will begin to stick in your mind after a while. Your spirit will start interpreting them with greater depth and understanding as you become more experienced.

—Cerelia

What's the Wheel of the Year spread?

You draw twelve cards, one card for each month, and arrange them in a circle. You then draw a thirteenth card to represent an overview of the year, and place it in the center of the circle. You read the cards in month order, and read the final card last. It's helpful to keep a record of which cards you drew for which months, so that you can check on the accuracy of your reading as the year progresses.

—Eileen

Can you create your own tarot spread?

Of course you can invent new spreads, why not? Use your intuition and creativity.

—Eileen

Can I buy a tarot deck, or do I have to wait for someone to give me one?

A tarot deck does not have to be given as a gift. Some Witches would have to wait forever to receive a deck that way! I would hate to think I had to wait to get a deck I really wanted, and had to hint to someone to buy it for me. One day in a shop I heard a young man saying that he couldn't buy his own deck, that it had to be a gift. (I think he was hinting.) I have also heard this online many times.

Although a deck is a very special gift, choosing a deck yourself can prove to be much more powerful. Many stores have sample decks you are allowed to look at and touch, to get a feel for which deck speaks to you. I pick my own decks. I hold them, and get a feel from them. I choose them. I don't hint. I buy.

—*Cerelia*

Can you recommend a tarot deck?

The Shapeshifter is a very nice looking deck, as is the Dragon deck.

—*Cerelia*

There are many of them on the market, all beautiful. If you have a particular affinity for dragons, fairies, a particular pantheon, or anything like that, look for a deck that represents your interest. The best all-around general deck is probably the classic Rider-Waite one, since almost everyone is familiar with it. The pictures can be read in their simplest forms without any guide at all.

—*Eileen*

How about The Mythic Tarot?

That's that deck that I use. I have been using it for over a decade. I find the book that accompanies it excellent for answering "Who" questions. When I asked it about my son, just before he was born, it gave me the card of Odysseus.

My son is a Gemini with red hair. Odysseus had red hair, and Gemini is the sign of the Trickster, which Odysseus certainly was.

—Eileen

How about the Tarot of Ceremonial Magic?

Lots of Witches will disagree with this, but I'd put it straight into the trash——as I would anything tainted by Crowley, his teachings, or the belief systems which spawned them. There are many magical systems, but that is one I find too negative for a Wiccan to access.

—Eileen

I have a Thoth deck. The book has very weird vibes.

If you get any kind of bad feelings from anything, be it cards, books, or whatever, don't hesitate to just get rid of them. There is always a reason why you feel this way. Going with your instincts is one of the first things to learn as a Witch.

—Cerelia

I know exactly what you mean about the vibes. I'd get rid of the book and the deck, and buy myself new ones. There are many beautiful decks on the market, including other Egyptian ones, and most of them come with a book.

—Eileen

Can you recommend a tarot book?

I have several tarot books at home, but the one I use every day is Nancy Garen's *Tarot Made Easy*. I also have Vicki Noble's *Motherpeace* book, *The Mythic Tarot* from Juliet Sharman–Burke's mythology deck that I use, and *A Keeper of Words*, from Anna-Marie Ferguson's Arthurian tarot deck. They're all good, but I think a general book (such as Nancy Garen's) would be best if you are mostly new to the tarot.

—*Eileen*

How do you store the cards?

I keep mine wrapped in a black cloth, in a black velvet bag. I also keep crystals in the bag with my cards, and sometimes use the crystals in spellwork.

—*Eileen*

What can you do when a reading predicts something terrible?

That's always upsetting, but the good news is that the future is a book which has not yet been written. The Tower is the worst possible card for me, followed by the Moon. Whenever one of them turns up in a reading, I do something to try to change the cycle that I'm in, or the life-thread that I am following. This might be doing something outward, if I have been in a contemplative phase; or doing something meditative and reflective, if I have been in an active phase. It might be staying in, if I have been going out a lot, or vice versa.

Even the mundane can undo a card's prediction: call different people, vary your normal routine, listen to new (or old) music, change your diet, take different routes, rearrange your furniture, and so on. Invite someone into (or out of) your life.

Make changes. Read the cards again after making some changes, and you may find that the frightening message is no longer there.

—Eileen

A strange discharge of energy happened during a tarot reading. Can you explain this?

Tarot readings can raise a lot of energy, even if you don't intend for that to happen. Many years ago, before I was disabled, a coworker asked me to read the cards for her. We were the only ones in the office on a Sunday, and I'd brought my cards. I'm not a reader. I never read for anyone else, but I helped her to draw a spread of cards, and read and interpret them.

It was dead quiet in the office, when we suddenly heard what we thought was a gunshot. (This was in Brooklyn, so gunshots wouldn't have been too unusual.) We then heard a strange crackling noise, and went to investigate it. The owner's office had glass walls. It was a self-contained room, set in the middle of the larger office space. There was a hole in the glass. It was safety glass, so it had begun crackling slowly apart, with the cracks radiating from the hole.

We thought at first this was a bullet hole and considered calling the police, but after looking around the office we determined that it could not have been caused by a bullet. The hole faced a wall, not a door or window from which a shot could have come. We then thought ricochet, but there was no entry hole in any of the windows or exterior walls of the office, and the door was intact.

The hair went up on the backs of our necks, and we started to freak ourselves out as we realized we absolutely could not explain why the glass was slowly shattering. We got so spooked that we locked up and left, with the glass continuing to crackle apart behind us.

The next time I went to the office, the glass had been replaced. We'd told everyone what happened (without mentioning the tarot cards), but I'm not sure if anyone believed us. It was very strange.

It is possible, of course, that there is a scientific explanation for what happened. There may have been some sort of air pressure or temperature difference between the glass room and the rest of the office that caused it, but I think we did it, by accidentally raising power during the tarot reading.

—*Eileen*

HEALING

Is it okay to cast healing spells for people?

Most Witches think that it isn't proper to cast a healing spell for someone unless they have asked for magical help. There are exceptions, of course, such as for your own child, or when someone is unable to make the request but you know they would welcome your magical help. The important thing is not to violate someone else's belief system with magical intervention.

—Eileen

I worry that even if someone asks me for my help as a Witch, the result will not be as they like and they will hate me for it afterwards.

It sounds like you might never feel you could ever do a spell. If that is so, it's okay.

If someone begged me for help, I would be there for him or her. In my opinion, the energies will only work for the good of the person who gives permission. This is why we never do any healing work without the person's permission.

—Cerelia

If a Witch refuses to cast the spell and the person dies the next day, is that the Witch's fault?

You never really know for sure. This is why working with magic or healing is very serious. It is work that should be thought out carefully. Most of the time we just need to follow simple common sense, but if all the choices or outcomes confuse or worry us, then I would suggest not doing any magic.

You have pointed out how serious magical workings are, and that they take a lot of thought and care. If you are an ethical Witch, your magic is done with a lot of love.

—Cerelia

Why do I feel exhausted after I cast a healing spell?

The usual cause of feeling tired after a healing spell is that you used your own energy. Using your personal power is a mistake in magic. You should instead act as a conduit for the healing energy of the Universe. Anyone who does psychic healing needs to take care.

—Eileen

How do I do this?

For any healing work, you need to raise energy (power), then channel it from whatever source(s) you usually use: Moon, Sun, wind, water, trees, animals, crystals, the ocean, the gods, or whatever. When you complete your spell or ritual, you ground the power and return it to its source. This is the safest way for any healer to work.

—Eileen

Why shouldn't we use our personal energy to heal someone?

We need to use the energies from the Universe, drawn through us, without using our own energies. We become ill if we do not do this, because we are depleting our own energy by giving it away. It just takes practice, to learn to use the energies from the proper place. Sometimes, when we are very involved in the outcome for someone we really care about, we forget this and may suffer the consequences.

—Cerelia

Using your own energy in a healing can be dangerous to your health. It can leave you open to taking into yourself the disease that you are trying to cure. Some healers will not work on their own loved ones, because they fear that they will overdo it out of love and become ill themselves.

—Eileen

How do we use the energies of the Universe to heal, but make sure that we do not deplete our own? How can we tell?

Sometimes we just mess up, especially when working with those we love, but a healer must learn to transfer energy, to channel it without using all of his or her own energy, and thereby run the risk of absorbing the other person's illness. Healing is not something that should be practiced without some training. It requires a lot of skill to do correctly. There are many healing techniques that Witches use. Using the aura is one of the most utilized ways. Other forms of healing include working with colors and crystals and gems.

As a healer, you are sort of like a hose through which the Universe can come. This is where you need to know if you are pulling from your own aura, or from Mother Earth herself. This is why learning how to do it properly is important. Healing is a lot more than just imagining; you are actually doing.

There is a vital force that exists in the Universe. It has many names, depending on the culture. Some call it Prana, and it is called Ki in Japanese. Healers have a natural abundance of this vital force, and they pass it on to others who need it. I can only explain this simply, as I see it. I am sure that other Witches heal in many other ways.

Energy is passed through the crown chakra, and is passed through the palms of the Witch to the person in need. The more that the Witch sends out that is good, the more he or she gets back, so it is a continual flow. We are sincerely connected to the Universe. Healing can also be done long distance. To me, when it is working properly, healing is a physical sensation of heat and love.

—Cerelia

Can Witches practice Reiki?

Reiki is a natural for Witches, since we already use energy to heal. Reiki has been known and used, under many names, for thousands of years in the East. It was kept such a closely guarded secret that it was virtually lost, until its modern revival.

This is exactly why I am a big proponent of "Guard the Mysteries—reveal them." Many magical adepts disagree strongly with me on this. They think that I share too much knowledge, but I think that secrets are negative and lost knowledge helps no one.

—Eileen

Can visualization be used in healing?

The human body has a natural propensity to heal itself. Creative visualization and energy work are very effective in healing because they empower the body to achieve what it is trying to do anyway.

—Eileen

I am ill, but the doctors say there is nothing wrong. Can I work spells to help?

You can seriously work with spells and healing techniques. There have been many cases (depending how many doctors you have gone to) where a woman is told nothing is wrong, when in reality, it's just that no doctor has been able to diagnose the problem.

I don't like doctors who say that nothing is wrong with you, instead of saying, "I just don't know." You know when something is not right with you. Except for people who may have mental problems, and may be constantly imagining things, most of us know when there is something wrong with us.

So yes, use the healing techniques and spells, but know that they are never recommended as a substitute for medical science. They are partners, so to speak. If you are seriously ill, don't stop trying to find the root of the problem. Yes, stress and other non-physical symptoms can make it hard for a doctor to find something physically wrong, but you know your symptoms and how serious they feel. Don't stop trying to find medical help.

We are still in human bodies. We have to follow the laws of nature and science and our bodies. There is nothing wrong with working with science and medicine as we know it, along with our spells and healing techniques. In fact, we strongly suggest it. Science and magic go hand in hand. You can also check into homeopathy. Please keep all of this in mind.

—*Cerelia*

What information is needed, to ask other Witches for help for someone?

With requests for energy and healing, it's helpful to include the person's first name and a general geographic location. This assists with directing the energy.

—*Eileen*

My son needs all the healing energies that you can send for his surgery. Can you help?

I can certainly sympathize with you and your son, after my son's accident and the last couple of operations he has had to have. This group of wonderful Witches have come through royally. My son had a broken femur, a rod put in his leg, and pins in a shattered thumb, but the doctor cannot believe that he has healed as fast as he has. He has surpassed the doctor's expectations, and he gives much of the credit for this to the Witches on this list.

One of his friends said that "Even your nose has straightened" (it had been broken but never reset). My son said, "Yeah, now if I could just grow my teeth back. . . ." (Well, we Witches can only do so much, after all.)

So everyone say a few words for her son tonight. I know he will receive much healing energy.

—*Cerelia*

Can healing spells be cast during the Waxing Moon, to gain health, and during the Waning Moon, to banish disease?

Yes. This means that healing spells can be done at any time.

—*Eileen*

Can I cast spells when I am ill?

Physical pain or discomfort interfere with concentration, and make it hard to focus on your objective. It is said that we should never work magic when we are ill. This is good advice, but it is not always practical. Casting a circle can require a lot of energy. Smaller spells, those worked without circles, can be better if you're sick but have a need to work magically. Witches with chronic illnesses save magic for our good days.

—Eileen

If I get sick, does this mean that I have angered the Goddess?

We all get sick sometimes. This is not a sign of the disfavor or abandonment of the Goddess; it's just a normal part of life. Being Witches doesn't mean that we will always enjoy good health. The only time we can take illness personally is if we inflicted it upon ourselves, such as lung problems for smokers, and so on.

—Eileen

My mother has dementia and cannot even drink or eat. Is there a spell I can do to help her?

Blessings to you and your mother. Remember that anything you do or say can be a form of a spell or ritual. Just being there for her and talking to her, even if you think she cannot comprehend, is a blessing and gift from you to her.

I am so sorry for your sorrow. Though it is a tremendous heartache, be glad that you have the opportunity to be with her and send her peacefully to the Summerlands. I was not that blessed when my mother passed away.

Don't worry about spells and such. Your actions and words speak louder to the Goddess than any spell could ever do.

—Cerelia

WORKING WITH THE MOON

Do you have to be outdoors to work with the Moon?

I love working with the Moon, and can't imagine working without it. This doesn't mean that I have to work outside, though. I know when the Moon is Full or New by being consciously aware of it all the time; and, of course, I have my calendar.

—*Cerelia*

Can you work with the Moon if you cannot see it?

I'm an urban Witch and can't see the Moon from my windows either. I use a calendar to follow its stages, and that works just fine for me.

—*Eileen*

I have the advantage of seeing the Moon most of the time, but some Witches do not. Don't feel you have to physically see the Moon to work with it. Your calendar should have the Full Moon and New Moon on it. Just follow that, and know that it is correct on the calendar. The Moon is still there, whether you can see it or not . . . and its powers are always there.

—*Cerelia*

How do we work with the Moon?

You can work with the Moon in various ways. You could begin a diet at the New Moon, for example, with your focus on the diet succeeding. You could also start your diet at the Full Moon, with your focus on your body growing smaller with the Moon as it wanes.

—*Eileen*

What are the stages of the Moon?

The New Moon (or Crescent Moon) is when the Moon starts to grow (wax), until it becomes full (Full Moon). Just think of waxing as growing, and waning (decreasing) as when the Full Moon starts to decrease in size.

—*Cerelia*

Is it crazy to consider myself as having a relationship with the Moon?

That sounds perfectly normal to Witches. Some of us are more sensitive than others to the enchantment of the Moon. Communing with the Moon, a prime symbol of the Goddess, is an excellent way to commune with her.

—*Eileen*

When should I cast my spell?

You go according to whatever feels right to you. We can cast spells whenever we like, but they are thought to be most effective when cast in accordance with the Moon. Some workings, such as banishings, are best performed while the Moon is waning. We can drive ourselves totally insane over astrological timing. It's usually a lot less stressful to just trust yourself and go with your gut.

—*Eileen*

If I'm not yet formally initiated, do I have the right to perform the Drawing Down the Moon ritual?

The Moon belongs to everyone, so of course, you have as much right to it as everyone else does.

—*Eileen*

—New Moon—

What does the New Moon have to do with spells?

The New Moon represents a new beginning and is very important. If you start your spell as the New Moon is starting to grow, your spell will grow along with the Moon, to be fulfilled when the Moon becomes full. Spells that take time to be fulfilled are best done at a New Moon.

—Cerelia

What sort of spells should I cast on the New Moon?

The New Moon is an auspicious time for beginning anything that you hope will grow and be successful.

—Eileen

New plans, new endeavors, your garden, and your spells, are all started on a New Moon. It is a wonderful time for all new endeavors: moving, love, your spiritual life, and so on. Witches also cut their hair (slightly, for growth) at the New Moon. You'll be amazed by how much it can grow by the following Full Moon. The New Moon is also a good time to look at yourself and see what changes are needed in you, or in your life.

—Cerelia

Is October's New Moon the last one of the Pagan year?

I count the Moons that way, starting and ending with Samhain, because this makes sense to me. You will find other Pagans doing it differently, often in accord with the particular culture or pantheon they mainly worship within.

—Eileen

───────WAXING MOON───────

When is the Waxing Moon?

The Waxing Moon starts out as the New Moon. It progresses to the Full Moon, hence the word waxing.

—*Cerelia*

What kind of workings should I do while the Moon is waxing?

The Waxing Moon is for spells of attraction or increase. For example, a money spell can be cast to draw money, a job, more customers, or whatever you need.

—*Eileen*

───────FULL MOON───────

What kind of workings should I do when the Moon is full?

The Full Moon is a major mojo night. It's great for every kind of spell, but especially good for bringing long spells (such as prosperity spells, or transformations) to culmination. It's also considered the best night for love spells and sex magic.

—*Eileen*

Aren't there names for each Full Moon? What are they?

Yes, each Full Moon does have a name. Those names differ from author to author, because there are so many different names for the Full Moon. Here is a list of some of the names:

January: Wolf Moon

February: Ice Moon, Hunger Moon, Wild Moon, etc.

March: Storm Moon

April: Growing Moon

May: Hare Moon

June: Mead Moon

July: Hay Moon

August: Corn Moon

September: Harvest Moon

October: Blood Moon

November: Snow Moon

December: Cold Moon

But remember that there are also other names for the Full Moons.

—*Cerelia*

Will a Full Moon spell work on a cloudy night?

This depends on you, on whether you feel like you can channel the Moon without seeing it. If it bothers you, wait for a visible Full Moon or wait for the next night, since many Witches consider the Moon to be full for three days (the days before and after the official Full Moon).

—*Eileen*

────── WANING MOON ──────

When is the Waning Moon?

The Waning Moon is the days following a Full Moon. The Moon decreases in size (as we perceive it), until the next New Moon.

—Cerelia

What kind of spells should I cast while the Moon is waning?

The Waning Moon is for spells of banishing, binding, or decrease. This doesn't mean we cannot work positive magic while the Moon is waning. We can banish disease, decrease unhappiness, bind a child molester, cast a money spell to decrease poverty or slow business, and so on.

—Eileen

────── DARK OF THE MOON ──────

What's the Dark of the Moon?

The Full Moon decreases in size, until it seems that nothing is there. This is the Dark of the Moon. Then the New Moon is exposed. It begins waxing, growing until it becomes full again.

—Cerelia

If the Moon is dark twice in the same month, is there a name for this?

The second Dark Moon in one month is called a Fairy Moon, or a Sidhe (pronounced "shee") Moon.

—Eileen

—————————BLUE MOON—————————

What's a Blue Moon?

Since this Moon-month has not survived in the solar calendar which we now use, there is no corresponding name. However, all cultures which used a lunar calendar had a Blue Moon, or thirteenth month. Some considered this time to be only a few days long. For others, it covered an entire twenty-nine days. Some cultures gave this month a name, but others considered it a dread or especially holy time that was too sacred to name. The second of two Full Moons in one month is also called a Blue Moon.

—Cerelia

A Blue Moon is the second Full Moon in one calendar month. Many Witches consider it an especially magical night.

—Eileen

What kind of spells should we cast when there is a Blue Moon?

Blue Moons are great for wish spells, but remember to be careful about what you wish for. It's a good idea to think a wish through before making it, to follow all the threads of its possible consequences, and to word it very carefully.

—Eileen

MENSTRUATION

Why do I seem to always get my period on or near the Full Moon?

That's why menstruation is also called moontime. The Moon rules tides, so Full Moon is the most natural time for menstruation to occur. Primitive patriarchal societies were frightened by the power they believed menstrual blood held, so that's probably one of the reasons why magic became associated with the Full Moon.

—Eileen

Why are we discussing menstruation?

This a very important subject to Pagan women. After so many years of patriarchy telling us that menstruation was dirty and that women were to be avoided at these times, it is important to have this discussion so that we can enlighten others to the fact that this is untrue. Female Witches have found that menstruation is not a curse, but a source of power. The human body is largely made of water. We all know that the Moon affects the tides, so we can see that it also affects our own bodies. We also know that the Full Moon affects everyone, male or female, in terms of emotions, temperament, and so on.

Since the Goddess is coming back into her own, the subject of women and spirituality has rightfully come to the forefront. A woman's menstrual cycle is directly tied to the Moon phases. The lunar cycle reflects a woman's cycle: Maiden, Mother, Crone; or New Moon, Full Moon, Waxing Moon. Some women start their periods around the New Moon, others around or on the Full Moon. Some women are more clairvoyant three days before a New Moon, or three days after one.

We should each learn at which phase of the Moon our own powers seem to be at their best. A book that goes into more specifics about what the Moon means to Witches is *Grandmother Moon*, by Z. Budapest.

—*Cerelia*

What does menstruation have to do with magic?

The old notion that women faint at the sight of blood is one of the most ridiculous things patriarchy ever came up with. This is from my poem "Cycles & Rain":

> come out to the forest clearings
> mistletoe and rowan trees
> if you have the heart
> who will you find there?
> women with their menstrual blood
> flowing down their legs
> women stamping, women steaming
> women singing to the rain
> women winding widdershins
> and banging tambourines

The reason all that nonsense got started was because the patriarchs feared menstrual blood, which was traditionally regarded as powerful magic. According to Robert Graves in *The White Goddess*:

> The magical connection of the Moon with menstruation is strong and widespread. The baleful moon-dew used by the witches of Thessaly was apparently a girl's first menstrual blood, taken during an eclipse of the Moon. Pliny devotes a whole

chapter of his *Natural History* to the subject and gives a long list of the powers for good and bad that a menstruating woman possesses. Her touch can blast vines, ivy, and rue, fade purple cloth, blacken linen in the wash-tub, tarnish copper, make bees desert their hives, and cause abortions in mares; but she can also rid a field of pests by walking around it naked before sunrise, calm a storm at sea by exposing her genitals, and cure boils, erysipelas, hydrophobia, and barrenness. In the Talmud it is said that if a menstruating woman passes between two men, one of them will die.[13]

That fear was why the Hebrews, for example, segregated menstruating women from the rest of the tribe. They didn't isolate the women in separate tents because they were unclean; the Hebrews did it to contain the magic they feared women could command at that time of their cycle. A patriarchal culture will never admit to that fear, of course, but there it is.

—Eileen

How can I get my body to menstruate at Full Moon?

Menstrual cycles can be influenced by many things. For example, women who work together often notice that after a while, everyone in the office seems to menstruate around the same time. To allow the Moon to rule your cycle, all you have to do is tune into the Moon and be mindful of the Full Moon approaching. Give it a few months, and you will see your cycle start to shift moonward.

I first read about this when I was a kid, in a novel. (I think it was *Even Cowgirls Get the Blues* by Tom Robbins.) The idea of menstruating in sync with the lunar phases seemed preposterous to me at the time, but now my period always seems to come at Full Moon. Remember that we're Witches, and we can do amazing things.

—*Eileen*

Is a Witch's body adversely affected during her menstrual period?

The thing to remember is that your cycle is not a curse. Women have been brought up to believe that a woman's period is a curse, and that is why so many women feel so tainted, drained, and dirty during their period. This is also why many Witchcraft traditions have a celebration of womanhood when a female child becomes a woman. This helps her feel empowered, not drained.

In Shamanism, menstruation is supposed to be a time of increased power. If you aren't a timid soul, it is said you should go sit on Mother Earth during your period, and let your blood run back into the earth (you could do this in a dress, discreetly).

—*Cerelia*

Do ovulation and menstruation affect women's magical energy?

Some yes, and some no. We're all very different when it comes to hormones and cycles and things. Moontime is Full Moon/full power for some Witches, the opposite for others, and some of us barely notice our cycles.

—*Eileen*

ANOINTING

Is anointing mandatory? How do we do it?

Like most things, different Witches have different ways of anointing. With candles, some Witches like to rub them with oil, some prefer to drip oil onto them, and some don't bother anointing candles at all. For anointing the body, altar, or tools, some Witches like to make the sign of the pentacle with the oil, while others simply dip their index fingers into an oil and touch whatever is being anointed. Other Witches do it differently.

I tend to be a minimalist in most things magical, so I'm not big on anointing myself or anything else. I'll rub an oil on my wrists or behind my ears more because of its magical smell than anything else. There is no right way or wrong way to anoint, just whatever works for you. Experiment with different methods, and you'll soon have your own way of anointing.

—*Eileen*

Where on the body do we anoint?

It's individual, like everything else. I like the third eye, and my pulse points if it's an oil whose smell I really like.

—*Eileen*

——————ASTROLOGY——————

Note: Astrology is a huge topic, but you will only find a very short section on it here because neither of us is an expert in it. Knowledge of the planets and how they affect life on Earth is useful to Witches: it helps us with our inner work, with knowing ourselves, and with counseling the people who turn to us for help. "As above, so below" is also one of our Mysteries.

—Eileen

Are we what our signs say we are?

Yes and no. Astrology isn't everything, because we're more complicated than that. Astrology is not always destiny. None of us ever fit our astrological profiles exactly. Some people are very much like the typical profile for their sign, but others don't fit it at all. The attributes put forth for the various astrological signs are just generally true, not specifically so. Moon signs and rising signs influence who we are almost as much as our Sun signs do, so that's why a comprehensive natal chart is necessary to understand yourself (or anyone else) astrologically.

—Eileen

Is there a simple book you can use to cast birth charts?

Yes. I use *Heaven Knows What*, by Grant Lewi. It gives extremely accurate readings.

—Eileen

Why doesn't anything I read about my sign fit me?

Find out what your Moon and Ascending signs are, and perhaps you will find your answers there.

—Eileen

*If I am a Pisces and my element is Water, does this mean I can't be
connected to Air?*

No. Your sign connects you to things, but it doesn't discon-
nect you from others.

—Eileen

What can astrology tell me about my baby?

A complete natal chart, one that takes all the planets and their
positions into account, is needed to really get a picture of
what might lie ahead for your child.

—Eileen

If my Sun and Moon are both in Virgo, what am I?

A double Virgo!

—Eileen

How can I learn more about astrology?

Many libraries carry astrology books. Focus on the serious
books, and you will learn a lot.

—Eileen

CLEARING

How do you purify your home?

I use white sage sticks to smudge my house for purification and protection. It has a beautiful and cleansing smell. It is burnt in a certain way throughout the rooms in your house, and the smoke cleanses the negativity out of your home. The sticks are very inexpensive.

—*Cerelia*

How do I clear my personal space?

Herbs such as sage, lavender, or rosemary are good choices to burn as incense for clearing. So is camphor, or even brimstone, if the problem is severe. Magical sweeping can also be used for clearing. You sweep toward the door, sweeping any negativity right out of the house. This can be done with a chant such as the traditional:

> *Besom, besom, Witch's broom,*
> *Sweep all evil from this room.*

You can even sweep yourself, to get rid of whatever you think you have been overlaid with. Laughter works, too, tear-streaming stitch-in-your-gut belly laughs that break up negativity and force it out of the house.

—*Eileen*

What's the proper way to smudge your home?

Exercise: Smudging is relatively easy. As with anything magical, strong intent is very important. When I do a whole house, I light the sage stick and wave out any flames. I tip the smudge stick up against the side of a bowl, to get it smoking.

A bowl, any kind of bowl that is heat proof, is used to catch any ashes that may fall on the floor while you walk from room to room.

Most smudge sticks burn slowly. I carry the bowl, the smudge stick, and something to act as a small fan. I carry it as high into the corners of the rooms as I can. I move the stick up and down, slowly fanning the stick to keep the smoke coming.

I usually know what I am going to say. In a trance state, I keep repeating it all the way around each room, in every corner and closet. I go to each room and do this, even in the hallways. If a room seems especially troubled, I will linger a little longer, or do the room a little slower.

If the smudge stick is still burning when I have finished, I set it down and allow it to burn itself out. I only use one stick for any smudge ceremony, so I make sure I have burned it all up. That is why small smudge sticks are better, in my opinion. Some Witches believe that you should stop smudging when the stick stops smoking.

I make sure that the whole house is done, and do not use that stick for any other smudging. I make sure it is completely burned up. That is me. I am sure that, as with any other kind of magical work, there are different ways to accomplish smudging.

—*Cerelia*

What can you use for the element of Air, to clear a sacred space?

A bell or a gong could be rung, or incense used to smudge the air.

—*Eileen*

How do I clear my new home?

I always use salt and water when I move to a new apartment, unless the place has such a positive vibe that I don't feel the need to asperge it.

—Eileen

What should my friend do about a ring with bad vibes?

It is more likely her imagination than an actual negative vibration from the ring. Her belief in its negative power could even be the cause of bad things happening. Try cleansing it for her in salt, or moonlight, or water, or whatever you like to use. You could also suggest that she just get rid of the ring.

—Eileen

We found a voodoo doll, with pins stuck in it. We pulled the pins out, but what do we do with them and the doll? We want to get rid of it without causing harm to anyone.

I'd put it in a container (bag, box, whatever) and fill it with salt, with the intent of neutralizing the doll by absorbing its energy and rendering it harmless. I'd put the pins in with it. Then I would get rid of it, get it out of my home and as far away from me as possible: throw it away, drive it to the dump, or whatever is the best method available. I would then perform some sort of purification of the place where I found it, and cast some extra protection around the house and everyone who lives there or visits.

—Eileen

Consecration

Do I have to consecrate my candles and tools and things?

Some Witches do not consecrate. I didn't at first, but then I began to feel a need to, because my tools and altar were out in the open. I became more sensitive to negativity and the energies of others who may come into my home. I felt that consecrating my things protected them from other people's negativity, from whatever else was going on, from whoever had been in the house, and so on. Consecrating candles cleanses them of the negativity of others who may have handled the candles before I purchased them. Consecration is a matter of choice, as with anything else.

—*Cerelia*

Every Witch has a different way of consecrating. Some Witches don't consecrate at all, feeling that magical use, or even just placing something on the altar, consecrates it. You don't have to ever consecrate anything. I never do. I simply use new tools, but most Witches like to consecrate magical things before use. So, consecrate things whenever you feel the need to do so.

—*Eileen*

Is there one correct way to consecrate candles?

There are different variations with different Witches. You will find that something is more appealing, or works better for you, than something another Witch may have told you. Use what works for you.

—*Cerelia*

How often should consecration be performed?

Whenever you feel the need.

—*Eileen*

——————GROUNDING AND CENTERING——————

How do I ground myself?

People often comment on how grounded I am. A big reason for this, I think, is the fact that I am almost always barefoot when I am at home, and that home is where I spend most of my time. So for grounding and centering, try working bare-foot. It's a great way to get in touch with Earth energy, and remain in touch with it. This can be especially helpfully to people with Air signs, or whose main connection is to Air energy.

—*Eileen*

How can I ground myself after a ritual?

Exercise: Stand with your feet firmly on the ground (or floor, depending on where you are), and imagine your feet growing roots. Imagine the roots going down into the earth, and attach-ing themselves into the ground. Hold this image until you feel grounded and stable. Then imagine the roots letting go, and relax. Have some juice and cookies to regain your strength.

—*Cerelia*

If all else fails, go outside barefoot. Physically touch the soil, or hug a tree, or use whatever medium of transference makes sense for you.

—*Eileen*

How do I ground power?

Every Witch has his or her own way of doing it. I am very connected with the Earth element, so I open my palms toward the ground and feel the power I raised flowing out of me, back into the Earth. Experiment, and you'll find the way that's best for you. Remember that we Witches are conduits for the energy, and must return it to its source when we are through using it.

—*Eileen*

Can energy be properly grounded if you are upstairs?

Yes. I'm an urban Witch and confirmed apartment-dweller, and I have no trouble grounding myself.

—*Eileen*

What are some quick things you can do to center yourself?

Read tarot cards, or burn incense.

—*Eileen*

Why should I ground and center?

Failure to ground power can leave the door between the worlds open, and cause strange things to start happening. Remember to always earth the energy that you raise, to return it to its source, rather than carrying it away with you. If you forget, do it as soon as you remember.

Grounding and re-centering is very important after any spell, ritual, or other working, especially when you are unaccustomed to raising and channeling power. This is why cakes and ale are traditional. It needn't literally be cake and alcoholic beverages, but ingesting simple sugars and carbohydrates is helpful with getting back to feeling normal.

—Eileen

————LOCATING LOST ITEMS————

How can I find a lost object?

When something is missing, what I do is to go back mentally to the last time and place where I know the object was, and retrace (mentally or physically) my steps from there. This has never failed to work for me, and it has also usually worked when I have done it for others. It's akin to taking someone through a guided meditation, as you help them to focus and guide their steps.

The most spectacular success I had with this method was in Los Angeles, before I became disabled. My company was doing the marketing for a building that was under renovation. A young workman had lost the master key to the building, after he had spent the whole day installing new locks in all the apartment doors. If he hadn't located the key, about one hundred locks would have had to have been changed, and he would surely have lost his job.

I got him to calm down, focus, and retrace his steps mentally. This worked so well that when we finished he was able to go upstairs, remove just one of the newly installed door sills, and find the master key under it. He was amazed by the experience, and kept asking me for weeks afterward how I'd done it.

The psychic component is also part of this method, since you have to feel your way back to the object, and trust that feeling as much, if not more, than your memory.

—*Eileen*

———————ORGANIZATION———————

What other skills should Witches have? [14]

Organizational skills are helpful in Witchcraft. How else to locate herbs in an overstuffed Witch's cabinet?

—*Eileen*

CHAPTER FIVE

Witchcraft

What is Witchcraft?

Witchcraft is a religion, one that is very much about service to others. In helping someone, you serve the Goddess. Witchcraft is physics, when you get to the level of quantum mechanics. Real Witchcraft would make poor drama, since there are few special effects. Magic takes place mostly in the mind, and is more often felt than seen.

—*Eileen*

You find, in time, that you live Witchcraft every day, even within your mundane life. It is always there, giving you answers (and questions) about the life we live. Witchcraft becomes such a part of your life, that you don't even think to call what you are doing or experiencing a religion. Witchcraft is life. We breathe it, and live it, every day.

Witchcraft is ultimately what I live in my life. It is the joyous celebration (and sometimes sorrows) that we all have to deal with in our everyday lives. Witchcraft is my breath, which to me is saying that I don't have to even think about it, in terms of calling it a name. I don't have to stop and think about why I am doing something. Witchcraft is me.

That is why it is said that you should live your faith, not just practice it. It is a shame that Witchcraft is so feared, when it is so beautiful.

—*Cerelia*

Why does the word Witchcraft scare so many people? My parents are petrified when I even say the word.

The word Witchcraft scares most people to death, due to hundreds and hundreds of years of bigotry and propaganda from the Christian churches. You can't blame your parents for loving you and trying to protect you, even in ignorance.

—*Cerelia*

What can you learn from Witchcraft?

Witchcraft helps you find peace within yourself, and a belief in yourself. It teaches you to take responsibility for yourself. It gives you a deep reverence for Nature, and teaches you that is where the true Goddess lies.

—*Cerelia*

What's the right way to practice Witchcraft?

There is no right and wrong in magic, so long as you harm none. Combine all the books you have read, then adapt, adopt, and reject. Reject whatever feels wrong for you, adapt everything that comes close, and adopt the things which feel just right. Witchcraft isn't static. Most of us find our practices evolving over the years, as we learn more and experience new things.

—*Eileen*

Isn't Witchcraft just for women?

Learn more about it, and you will see that this isn't so. Reading books written by male Witches might help you to have a better understanding.

—*Eileen*

What's magic?

You have to know the importance of the Universe and all of Nature, before you can even begin to talk about magic. Learn the spiritual side first, before wanting to know what magic is.

—Cerelia

To Wiccans, magic is a sacred gift of the Goddess (the Universe). We do not insult her by misusing magic. We do not use it to cause harm, nor do we waste it on trying to perform parlor tricks or stage magic. For Wiccans magic isn't about power, it's all about the Goddess.

I believe that science will eventually explain how and why magic works, but that will not diminish magic one bit. Understanding the geology or astrophysics of the Moon makes it no less beautiful or mysterious when it shines brightly in the velvet sky, or peeps out through a veil of fog.

One of the most interesting conversations of my life was with a physicist from China. We somehow got to discussing quantum mechanics. He spoke in scientific terms, and I spoke in magical ones. After a bit, we both realized that we were describing the same things, just using different names for them. I was never a scientific person, and never took a physics course in my life, but I was able to discuss quantum mechanics with a physicist because I understood magic.

He was amazed, too, and told me that it was difficult for him to find other scientists who could understand what he was talking about. I have never forgotten that conversation, because it was such a revelation to me. Esoteric thought is esoteric thought, I guess.

Physical effects are often seen in magic, such as candles burning brighter, or longer, because magic is the manipulation of energy. Things which don't usually explode are liable to do so. Magic releases a lot of energy. Things often shatter, especially in the beginning. Nothing to worry about, it's just magic.

—*Eileen*

Every thought is magic, so be careful what you think.

—*Cerelia*

Are magic and Witchcraft supernatural?

Witchcraft is not supernatural. Quite the contrary: it follows the laws of science (although science does not recognize some of the magical workings that we deal with . . . yet). For example: we can't physically fly, we can't change our eye color, and so on. We work with the unseen forces of the Universe. People use the word supernatural for things they cannot see or readily prove. To Witches, the energies we work with are very real, and very natural.

Because magic is not supernatural, it stands to reason that magic and science go hand in hand. Remember that Witchcraft is based on science. If something isn't scientifically possible, it isn't magically possible (except that science hasn't yet discovered some of the things that it cannot see).

—*Cerelia*

Magic is the manipulation of energy to manifest a desired result. Energy is all around us: wind power, solar power, bio energy, and so on. Magic is therefore natural, not supernatural, and subject to the laws of physics (bearing in mind that we do not yet completely understand those laws). The Sun, wind, the Moon, storms, earthquakes . . . all of these can be used magically.

Because it is natural, magic can only achieve things which are in accord with the laws of physics (no flying on brooms, no changing into animals, no turning invisible, and so on.) Quantum mechanics is the branch of physics to investigate for a better scientific explanation.

—Eileen

What advice can you give me about magic?

Don't get hung up on the details and the mechanics of magic. Get in touch with the Goddess, trust yourself, listen to your inner voice, and go with the flow of life and magic.

—Eileen

What's intent?

As we've said many times, tools and circles are not the magic . . . you are. Your intent. If your spell fails, it may be that what you were working for was not as important to you as you thought it was. You didn't really feel the intent of what you wanted, or were working toward; therefore the spell didn't work, didn't come about.

Major intent fills us with such emotion that we feel consumed with it. It is done from the heart. That is pure intent, an intent or feeling that is so overpowering that you are filled with it. You feel it with every fiber of your being. The tools and such help you to focus, but remember where the true magic lies, in the intent!

—Cerelia

Magical techniques are tools. Intent is what makes magic positive or negative. If you cast a healing spell for someone you hate, and have that hatred on your mind or in your heart while you say the healing words, or burn the healing herbs, you're probably doing the person harm.

—Eileen

How can I explain magic to a scientist?

Explain magic in terms of physics, how a particle under study changes its movements because it is being studied. We call that magical attention. Help the scientist to design some experiments, some ways to measure magic (but don't ask me how to do that, because I'm definitely not scientific).

—Eileen

Why can't scientists or rationalists understand that in studying the Craft, as with all religions, you work on faith and this can have great personal meaning?

I think science makes strides every day, but to many scientists, if they can't prove something, or have tangible evidence of it, it isn't real and it doesn't exist. They never admit it when what spiritualists have been saying for many, many years is really the same thing as what they now call a "scientific discovery."

—Cerelia

What's an adept?

A magical adept is a person, Witch or otherwise, who knows how to channel energy and use it.

—Eileen

What's sorcery?

Sorcery deals with the supernatural.

—Eileen

What role does polarity play in Witchcraft?

Although we look for equality between men and women, we must also celebrate the wonderful differences, and the power of that energy and magic between them. It's very magical, and very powerful.

—Cerelia

Neither gender is more important than the other. They are equal, create balance and polarity: yin/yang, yoni/lingam, anima/animus.

In Classical Wicca, polarity is expressed in strictly male/female terms: Covens must have a high priest as well as a high priestess; male and female working partners for rituals; male teachers for females, and female teachers for males; and so on. I disagree with that interpretation of polarity. I reject its implicit rejection of homosexuality. Polarity takes many forms, and not all of them are gender-based.

We all contain both energies, anima and animus. Females getting in touch with their male selves, and males with their female selves, is an important part of the inner work it takes to be a Witch. This has nothing to do with being gay or straight, it's about knowing your whole self.

The Goddess unifies all opposites, as Starhawk pointed out. The Goddess is the sum of polarity. She contains male and female energy. She is Balance itself.

—Eileen

We need opposites to keep the world moving and multiplying. To keep the magic flowing.

Exactly. This is the yin and yang of being, without which there could be no balance.

—Eileen

What's the role of sexuality in Witchcraft?

Sex is a very important aspect of Witchcraft. Sex is the beauty of life. It is the true magic of the Universe, the interconnection of every living thing. Sex, and the energy of the female and male, are very powerful magic. They are a part of any tradition of Witchcraft. There is nothing wrong with it. The Great Rite is a very beautiful and powerful ritual, when it is held in high respect, and especially when worked between a husband and wife, or any loving couple.

—Cerelia

The absolute truth of our bodies is a source of spirituality in Wicca. We're mammals, and no amount of fasting or celibacy will change that. Desire is the force that holds the very atoms of being in place. The Universe would fly apart without desire.

—Eileen

Are drugs used in Witchcraft?

Some trads and shamanistic practices work within a boundary of usage, but this is very dangerous and it is not used just for kicks. Don't think you have to use drugs to be a Witch or to work with a Coven. There are other methods to reach changes of consciousness.

—Cerelia

Drugs can open your third eye, as my youthful experiments taught me, but they can also kill you, drive you mad, or get you incarcerated. There are much easier ways of opening your third eye, such as meditation.

—Eileen

—————————Book of Shadows—————————

What's a Book of Shadows?

It is an account of all your rituals, spells, herbs, and so on. It holds names of deities, and correspondences you have had great success with. You can put anything in a BoS that has aided you in your search, and in your practice of magic.

• *—Cerelia*

A Book of Shadows is a never-ending book, since we are all works-in-progress. In some traditions the BoS only contains rituals. In others it is secret, the repository of family or clan spells, rituals, and so forth. Solitaries have no tradition they must follow, so for us the BoS is usually a grimoire of spells, rituals, and magical information. Mine is heavy on herbalism, but another Witch's might contain mostly lunar lore and magic, mythology, or only contain spells.

—Eileen

Why does a Witch make a Book of Shadows?

A BoS is very important to keep all your information in. As a novice you will need it right at hand for spells and rituals, until you either memorize them or become adept at making them up as you go along. It is also for keeping a record of the spells that you have performed, and whether they were a success or not. Use your BoS for writing down what you thought you did right, or wrong. It is quite difficult to keep it all in your head.

—*Cerelia*

What's the importance of a Book of Shadows?

As for the Books of Shadows, they are just words. It is the practice of using what is in the BoS that is the power. The power is in you, but some Books of Shadows hold very powerful rituals passed down from Coven to Coven. Other Books hold a solitary's personal account.

—*Cerelia*

Should a Book of Shadows be handwritten?

I think so, but it's a personal choice whether you keep a handwritten Book of Shadows, or keep it on your computer. I keep both. I have a lot more information in my computer than I do in my BoS, but there's no magic in the computer. I wouldn't cast a spell atop it, as I do with my Book.

—*Eileen*

As we always say, the choice is yours. Neither is more right or wrong, but this is how I feel about it. I have both, my own BoS, and a computerized one. The computerized one contains loads of information about everything, including some things that I probably wouldn't put in my personal Book. The reason that most Witches prefer the handwritten one is for the simple fact that it is in your handwriting, so it is more attuned to the personal you.

There is power in a part of us that seems to come through in our own handwriting. If we found a BoS a hundred years from now, would you feel closer to the writings and presence of a Witch and her spells in her own handwriting, or all typed out? I guess the answer is always an individual one. I just know how I would feel.

—*Cerelia*

Is it okay to let people touch your Book?

It's best for no hands but those of Witches to touch a grimoire, in my opinion.

—*Eileen*

Can you make your BoS out of things you download from the Web?

I think it's great to have a lot of information from the Net. This is how many Witches get started, but a true BoS contains your very own workings, those which you have personally conducted: your own rituals, in your own words. Your BoS should be something that you would be proud to hand down to someone you loved and trusted, not just a bunch of Web-sites downloaded. Web downloads are a great way for people to get started, but being a Witch is about you.

I know some Witches who do their BoS typed into a binder. No one can say this is wrong. I find this much more appealing than in the computer. It's just what appeals to the individual Witch the most. At least, this way, it would be your own workings. Web sites vary so much . . . while there are some wonderful sites, most are filled with a lot of misinformation. I trust books much more, because reputable authors have done much research, whereas some sites are set up in a short time, and usually just contain information stolen from another site.

I guess the point I am trying to make is that your own personal BoS that you can hold in your hands, fill with your own experiences and spells and recipes, and so on, is the one that you will cherish for the rest of your life. You will be proud to hand it down to someone special.

—*Cerelia*

What if I lose my Book?

A lost or stolen Book of Shadows isn't gone, it's in your heart and mind and memory. What we learn matters more than what we write down. I'd miss my grimoire if it were lost or stolen or destroyed, but not having it wouldn't make me any less spiritual, any less a priestess, or any less a Witch.

—*Eileen*

——————ALTAR——————

What should an altar be made of?

Whatever is available to you, whatever looks good and feels right to you.

—*Eileen*

Where should the altar be placed?

Personal preference rules, or the physical reality of our dwelling places. My altar currently faces South, simply because it is the only wall suitable for the altar. I am not comfortable with my altar facing that direction, though, so I have seldom used it as I did before I moved to this place. I prefer to have my altar face North, my personal power direction. *Ç'est la vie*. Life, and magic, continue nonetheless.

It's great when you are able to place your altar in whatever direction feels most powerful to you (East or North, for most Witches), but this isn't always possible. It's fine to place your altar in whatever space is available to you, and use and enjoy it wherever that may be.

Fire safety should always be a consideration in altar placement. Never place an altar in front of curtains or wall hangings, in case a candle or something else you happen to be burning gets out of control.

—Eileen

The altar and ritual tools are always placed inside the circle before casting. You can place the altar in the center facing the North, a direction of power, but some Witches prefer the East, where the Sun and Moon rise. Everything you need to work with should be in the circle before casting. Don't forget the matches, an easy thing to forget.

Altar placement matters, if where it is placed bothers you. Use what feels natural to you. Any way the altar faces is acceptable. The direction of power is one that you feel and decide for yourself. Most Witches start their circles facing the North (the direction of power), or East (the sign of new beginnings, because the Sun rises in that direction).

—Cerelia

If my altar is against a wall, it cannot be in the middle of the circle when I cast one. Is this a problem?

Nope. Altars usually get placed on walls. Just envision the sphere of energy encompassing the altar, when you cast your circle.

—Eileen

My altar sits against a wall, as altars usually do. I have built-in wooden cabinets, which my altar sits between. I do not cast that many circles any more, but when I do, I use a portable altar that I can take up and put away. I visualize a protective sphere when using the altar against the wall.

If I were outside I would use a portable altar, and cast the circle physically. If you do not visualize well, use a portable altar so you can physically cast the circle. Otherwise, you could visualize the circle going around your altar space, since you are not able to physically make a circle.

—*Cerelia*

How can you keep your altar safe from children and pets?

My altar is a high altar, on top of a tall black lacquer media cabinet. I like it because it's too high for small children to reach the top of, and the rest of it serves as the storage place for all my many herbs, candles, and other Witch's supplies.

An upper shelf of a bookcase would make a good living room altar in a home with small kids. I'd have used something like that, if I hadn't happened to have had the cabinet. Even with its height, I keep my sword in a closet. There's something about boys and swords, so I know there's no way my son could resist it if he could see it.

—*Eileen*

Even if you just put up a couple of candles, some flowers, and a picture or two in your living room or wherever the kids can't reach, this will help you focus on your new path all day long. It teaches the kids about how special an altar is, so they can learn the beauty and sacredness of it as they grow (and maybe little hands will learn to leave it alone until mom says it's okay).

—*Cerelia*

Is it wrong to allow your pets to investigate your altar?

Nope. It's also okay if they eat your offerings. Just be careful of putting out things that might harm them, such as toxic herbs and lit candles.

—Eileen

What if you can't let anyone see your altar?

My altar, with a few things hidden away, just looks like part of my home decor when I'm not using it.

—Cerelia

That's how it was for me, when I lived in Egypt. I used trays then, for casting spells. Whatever works.

—Eileen

What are altar tiles used for?

Altar tiles are for fire safety, decoration, magical or religious symbolism, and so forth.

—Eileen

I have a hard time getting fresh flowers all the time. Can I use silk flowers on my altar?

You don't have to use flowers at all. I love them myself, but only use them when in season, out of my own yard. I only buy flowers on Sabbats, and I use a few silk flowers in between time.

—Cerelia

What size should an offering plate be?

That's totally up to you. It could even be a bowl.

—Eileen

Must an altar cloth be used?

I never use one, because of my concern about fire safety. I like to burn things atop surfaces that will not catch fire, such as marble, stone, and glass. This is one of those "each to his or her own" things, though. Once in a while I will use a cloth while decorating for a Sabbat or ritual, but if so, I remove it before I start burning things.

—Eileen

Must all the elements be present on your altar?

Again, personal choice.

—Eileen

What color candles should I use for the Lord and Lady, on my altar?

Whatever colors feel right to you. I like poppet candles to represent the Lord and Lady, the candles made in human forms.

—Eileen

The altar candles are traditionally red and green, the ancient magical colors for Nature: red for the God, and green for the Goddess. This can differ from Witch to Witch, though. I prefer white or silver for the Goddess, and red or green for the God. The Goddess candle is placed on the left, and the God candle on the right.

Another combination that is used is yellow or gold for the God, and white or silver for the Goddess. A reason for not using gold and silver candles, depending on where you get your candles, is that they tend to be more expensive . . . and I burn way too many candles for that!

—*Cerelia*

What stones should we have on our altars?

We don't need any stones for our altars, but we can use them if we like. If you use something to represent each of the elements on your altar, a stone (or a group of stones) can be used to represent Earth. Some Witches like to use flat stones as offering plates, or even as mini–altars.

—*Eileen*

How do you clean your altar?

I usually just dust and polish, rearrange things, wash and refill my chalice, and so on. Some Witches have a special altar oil they anoint their altars with, but that sounds too messy for me. I also do something with my altar that will make most Witches shriek in horror: I allow my cleaning woman to clean it. I feel like its energy is too strong, and too firmly set, for this to disturb or diminish it. I have been blessed with cleaning women who have good vibes in recent years, but if I disliked the woman I wouldn't allow her to touch the altar.

—*Eileen*

Is it okay to have your altar in your bedroom?

The most powerful energy, to me, is sexual energy. It can be worked with in many ways, so I do not see having the altar in the bedroom as a problem. Sex between a husband and wife is a pure, powerful energy, nothing to make any altar or spell impure.

If having the altar in the bedroom bothers one partner, the feelings of both partners have to be considered. If one feels strange about having the altar in the bedroom, there will be negative energies expressed on that partner's part, whether they mean to or not.

We have to follow what feels right to us. If one partner is strongly against having the altar in the bedroom, make a portable altar, one that you can put aside in the closet or wherever. Use it only when you are able, because you do need your privacy from all of the noisiness of everyday life. An altar doesn't have to be big and grand, just what you think you need.

—*Cerelia*

Bed, computer, altar . . . my bedroom is my sacred space. Sex is sacred in Wicca, so having your altar near you bed adds to the magic.

There are magical traditions, such as in ancient Egypt, in which you have to be in a purified state to practice magic— abstaining from sex, bathed, and with an empty stomach— but Witchcraft isn't one of them. We can even use sex to raise power for spellwork. Ultimately, our bodies are our altars.

—*Eileen*

Is it possible to have an altar at work?

Cerridwen Iris Shea wrote in "Integrating Work and Magical Life":

> When I worked in an office, even as a temp, I had a portable altar that I would take with me, wherever I worked . . . I carried with me a small square of blue velvet. On the velvet, I placed an oversized clam shell. Inside the clam shell I set a scented tea light (air and fire), a small pine cone, and several crystals. I did not light the candle, but I liked having it there. No one ever challenged me (and I temped at over a hundred corporations over the years, all across the country). I often received comments about how lovely the set-up was! It was something wonderful to have—a place of retreat on a busy desk. No matter how stressful things got, I could always look over at my mini-altar, take a few deep breaths, and come back to center.[15]

We have to be reasonable in what we expect in terms of accommodation, though. We wouldn't object if Christian coworkers had small crosses or religious icons on their desks, but might feel otherwise if they had huge crucifixes or the Stations of the Cross over their desks.

—*Eileen*

I can't have a permanent altar. It is also difficult for me to create sacred space, to keep it cleansed and consecrated.

A Witch's Box might be a good solution for you. It's just a box, of whatever size and type appeals to you, that contains all of your tools and other working supplies (candles, incense, oils, and so on). Depending on what type of box you select, it might also serve as a portable altar. You cleanse and consecrate the box in whatever way you like, and only use it for spells, rituals, worship, meditation, and so forth.

—*Eileen*

TOOLS

Do we need tools?

Some Witches are very adept, and they take to magic quickly, without the help of tools. Tools are just that, helpers. They help focus and are enjoyable, especially to a Coven or other group of Witches working together.

Ritual and tools are very important to a beginner. That is where it all starts. Many Witches continue using ritual, but after a certain time, some Witches become adept enough that ritual is used only because it is enjoyed. It doesn't make you any less of a Witch if you decide not to use tools or elaborate rituals. The magic is not in the ritual, it is in the Witch.

We always try to assure new Witches that although tools help and aid you, they are not necessary. They are excellent for training a new mind in magic. That is their purpose. After that, when one becomes more adept, you choose when and if you want to use them. After one becomes adept, tools are used mostly because they are enjoyed.

—Cerelia

Tools are just props and not that important in spellwork. Props are optional. We use candles and things because we like them, rather than because we need them. Props aid focus, that's all. You only need whatever tools you feel you need. The magic is in the Witch, not the spells or tools or candles. Some Witches work without any tools at all.

Tools are not needed to worship, to commune with the God or Goddess, or even to work magic. This is a personal choice. I still don't have a cauldron, and still use an old bronze letter opener for an athame, but I love incense and have several censers. Tools come when you need them.

—Eileen

If tools are not the important part of magic, what is?

My favorite word . . . intent! It wouldn't matter if you had five of every tool imaginable, because without intent, they are all powerless. They serve a great purpose for a new Witch though, to help train and focus your mind through ritual. The magic is in the intent, not in the tools.

Intent! Nothing to be scared about. Tools are great, especially to get started with, but some Witches are naturally adept. Other Witches, after a long time, are able to do their magic quickly, by only thinking about it. If you plan it and think about it for a day, you are actually doing the ritual as you think about it. Intent, that is the magic; not the tools.

—Cerelia

Where do I get my tools?

Use what you have, or no tools at all, or acquire fancy ones when you are able to. There are many traditions and many superstitions about tools. I think it's fine to acquire them however they come to you, and see nothing wrong with buying them.

—Eileen

What do I do if I cannot afford to buy tools?

Tools can be easily acquired right in your own kitchen. I still use a goblet from the kitchen for a chalice.

Athame: Have you got a fancy cake server, or letter opener?

Chalice: Use any goblet.

Cauldron: A big old cast iron pot will work great, and any stock pot will do.

Censer: Use a pot of dirt.

Wand: Get a tree branch, or a piece of driftwood.

Pentacle: Draw a pentagram on paper.

Book of Shadows: Any blank book will do.

Use what you have around you, then trade up to fancier tools if you feel you still want them later on. In terms of other magical supplies, I often say that a Witch can accomplish almost every imaginable type of working with a basic kit of white candles, sandalwood incense, an amethyst, and some rosemary.

The tools are fun, but they're only props. Being a Witch doesn't take money, it takes time and dedication to the path.

—Eileen

Does a wand have to be straight?

Druids sometimes used a curving yew rod hung with tin-kling bells, and ur hekau (the mighty one of enchantments), the Egyptian wand, was curved at the end where the ram's head was.

—Eileen

What if I have to hide my tools?

Athames and swords can look scary to people who don't understand their purpose. A letter-opener athame could hide in plain sight though.

—Eileen

What's a pentacle used for?

It is a Witch's symbol of protection, and is very powerful. Placed on your altar, it can also be used in the magic you may be doing. You can also use it in meditation practices.

—Cerelia

What's the difference between a pentacle and pentagram?

One way of remembering is that a pentagram is drawn. A pentacle is the same symbol, but it is called a pentacle when it is a round disk, which is inscribed with the pentagram. For example, on a necklace it is called a pentacle.

—*Cerelia*

Have you heard of just the five-pointed star being called a pentacle?

Without the circle around it, I have seen it used as a Pagan symbol.

—*Cerelia*

How does magic work?

MAGIC

You, as individuals, have to do the work. You have to learn how powerful intent and will are. I can give you some basic tools, but I can't transform your mind. You must do that. You must work at that. You must want this magic in your life, want it so badly that you work at ritual and intent until you do not need the rituals or tools any more. That is personal work.

Magic has always been synonymous with superstition and stereotypes, with Witches with warts and snaggly teeth, and so on. The magic of the twenty-first century is about your will, and very importantly, your intent. You bring about changes within your own consciousness. You find out more about yourself, about who you are. This magic can have a spiritual intent. I believe that as you tap into your own psyche, you also attract energies from the Universe. That is why being careful with magic is important.

We can enter consciousness where we truly experience the gods and goddesses, whatever we perceive them to be. Changing this consciousness at will is called magic. To change this consciousness at will is not easy. This is why emphasis is sometimes put on a certain type of clothing, tools, and so on. They help Witches to invoke the sacred energy they are looking for.

Focused intent enables the Witch to change consciousness at will. Maybe sacred names and intoning are used, as in the Kabbalah, or drumming, as in shamanism. Different belief systems bring about the shift in awareness in different ways. Different traditions are just that, different. None is any better than others. It is a personal choice. The belief is that chanting the name of a god or goddess captures the very essence of that deity, and by doing so you are tuning into the associations of these sacred deities.

Instead of the Western attitude of submitting ourselves to a god so that he can bestow his grace or wrath as he deems fit, we become the center of the Universe. All the rituals, all the spells, are but concentrated will. We believe we can will to effect anything we want.

To anyone who says, "I do not use rituals or spells," I say, "Good for you." But we wonder if they are talking about the change of conscious awareness that I am really talking about, unless they have been a Witch or Shaman for many experienced years.

There are different types of Witches. Yes, there were those who just lived a very earthy type existence, living with the land, herbs, flowers, and so on, but there were also those who were so much more. An individual Witch just has to know how far he or she wants to go. There is nothing wrong with a wonderful, spiritual, peaceful life as that type of Witch, but there is also nothing wrong with knowing there is more, and trying to find it. I have my limits as to what I will work with. That is my right as an individual Witch. What works for you is what you will choose.

I believe that magic is channeling into conscious awareness a specific type of deity energy, from the collective psyche. These energies are real. Deities are there to help focus the intended energy. I can tap into the energies that each deity may represent. Knowing their lore and such is important, for tapping into their specific energy. They can represent many situations in our lives.

To me, whichever way you believe is never the issue. The common thread shared by these beliefs is that we believe in powers with whom we can relate. This provides knowledge and wisdom in our own lives. What you feel comfortable working with is a personal choice. The biggest affect this has on our very being is that we learn to not feel alone. We learn the Mystery, that we are all very deeply connected.

—Cerelia

How is magic perceived?

Scott Cunningham is very definite, in his books, about being able to see energy when you work with it, but we all experience magic differently. Some Witches sense it, some hear a humming or feel vibrations, others are visual, and some Witches even smell magic. This can relate to your element, which is often related to your astrological sign.

Whatever you experience is normal, because we each have different gifts. I'm very tactile, so I seldom see energy. I tend to sense things physically or in a psychic way, rather than see, hear, or smell things as other Witches do. I feel magic. It starts as a sort of psychic tingling, then becomes a whole-body physical sensation as power raises.

Don't feel like you're doing it "wrong" if you don't see anything when you make magic. Keep studying. As you learn more about yourself, many of your questions will be answered. Understand, though, that this is a process, that no adept ever finishes studying.

—Eileen

How do you learn to alter your consciousness?

Yoga is one way. So is a good Coven, if you are able to find one, as is a drumming group, if you have one to work with. Read everything that you can get your hands on that opens your mind to all the possibilities. Otherwise, you can alter your consciousness the good old-fashioned way, by working on your own.

Discipline is very difficult when you work alone, but with the right attitude and endurance, you can learn to do it even if you are a solitary practitioner.

—*Cerelia*

Can I learn to do magic by myself?

By reading and working yourself, you can learn to connect. Some Witches do it easier by themselves, while others need more help, and need to work with others. That is why a Coven is so important to some Witches, but not important to others. Finding the connection is not always as easy as it sounds.

—*Cerelia*

Can anyone learn to practice magic?

Everyone has the capabilities, but some are more naturally adept than others.

—*Cerelia*

Anyone with basic intelligence who is willing to spend the necessary time in study and practice. Witches have no monopoly on magic, and people of every faith can and do learn to use it. The greatest magical adept I have ever encountered was a Muslim sheikh, my late teacher.

—*Eileen*

Is there a connection between magic and religion?

Magic is worked within many different types of religions, yet that still isn't a requirement. I believe that everyone who works with magic has some kind of spiritual support system they believe in, no matter if it has a name or not. This is how we find that special place, in our minds, that helps us attract the energies of the Universe. There are many ways to achieve this.

—*Cerelia*

Working magic may attract energies and entities.

True. That's why we keep our homes protected, to try to keep anything unwanted from getting in.

—*Eileen*

What will magic do for me?

When magic comes into your life, it pushes some things out. Like the goddess Kali, it burns away things that aren't worth keeping.

—*Eileen*

What's the best way to use magic to help yourself?

The Law of Three: the more we help others, the more we help ourselves.

—*Eileen*

POWER

How do I learn to understand the true power of magic?

I believe that spirituality, in whatever way one may believe, opens a place in the mind. This is the place we need to get to in order to understand and explore our interconnection. We can get there through meditation, chanting, rituals, and so on, but understanding of the Universe and its connection to everything is very important. This is what makes your magic work powerfully.

It may sound easy to say, "Yes, I believe in the beauty and the interconnection of the whole Universe," but this goes way beyond simple words. You must really believe it and feel it. To really believe it, to experience it and to live it, is not as easy as it sounds.

—*Cerelia*

Where's the power then?

The only power worth having is power over yourself and your own life. Learning this can be the work of a lifetime.

—*Eileen*

Intent! I don't believe anyone is granting me permission. I don't believe in a pre-determined life. I can change my life for better or worse, any time I want. It is always the power of the intent. Attaining the power of pure intent is not easy. Yet sometimes, when it is pure and from the heart, it is the easiest thing in the world.

—*Cerelia*

How do I raise energy, or power?

Exercise: The simplest way to begin is with your hands. Be in a quiet place where you will not be disturbed, perhaps with some incense burning or some soft music playing. Hold your hands several inches apart, with their palms facing. Move your hands around a bit, until you begin to feel something in the air between them. That's energy: the energy you can use to make magic. Be patient, and keep repeating this exercise until you are proficient at it. Don't forget to earth the power after you finish, by holding your palms downward and sending the power you raised back to Mother Earth.

—Eileen

Raising power must be learned. Cunningham makes magic sound easy. In a way it is, but in another way, it is very difficult. He is trying to encourage, instead of discourage. The most difficult part is getting your mind to believe that what you have been told all your life is pure nonsense.

—Cerelia

Witches don't require thirst, hunger, or the self-infliction of pain to raise power. We have a different way, one based on desire and acceptance rather than pain and denial. Why hurt yourself in an effort to command or persuade the Universe to do your bidding, when we have only to open our minds, open our hands, and accept what the Universe offers us?

Candlelight and incense work for me. So does poetry. Creation is a magical act, so I often use poetry to raise power. We are all different, and must each find the way of raising power that works best for us. Experiment. Remember that to focus on power can be to miss the point of power entirely. Focus on the Goddess, and how you can use the power to serve her.

—Eileen

How can I tell if I am raising enough power?

If your spells work, you're raising enough power.

—*Eileen*

How do I control the power?

Don't even think about controlling it. Focus instead on channeling it. Make your body its conduit, then return it to its source.

—*Eileen*

How serious is magic?

You have to differentiate between magic and common sense. If you are foolish with money, you will always be in debt no matter how many prosperity spells you cast. A healthy, balanced diet and sufficient exercise are more sensible than spells for weight loss. You have to be careful with spells like that, and be sure to cast them in a way that harms none.

Here is an example of the kind of thing that could go wrong: you cast a spell to lose weight, then you get cancer or another disease with an associated wasting syndrome. You lose a lot of weight, but certainly not in the way you meant.

Respect the power of magic, even when casting insignificant spells. Be very cautious about when and why you cast spells. Only use the power when it's absolutely necessary, and be very sure about having good reason to do so when you manipulate anyone or anything. I will bet that I cast less spells in any given year than most novices do. I save magic for the big stuff, save it for important things which cannot be dealt with any other way.

—*Eileen*

Understand the seriousness of magic, and why it is important to cast only well-thought-out spells, with all consideration of what could happen. It is important to cast spells with integrity, and only when needed. Do not take your magic lightly, nor the spells or rituals you cast. Try to think about those shadows you may be casting without realizing it.

—*Cerelia*

How can I make my magic stronger?

Self-discipline and meditation are ways to strengthen your will, and therefore your magic. By self-discipline I don't mean anything dangerous or esoteric. There is no need to stick your hand in candle flames, or starve yourself. Simply keeping your word, actually doing the things you say you will do, is an excellent way to exercise your will.

—*Eileen*

Will I get everything I ask for?

If we don't get something we desire, or do not receive the results we want, it should be respected as something not in works with the Universe right now. Perhaps the energies are too strong against whatever we are asking for, or there are also many others who are working with these energies. It could also be that our intent is not strong enough to bring it about. Any further interference can cause more harm than good. I don't believe we can put blame on anything when our workings do not come about, or praise anything when we do get our spells to work.

I am very afraid to cast spells for others, or myself, without putting much thought into what I am asking. This is because I never really know, even with all good intent, what energies I may be messing with.

When the Universal energies give us a flat "No," we must learn to leave it alone at this time. When it says yes, a thank you to the Goddess (or Universal mind) is always appropriate. Or however you may view it.

—*Cerelia*

—Black Magic—

What is black magic?

Black or dark magic is used to do others harm. It is using any means, no matter what, to help yourself or someone else without regard for any living thing.

Using the phrase black magic is stating that your intention is evil, or that you do not care who gets harmed in the process of your spell. To me, the phrase black magic describes the negative or evil path.

—*Cerelia*

Black magic is manipulative and harmful, such as a spell that is cast with the intention of hurting someone or something: causing illness or injury or failure, disrupting relationships, creating chaos just for the hell of it, and so forth.

—*Eileen*

What makes magic dark?

I equate dark magic with the outcome of what someone is desiring. That is what makes it dark or light. Witches can work with the dark aspects any way they like, but they must take responsibility for whatever the outcome may be. This is especially true if they do not care to integrate and balance the dark and light sides of themselves.

Magic can also be dark because of the means by which those practicing it wish to attain something, such as through harming another, or via sacrifices. These are the traps of dark magic. Magic is not dark because we have negative emotions or feelings, that is what being human is.

—*Cerelia*

Is it evil to work with the darker aspects?

The intent of the practitioner, not the ritual itself, is what makes magic evil or not. When I speak of dark, I am speaking of different planes of reality that a Witch may enter and leave.

Some Witches work with different entities. Some of these are dark and can be dangerous, if the Witch has not been taught properly. Castenada spoke of inorganic beings, which I have encountered. Though I learned not to be afraid, I also knew it was time to quit for a while. To me, evoking entities is dark. You are bidding their presence, and you demand that they help you succeed in whatever outcome you want.

There is also the darker side of ourselves. We all have one, but a Witch can learn to balance the light and the dark.

—*Cerelia*

Isn't black magic just the side of us that most people decide not to deal with?

There is no question of if we have a dark side, because we all know we do. Wiccans learn to integrate the dark and the light to work our magic. Ethical Witches do, anyway. Witches cannot ignore the darker sides of ourselves. To do so could be very damaging to our own psyches. To me, the phrase black magic describes the negative or evil path, not our darker side.

When we call what we practice white magic, we are not saying that we do not acknowledge the darker side of ourselves. We acknowledge that we work to integrate both the dark and the light, for the good of ourselves and others.

—*Cerelia*

So how do you view the dark side in each of us?

In my opinion, the only way to get to our own power is to work through the negativity and pain in our lives. Everyone has their own personal pains and problems. That's understood. Wiccans do not see just the happiness in life. How could any human being do that? You have to feel all the other sides of life to balance the light and the dark.

—*Cerelia*

What does it mean to work with our dark side?

Everyone has a dark side, but we can learn to work with our feelings and sort them out, instead of using them to make dark things happen. If we do not investigate who we are, we will never understand the powers within us. Using negative aspects of ourselves, such as anger, lust, or greed, with raw intent is where we fall into the traps of dark magic.

We all feel angry at times, or very emotional over a situation, or have our sexual energy very high. A lot of stored up energies and powers occur at these times, making them a very good time to work magic, in my opinion, because our energies are at their height. But, with much studying and dedication and practice of the Craft, you learn to really know yourself.

When Witches learn to integrate all of their feelings for the good of themselves, others, or the situations they are in, they learn control. Control is power in itself; not using magic helter skelter. We acknowledge that the darker sides of ourselves are there, of course they are, but as we investigate or search within our own souls, we learn how to work with our whole selves. We learn to not just work with the light side, but to integrate our whole beings, bringing them into balance.

This is why magic and ritual take practice and understanding of oneself as a Witch. Witchcraft is pure psychology in motion, working within ourselves. This is quite exciting, but the true magic is the power of balancing them. You either care about integrating yourself as a whole, or you work with whatever raw or dark side of the Craft you choose. This is where the choice of what kind of Witch you want to be comes into question. That is definitely something to think about.

—Cerelia

How can we really know that black magic is wrong, unless we learn about it?

I agree that just because someone says that something is wrong, or is definitely bad, as with black magic, you don't have to take it in blind faith. But I also think that the words *black magic* alone tell you more than most people want to know. I worry about those Witches who have a need to find out more about something that is obviously harmful. Black magic is very seductive.

How do you really know, without doing some research first? Yes, just for your own education, and to be able to say honestly that you know what you are talking about, some research is smart.

The same can be said for the vast amount of knowledge that we all need, but Witches need to use care and caution in choosing what we are interested in.

The problem lies with "after." After reading and becoming educated about this type of magic, you may begin to think, "Hey, this isn't so bad," or that this kind of magic should be okay. You can get sucked in before you even realize it. You do have to know when you are being drawn in. You have to make your own choices.

Evil is very powerful. It is something that we should be aware of, and recognize. We need to recognize its power, so as not to succumb to it. Evil's power has been shown throughout history. It is very seductive and sneaky. Evil can quietly come upon us, without us ever realizing what we have been working with.

Realize that there are some Witches out there who would like to help, who want to save you the bother of messing with something that is definitely of no benefit to you. The choice is always yours, but forewarned is forearmed.

—Cerelia

I dabbled in black magic when I was young and stupid, but I have since learned better.

Don't feel bad. Lots of white Witches learned that lesson the hard way.

—Eileen

Defining something as positive or negative is very hard to do.

I think there is a voice in most of our heads. It truly tells us, if we listen, what is acceptable. Those who do not listen, make dark choices.

—Cerelia

Sometimes I feel so angry. How do I make sure that I don't harm anyone while doing rituals and spells?

We all get angry, or sad, and we have hateful and sometimes really atrocious thoughts. We feel like we would really like to cause harm to someone at times. Does this make us horrible people or Witches? Of course not. It makes us human. Knowing how to work with these energies is what makes your magic light or dark.

As ethical Witches, we learn to integrate these emotions and thoughts into a more positive way.

—Cerelia

What is necromancy?

Necromancy is conjuring the dead to use for divination, either using a dead body to raise, or to bring a spirit forth from a dead body. It is disgusting, and the most horrible of magical rites.

—*Cerelia*

What is chaos magic?

Chaos magic is nasty stuff. Usually it means using magic to create disorder. Chaos magic is generally black, such as sending pain through the Internet. It tends to be big but sloppy. Wiccans and others on right-hand paths would do well to avoid chaos magicians, because it is so easy for them and the people around them to get caught up in the vortex of what they create, intentionally or otherwise.

—*Eileen*

Why shouldn't I be friends with someone who practices black magic?

We don't avoid evil because we fear it, we avoid it because it's harmful. Germs exist, too, but we don't embrace them because they will make us sick. There are many ways to be a Witch, but if you're Wiccan you follow the rule of "harm none." Black magic is always harmful. Doing harm is its reason for being. Would you want to associate with someone who molested children, or spread computer viruses, or poisoned drinking water?

One very good reason for not associating with people who use black magic is that you definitely don't want to be standing near them when the Law of Three rebounds on them.

This is a lesson that can be a hard one to learn. I cannot say this loudly or often enough: anyone who uses black magic is not your friend.

—*Eileen*

How can I help friends who have gotten into black magic?

Break all contact with such people until they come to their senses and stop. They have chosen a dark road, one that you cannot follow them down without getting hurt in some way. Walk away, if you want to protect your family. Break all contact. Light a candle for them, make a wish that they will find their way back to the light, and walk away until they forswear black magic.

It will hurt to do this, and you will still have the impulse to help them, but your first duty is to yourself and your family. In the meanwhile, it might be a good idea to cast some protection spells around yourself, your family, and your associates.

—*Eileen*

Curses

What's the deal with curses?

Curses aren't all they're cracked up to be. They generally only have power if you empower them by believing in them.

—*Eileen*

How can you tell if you have been hexed, are a victim of circumstance, or are suffering a backlash from your own actions?

Those are things for a Witch to reflect on. Did I cause myself harm? (This is usually what happens, ninety-nine percent of the time.) Sometimes you can't be sure, but it is very convenient and careless to always blame all bad events in our lives on hexes and curses. Any Witch worth her or his salt usually knows when she or he has made a mistake in judgment. Common sense is very important. If you believe in someone else's powers to do you harm, more than you believe in your own powers to protect yourself, you have lost the battle right from the start.

—Cerelia

Sometimes things just happen, without human agency. Trying to figure out whom to blame for something is usually a waste of time. It's generally best to just deal with what is, as best we can.

—Eileen

Terrible things have happened, since a black Witch cast a spell on me . . .

Where thoughts go, energy flows. If you spend a lot of time thinking about what you think some other practitioner has done to you, you feed (or even create) the negative energy.

Power belongs to the Universe. No one can take it from you. That spell will only work so long as you believe in it. What he has done is steal your belief in yourself from you. Refuse to be his victim. Laugh at the spell. Laugh at him. Call upon whatever god/dess you most believe in to unbind you. Break all contact with this person, and stay away from black Witches in future.

Dion Fortune wrote that crossing running water, such as a stream or a river, was a surefire way to get a Witch off your trail. I tend to doubt that, but you might want to try it.

—*Eileen*

—————————MAGIC CIRCLES—————————

Do we have to cast a circle in order to cast a spell?

You can do candle magic, or other types of spells, without ever casting a circle. When a Witch becomes adept, spells can be cast at a moment's notice, within the mind, without any tools, and without casting circles. For an adept, the protection of a circle is there in a second's notice, if not there all the time, because of the Witch's visualization skills.

—*Cerelia*

I notice that the longer I practice magic, the less I need to cast circles to manifest results. Simply turning my magical attention to something is sometimes all that is needed.

—*Eileen*

Why are circles cast?

Circles are created to contain energy, and also to protect us from unwanted energies. Most Witches know that there are energies and elementals out there that have to be dealt with. We must be careful, because while we are concentrating on the ritual aspect, we are not always focusing on protecting ourselves. A magic circle is also a sacred space where we are inviting the Goddess to join us.

—*Cerelia*

Non-Witches use circles to protect themselves from the forces raised (or roused, if working with dangerous entities). Witches use them to amplify power.

—Eileen

How should I cast my circle?

It's your circle, so you cast it whatever way feels right to you. Experiment, until you find what works best for you. Each Witch usually has his or her own way of casting a circle. Mine is very simple: I face each direction in turn, holding my sword, and call the Lord of that Watchtower. I always begin and end with North, but some Witches prefer East.

—Eileen

Who are the Lords of the Watchtowers?

They are personifications of the cardinal points, N, S, E, W. They form the square (or cube) in which the magic circle (sphere) is cast.

—Eileen

What size should my circle be?

Cast it however large or small feels right to you. When working in a small space, cast a sphere just big enough to contain yourself and whatever you are using as an altar. Lots of Witches, particularly urban Witches, work magic successfully in very tight spaces.

—Eileen

Should we mark the outline of the circle?

I seldom do. At most I place candles or crystals of different colors at the quarters; but if you have trouble visualizing your circle, by all means marks its outline.

—*Eileen*

When I cast my first circle, whom should I invoke for protection?

I just use a generic Lord of the Watchtower of the North, East, etc. You should use whoever you would feel protected by.

—*Eileen*

When is it appropriate to cast a circle?

Casting circles is not necessary, but for a new Witch it helps with learning to focus. Some Covens and groups enjoy the ritual of casting a circle, and it does raise a lot of power within a group of practitioners. The intent is the magic, though. This is something to always remember.

Though circles are not always necessary, to me it depends on the intensity of your spell or ritual. I do candle spells, which can be very powerful. I do not cast circles every time I work with candle magic, but my intent is there to keep myself safe.

—*Cerelia*

Trust yourself, and only cast circles whenever you feel you need to cast them.

—*Eileen*

How do I know if I cast the circle the right way?

Once again, if your spell works, you cast the circle properly. Some Witches will tell you a lot about how things are "supposed" to be done, but I strongly disagree with that approach. We are all different. We work best when we work to our strengths, and do things in the way that feels right to us. If your spells work, you're doing them in the way that is right for you.

—Eileen

Don't I need three more Witches to cast a circle?

It does not take four Witches to cast a circle. A lot of nonsense and magical misinformation get around, things which new Witches and young Witches sometimes take as fact.

—Eileen

(See also Entities on page 175.)

EARTH

(See also Grounding on page 246.)

What are correspondences for Earth?

The North; the pentacle; the female principle; fertility; darkness, quiet; practicality; thrift; acquisition, patience; responsibility; boredom; stagnation, the materialization of cosmic
powers; the color green; the metal gold.

—Cerelia

What can I use to represent Earth?

You can use salt, or the earth (dirt) itself.

—Cerelia

Rocks, stones, crystals, ivy, grain . . . those say Earth to me.

—Eileen

What's Earth magic?

Earth Magic encompasses many things: herbs, stones, kitchen
Witchcraft, magical powders, even global workings.

—Eileen

Can Earth magic be practiced indoors?

Don't let the weather stop you. I'm basically an Earth magic Witch, and I always work indoors.

—*Eileen*

Air

What are correspondences for Air?

The East; the wand, sword, or athame; the male principle; intellect; energy; endeavor; sociability; squandering; frivolity; the expression of the magicians's will; the color yellow; the metal silver.

—*Cerelia*

What can I use to represent Air?

Incense.

—*Cerelia*

On my altar, Air is represented by a tall container full of joss sticks, feathers, and a cloisonné butterfly. Insects and birds represent Air, for obvious reasons.

—*Eileen*

Incense

Why is incense used for magic?

The smoke represents Air. The smell of incense also helps in awareness shifts, so it has two purposes.

—*Cerelia*

Could you give me an example of an Air spell?

Example: Any use of incense is a very simple Air spell. One example would be to write down your wish, start some incense burning, then set the paper ablaze (in a fireproof container, of course) and waft the smoke of the burning paper skyward, with the incense smoke, as a way of sending your wish or request to the Universe. Some Native American nations use bunches of sacred feathers to direct smoke in this way.

—Eileen

How do you burn incense?

Incense cones and sticks can usually just be lit with a flame. The cones burn hot at the bottom, so it's best to set them in a metal censer or other container that will not burn. I like to use fruit charcoal for burning loose incense, by heating it on the stove until it's glowing hot, but this is somewhat dangerous. Magical supply shops sell packages of the safer self-igniting charcoal. This type doesn't work as well as pure charcoal, but it's a lot easier to work with. You just touch a flame to the charcoal disc, drop it into a censer, and wait a moment while the flame sparks across the tablet. I always notice the charcoal smell behind the incense, but most Witches don't seem to mind it.

Whatever kind of charcoal you use, burn it in a metal censer that has a layer of sand or salt beneath the coals to absorb the heat, and place the censer on a surface which will not easily burn.

—Eileen

Incense helps me to shift my awareness.

It does so for me as well. Incense is the quickest method for me to get in a magical mood. I like to burn it before I read the cards, and for many other reasons besides spells.

—*Eileen*

Is there any danger to using incense?

Some people are allergic to it. As much as I love incense, I don't burn it if my sinuses are infected, or if my son has a cold. If incense aggravates your lungs, you could simmer herbs instead of burning incense. A pot of water, a handful of herbs, clouds of steam . . . this could even be therapeutic, depending on which herbs you use. There are also several methods for getting essential oils to scent the air. Placing a few drops of an oil on a hot light bulb is perhaps the simplest. Another alternative, with allergies, is to burn incense outdoors.

—*Eileen*

I cannot wear perfume, or burn too much incense, due to headaches. Those Witches who are terribly afflicted by smoke and smells from incense could use a feather to represent Air. There are also lighter fragrances of incense, such as sandalwood. Experiment a little, if you can.

—*Cerelia*

So maybe we shouldn't use incense at all then.

I love incense and don't plan to ever stop using it, despite chronic sinus problems. I use common sense when burning incense, though, like opening the windows for ventilation. I will not burn anything if anyone in the house has a cold or other respiratory complaint, and I only burn incense when my son is asleep in his room with the door closed, or at school. I didn't burn it at all when he was a baby.

If I feel a need for billowing clouds of frankincense, I take my brazier out onto the balcony. I do this at three or four in the morning, so that I'm not annoying my neighbors with the smoke. Moonlight, frankincense, silence . . . it works for me.

Less is often more, when it comes to incense. If we're judicious in our use of it, and careful of how it might affect others, I see no reason for us to deny ourselves incense.

—Eileen

How many sticks of incense should you burn at a time?

One stick, or three, is what I usually use. I burn three when I want to mingle scents for magical reasons, or just because they smell good together. Try amber and green tea, for sacred space and general spirituality.

—Eileen

How can you avoid getting burned when using a covered censer?

Use tongs. I usually bring the censer to the stove, hold the charcoal with tongs, light a burner, touch the charcoal to it, and drop it into the waiting censer. (This is urban hearth magic.) The sides of a metal censer will quickly get too hot to carry it to the altar, so I put mine atop an alabaster vase before I start this whole operation. I hold the cool stone to carry the censer to the altar, sprinkle incense or resin or dried herbs over the charcoal, cover the censer, and I'm ready for my working. The tongs can also be used to lift the hot cover off, if you want to add more incense.

—Eileen

Do we have to use incense?

I must have missed the memo on that.

—*Eileen*

Who said that anything was mandatory? Tools are just that: tools. When we do not need them any more, we may decide not to use them. The intent is the magic, not the candle, not the incense.

—*Cerelia*

What are smudge sticks, and smudging?

Smudge sticks are bundles of dried herbs, usually sage or sweetgrass, that emit a lot of smoke when burned. You smudge to displace negative vibes, or to banish something or someone. The smoke is positive energy that drives negative energy out.

—*Eileen*

Smudging is burning sage and letting the smoke purify and cleanse your home, or whatever you are trying to clear.

—*Cerelia*

What kind of spoons make good incense spoons?

I use a set of sterling silver demitasse spoons with botanical motifs (flowers) on their handles. You should use whatever appeals to you, whatever works.

—*Eileen*

FIRE

What are correspondences for Fire?

The South; the sword or athame (in some traditions, the wand); the male principle; action; courage; defense against hostile forces; struggle; animosity; jealousy; anger; the color orange; the metal gold.

—Cerelia

Fire is also associated with healing (Brigid) and blessings (Kali), because it can burn away disease, negativity, and so forth.

—Eileen

What can I use to represent Fire?

Candles.

—Cerelia

What's the best way to ignite things?

I dislike matches because I associate them with cigarettes, but I like working with sulphur—you can't make brimstone without it, and it's good in banishing recipes. To each his or her own. My method of preference is to light candles and incense from the gas flame on the stove (urban hearth fire), so it's always a problem for me when I live in a place with electric stoves. One adapts, and one goes on.

—Eileen

My candles set my altar on fire, and I have been afraid to work with fire since then.

You have learned the most important thing about fire: to respect it. Use extreme fire safety (flameproof containers, water or fire extinguisher on hand just in case, but mostly use respect and total attention) and try working with fire again. Tea lights or votives are the safest candles to start with. Put them in glass cups, atop coasters or saucers or anything that cannot catch fire. Be careful of swirling robes, swinging hair, hanging sleeves, and so on.

—Eileen

What do you do if you can't burn things because it sets the smoke detector off?

That happened to me once, in an apartment that I lived in years ago. After that, I put anything I wanted to burn as part of a spell into the trash chute, because the trash got incinerated in the basement. The spells I cast using the trash chute worked just as well as the other kind.

—Eileen

Candle Magic

What's the proper way to light a candle?

I only light a candle with another candle, one that I use only for the purpose of lighting my ritual candles. It is always white or silver.

—Cerelia

Must a candle burn all the way to the bottom?

Different Witches feel differently about that. I always burn a candle until it extinguishes itself, if it's for a spell. But if I am burning a pillar candle for no particular reason, I will blow it out before I leave the house or go to sleep, and light it again another time.

—Eileen

You can do anything that feels right to you. I burn a candle all the way down for one spell or ritual, because I believe that this is needed. You may not believe this. After so many years of doing things the way I do, I can't tell anyone else that their way is wrong. Sometimes I don't even remember why I may do something differently from other Witches.

I cannot blow out a candle, because it feels like I am blowing away all the energies I am trying to attract (like, poof, they're gone), so that is why I don't. I hardly ever put myself in that position, though, because I always (unless there is an emergency) let my candles burn out on their own. That's not easy, since I love long tapered candles, so I make sure I am going to be home and awake before lighting candles.

As I said, do whatever works for you. You have it in your mind a certain way. Your mind believes this, so it would work for you, but not for me. The power of the mind is different for each of us.

—Cerelia

What's the proper way to extinguish a candle?

Of course, the best way is to let them burn out, but if I must extinguish them, I never blow out my candles. I either use my snuffer or wet my fingers and pinch them out. If you don't want to burn a candle for eight hours, use a small taper or a votive. If you can't stay with the candle, extinguish it before leaving.

Blowing the candle out does the same to the spell. I have had to leave in a hurry and had to pinch the candle, or use a snuffer. I did relight it to continue the spell when I came back. There may be other Witches who do it differently, but this is my way.

Here is Raymond Buckland's way of putting out a candle: "It is best to light a taper and then light the candles on the Altar from this, in the order noted. At the close of the ritual you may blow out the flames—in reverse order to that of lighting—or you may put them out with a candle snuffer. Do not pinch them out with your fingers."[16]

This is what Silver Ravenwolf has to say about extinguishing candles: "Do not pinch it, as you pinch out the desire, and do not blow it out, as you blow the desire away from yourself. Use a candle snuffer, or wave your hand over the candle to create enough draft to extinguish the candle."[17]

Scott Cunningham says to use a snuffer, or your fingers. So you see, this is just a small sample of opinions on the subject. I like to go back in time to the people who revived Witchcraft in modern times. And now I can't remember why I might do something the way I do. I think the main consensus is to use a snuffer or let candles burn out. Some spells which require intense concentration require you to extinguish the candles as soon as you are no longer able to concentrate. Then you do have to make a choice.

For those of you who like to blow out the candles, the only suggestion for blowing them out is to be sure to blow them out in reverse order of lighting them. If you are one of those Witches who just can't decide what is right for you, buy a snuffer. They are inexpensive, and will put your mind at ease.

—Cerelia

What does it mean if you try to extinguish a spell candle, and it won't go out?

I'd take it as a sign of the spell working, working strongly.

—Eileen

If the candles keep extinguishing themselves, does this mean that your spell is not meant to be?

First I'd check for drafts, in the place where I burned the candles. Absent drafts or some other explanation, I'd take it as a message.

—Eileen

What sort of candles are best to use?

A candle made by a Witch with magical intent will definitely give extra oomph to a spell, but plain old candles from an ordinary shop will also work just fine, if your intent is clear and your will is strong.

—Eileen

What kind of candles do you use?

I love long tapers. I start them early in the evening and let them burn out on their own. If you can't do this, you can snuff them out when you need to. Votive candles and tea lights burn quicker.

—Cerelia

I like short candles, 2- or 3-inch candles that burn all the way down before bedtime. One thing you may notice as you go along is that when a Witch burns a candle with magical intent, it might burn for many more hours than that type of candle is supposed to burn. I won't leave a candle burning while I sleep, and feel like it adversely affects the magic to blow a candle out, so I try to use short candles.

Tea lights and votives are other kinds of small candles that are usually inexpensive, as are the Sabbath candles sold in Jewish neighborhoods. I like votive candles. I burn them in glass custard cups, on top of a glass pentacle, but I still won't leave or sleep while they're burning.

—Eileen

What are votive and pillar candles?

Votive candles are very small, 2 to 3 inches high. They are usually burned in small glass containers, or candle holders that are made for votives and tapers.

A pillar candle is tall and round. I have one that is about 15 inches tall. They come in a variety of heights and widths, but they are considered large candles, in any respect.

A votive candle will burn in a few hours. I use my blue pillar candle for ongoing spells of blessings, protection, and good fortune for my family, friends, and myself. I burn it at different selected times, for a couple hours at a time. It would take a very long time to burn a pillar candle completely down all at once.

—Cerelia

What color candles should a Witch keep in stock?

Candle colors can vary as to what they may mean, psychologically, to different Witches. Here is a list of the candles and colors that are normally accepted. These are the candle colors most commonly kept by Witches:

White: Monday
This can be used as a Goddess candle. White is the perfect balance of all colors. It can be used to symbolize purity or spirituality. A white candle can also be used in place of any color candle, if you happen to not have the color you want.

Red: Tuesday
Strength, health, and passion

Light Blue: Wednesday
Peace, patience, and understanding

Dark Blue: Thursday
To banish depression and negativity

Green: Friday
To attract money, fertility, and luck

Black: Saturday
To repel evil and negativity

Yellow or Gold: Sunday
To attract charm, confidence, and creativity

Candle colors are there to work with, pertaining to what certain colors represent to you, such as green for money. Most colors are basic, but if you firmly believe a certain candle color means something to you, then that is what it means.

The magic is in what you believe to be true. Tools aren't really necessary, so nothing is "wrong." It is your own mind and psyche you are working with. Use what works for you, and what you enjoy. I enjoy candles and all their colors, so that is what I work with.

Your intent is the most important thing. Just relax and enjoy yourself as you choose what feels right to you. Remember that Witches can vary on which colors, correspondences, and so on, that they may use. If something feels more right to you, then use that. Correspondences are very interesting, and a study in themselves. A few good books will help you to get started, and then you can decide what works for you.

—*Cerelia*

Can a cracked or broken candle be used in a spell?

I wouldn't use a such a candle for magic, but that's just me. If I made candles I would add broken ones to the pot, and melt them down. Otherwise save broken candles for power outages, when you just need candles for light.

—*Eileen*

Do I need to use new candles for each spell I do?

I believe you do. You would not want to use the same candle for different spells.

—*Cerelia*

Can I use a candle more than once?

Most Witches use a candle for only one ritual or spell, and burn it down completely. The exception is a special candle, such as my huge pillar candle, which I burn on occasion for healing and protection for my family and loved ones. That is why shorter candles are easier to work with, if you cannot burn your candles all the way down for one spell.

—Cerelia

This is something that different Witches feel differently about. Some say you should never re-use a candle, and instead melt the wax down and make a new one. Other Witches say it's fine to re-use candles. I would re-use candles (such as big pillar candles) for rituals, but would never use anything but a new candle for a spell. What do you think? Go with whatever feels right to you.

—Eileen

Why do Witches cleanse or consecrate candles?

Witches cleanse candles because candles have been through a lot of hands before we buy them. When we cleanse a candle, we are getting rid of any negative energy that may have become attached to the candle by the people who handled it on its way to the store. Candles are also touched by a great many people in stores, so that is why so many Witches feel a need to cleanse and/or consecrate not only candles, but any tool they may buy. Remember though, that all Witches have different ways of conducting themselves in how they handle their tools, candles, and so on.

—Cerelia

Do I have to dress or consecrate my candles for spells?

I do this, but some Witches do not. Consecrating a candle forges a magical link. A spell begins as a thought, and dressing a candle is part of that thought.

—Cerelia

How do you dress a candle?

Exercise: When I consecrate my candles (or whatever else), I use rose oil, my personal favorite, but you should use whatever calls to you. I hold the taper, and dab my finger with the oil. If I am doing an attracting spell, I would rub the oil from top to middle, and then bottom to middle. A banishing spell would be middle to top, and then middle to bottom. I then say "I consecrate this taper (or whatever I am consecrating) in the name of the Goddess."

—Cerelia

A topic that Witches can really get into a snit about is how to dress candles. You can find all sorts of advice on how it must be done, but there are plenty of Witches who cast powerfully effective spells by doing it differently. Or without dressing their candles at all. Or without even using candles.

I carve candles more often than I dress them with oil, but when I do dress a candle, I usually drip the oil onto it and let it dry overnight.

—Eileen

Where/when should we buy candles?

For anyone living in an area where Pagan supplies are hard to come by, remember to buy black and orange candles at

Halloween, while they're in all the shops. They usually go on sale November 1.

Yule is a great time of year to buy candles, since they are so plentiful. Lay in lots of bayberry candles while they're available, if you think you'll be doing wealth and prosperity spells over the course of the year. Remember that cinnamon candles have many, many uses, and do hit the shops right after Christmas, when candle prices fall drastically.

By planning ahead, buying things while they're in season and storing them until needed, you can keep yourself stocked up: fairies at Christmas, if you're into Faery Wicca or fairy magic; red, green, and gold candles at Christmas; other colors candles for your national day; flower wreaths at Easter; twinkly lights at Christmas, for fire festivals; witchy stuff at Halloween; and so on. My father gave me a small Witch doll with red hair. He got it in his pharmacy, from their Halloween display, but I keep it on my computer all year.

Christian holidays may dominate the market in many countries but look to other sources as well, such as ethnic neighborhoods and minority religions. You can get nice altar items for harvest festivals from shops that sell Kwanzaa merchandise. Many people practice Santeria in New York, and there is much to interest a Witch in a Santerian botanicá. If there are Hindus, Native Americans, or other Pagan peoples in your area, look to their shops for supplies.

Try Judaica shops, too, if there are any where you live. I often use the Sabbath candles, which are available in the Jewish shops in my neighborhood, for spells. Sabbath candles are great. They come in many colors, and are usually a lot less expensive than the candles sold in Witchcraft and New Age shops.

—Eileen

What kind of candle is good for spells of attraction?

I use small gold birthday candles to represent myself. They work very well.

—Cerelia

What kind of candle is good for creative blocks?

Try a cinnamon candle for that. A big candle is fine, one that you can burn whenever you need inspiration. Can't find a cinnamon candle? Add a few drops of cinnamon essential oil to the liquid wax of a glass-encased (seven day) candle after you have started burning it. You can also burn powdered cinnamon or even cinnamon sticks over charcoal, but it takes a bit of practice to work safely with charcoal at home.

—Eileen

What kind of candles should I use when someone dies?

The "best" color is whatever color feels right to you. You can never go wrong with white candles, which are always appropriate. Pale blue represents peace to me, so that's why I like pale orchid-blue candles for those who have left or will soon leave. I think of them as Peaceful Passage candles.

—Eileen

What if a spell calls for a black candle, and you don't have one?

A white candle turned upside down represents a black one. Just cut into the wax to expose the wick.

—Eileen

Are there any dangers in using candles?

It goes without saying that all of us should have strict safety procedures in place whenever we work with fire, and never leave candles or anything else burning unattended. I would never leave a candle burning if I left the house or went to sleep. I never do spells that require candles to burn all night, but if I did I guess I'd buy the electric kind and say that would just have to do. An electric candle just isn't the same, but it's better than a fire.

—*Eileen*

Some people prefer not to be around any kind of lead exposure. The metal piece at the bottom of some kinds of candles can leak lead into the air, when burned. We also have smoke with our candles. Fragrant candles are not good for us or for our pets, so Witches should be aware of that. Some say that there can be allergic reactions to scented candles in pets, and that if the reaction is serious enough it can swell the throat closed and suffocate the pet.

As with incense, I burn candles only when I need to do some magical work, not every day of the week.

—*Cerelia*

What do you do if you cannot burn candles?

Then don't use them. It isn't like it's a requirement or anything. Herbs that correspond to Fire might be good substitutes. Witches often place candles to mark the quarters; you could use any herb of Fire instead. Many of us like to keep something that represents each of the elements on our altars, and it's usually candles for Fire. You could use herbs instead.

—*Eileen*

————————Water————————

What are correspondences for Water?

The West; the cup, chalice and cauldron; the female principle; body fluids; magical brews; the rhythms of Nature; emotions; sensitivity; receptivity; instability; indifference; the color blue; the metal silver.

—Cerelia

What can I use to represent Water?

Traveling water (fresh running water) is preferable. I use river water from the springs that come down from the mountains. Water from a brook would be good, too.

—Cerelia

How can I get in touch with the element of Water?

Reading myths about the ocean, or myths of merfolk, marine life, or water deities, might inspire you.

—Eileen

————————*Holy Water*————————

What should I use for holy water?

There are many different kinds of holy water. Some Witches like to make it, while others prefer water that has been blessed by Mother Nature in some way. Rain water and melted snow are popular for use as holy water. So is pure water from natural sources, such as springs and brooks. Water from sacred places can also be used, such as water from a well that is used as a devotional site.

Dew can also be collected and used as holy water. Dew collected on Beltane morning is traditionally considered magical, and water from the first rain in May is considered sacred by many Witches. Urban Witches usually go for bottled spring water.

Basically, whatever kind of water seems sacred to you is holy water. I like melted snow for holy water. Also called shape-changing water, it's great for spells involving transformation of any kind. (If you live in the tropics, you could melt some ice instead.)

Being a city Witch doesn't give me much of a chance to collect dew or other naturally occurring waters, so I like to use rosewater, which is available in gourmet shops and Middle Eastern grocery stores. I like to fill my chalice with it and offer it to Isis, whenever I want to thank her for something. Rosewater is a favorite of mine. It's possible to make it, or other types of flower water (lavender water and orange flower water come to mind), but I always buy it.

Florida Water, sold in botanicás, occult shops, and catalogs, is water with alcohol, floral essences, and other essential oils added to it. Florida Water is used to cleanse negativity or bad vibes away. Again, each Witch has his or her own recipe for it.

—*Eileen*

What's the difference between our holy water, and the holy water of other religions?

Catholic holy water, as I remember, is just ordinary water that has been blessed by a priest. We are all priests and priestesses in Wicca, so we can bless our own water.

—*Eileen*

PSI-MAGIC

Can intense visualization be used to cast spells? Is this as powerful as the traditional way?

Absolutely. It's called psi-magic. Most Witches consider it advanced work.

—Eileen

Some very powerful Witches have only to think about what they want. Their intention is so powerful that this is all they need. This is, really, what I think most Witches are working toward. We start out with the props and tools, and end up not needing them. Though some Witches still consider it very enjoyable to cast spells and circles, they may only do them on special occasions.

—Cerelia

Can you give me an example of psi-magic in action?

Here is a way to use psi-magic to deal magically with situation such as hearings, court cases, and so forth. It's definitely manipulative, so you have to decide whether your situation warrants such a use of magic or not.

Exercise:

1] Try to identify the decision maker(s): judge, jury, doctor, panel, chairperson, or whoever.

2] As you testify (or while your lawyer presents your case), focus on the decision maker(s). Concentrate on getting your message through to them, on getting them to see things from your perspective. Try to access whatever is fair and honest in them, and reach that. Get a feeling for the decision maker(s), for his or her energy pattern, and try to touch it with your own energy signature, in a benign way.

3] If the decision was not rendered immediately, continue to do this same work after you go home. Keep it up for as many days as it takes for the decision to be made. Focus on maintaining a connection between the decision maker(s) and yourself, a positive connection that will enable the decision maker(s) to see things from your point of view.

4] Keep your goal in mind, and manipulate the energy toward manifesting your goal.

—Eileen

I want to help my relative to get well, but I'm not sure how. If I light a candle and meditate, would this be enough?

Psi-magic is simpler, and works powerfully well.

Exercise: From time to time, when you have the time and peace to focus on it, think about your loved one's illness or physical problem, and direct healing energy to the specific body part involved. How you do this is up to you. Picturing colored light surrounding the body part is perhaps the most common method, but you should do it in whatever way makes the most sense to you. Be very careful, however, to channel energy when you do this. Using your own energy can drain you, or make you ill.

—Eileen

SPELLWORK ——————ABOUT SPELLS—————

What is a spell?

A spell is a prayer. Spells needn't be ceremonial in nature in order for them to work. Wishes and words and thoughts are all spells, when intense enough.

"Spells and charms worked by Witches are truly concrete poetry."[18] Starhawk is so right about that. This was what first drew me to Wicca, and why I often use poems as spells.

—Eileen

A spell begins with a simple thought. If you believe in yourself enough, and the energies that be, that is enough. A prayer is a spell. The amount of preparation or lengths you want to go to, that's up to you. Sure it can be all grandiose, but it can also be as simple as a prayer. The power is in you, not in fancy words. Your intent is what gives your spell power. Just by lighting some candles and speaking to the Goddess with all the emotion you can muster, you can bring about a great many changes.

—Cerelia

What's the difference between a spell and a prayer?

Call a spell a prayer. We've all had practice at that, and it's really the same thing, except that you are trying to guide favorable energies toward you, rather than asking a god for his permission. You are not asking for something. You are working with the energies, to bring the thing to you.

—Cerelia

What do I need to cast spells?

You need very little to cast a spell. Tools are a way of capturing a Witch's attention. They help to focus on what is at hand, but belief is the most important tool. You can have all the expensive tools in the world, but if you do not truly believe in yourself and the magic within, little will be gained. This is why the spirituality behind Witchcraft is so important. You learn that this is where all your powers lie.

When you are able to get a couple of books, try to get *Wicca: A Guide for the Solitary Practitioner* by Scott Cunningham.

Earth Power by Scott Cunningham is also good to show you how simple and inexpensive it can be to cast spells with a tree, a stone, or water. I also recommend Eileen's book, *The Wicca Handbook.*

—Cerelia

How do you feel, when you cast a spell?

Different spells affect me in different ways. Some leave me feeling energized, while others exhaust me. There have even been spells where I didn't feel much of anything while I cast them, but the spells worked beautifully.

—Eileen

How long does a spell last?

The length of a spell's effectiveness varies widely, from a few hours to eternity. Focusing on how long you want your spell to last, while you cast it, affects this.

—Eileen

How long does it take for a spell to work?

Some spells work immediately, while others can take months to manifest.

—Eileen

What advice do you have on casting spells?

Keep your spells simple, and from your heart. Be patient. When you are casting a spell, you are affecting yourself. A Witch must develop a strong, loving, responsible character, in order to invoke these same powers. We do not want to invoke weak, uncaring, or irresponsible powers. We cannot invoke what we are not. You have to first find the magic within yourself, then you can pull whatever energies that are in sympathy with yourself to yourself very easily. This is really hard to explain. I hope it has made some sense to you.

—Cerelia

What's a good first spell to begin with?

Don't be afraid to start with simple blessing or protection spells. Every time you said a prayer as a child, you were working your magic.

—Cerelia

How about trying something that is both positive and useful, such as healing, blessings, purification, and so on? Start with something you actually need, but something simple.

House blessing spells are good starter spells, since there is very little that can go wrong with them. Consecrating tools is also fairly simple. We can all use all the blessings we can get, so a house blessing spell is never wasted.

—Eileen

What measure do I use when a magical recipe calls for, say, three parts of this, and five parts of that?

When a recipe says "parts" it can stand for anything, for whatever quantity you're using. Example: 5 spoons of cinnamon and 3 spoons of ginger, or 5 cups of cinnamon and 3 cups of ginger. You needn't use measuring devices in that case, any spoons and cups from the kitchen will do. The proportion of ingredients in relation to one another is what matters.

I love recipes that measure things in parts, since I'm a "pinch of this, and dash of that" type of cook. The skills needed to make magical recipes are pretty much the same ones required in cooking.

—Eileen

Are we allowed to cast practice spells?

This is something that other Witches will have different views on, but I consider magic way too sacred to waste on "practice" spells. I never cast spells without very good reason. The notion of casting spells for practice, or just to show what you can do, makes no sense to me.

Some British television show once asked me if I would appear on it regularly (not realizing that I lived in New York) and cast spells, to show people how it's done. This was out of the question because of geography, but I would have said no even if their studio had been located in my building. How could you cast a spell just to show how to cast a spell? Think about that. It certainly gave me pause.

—Eileen

When I do spells, does it affect anyone else?

Witches have to think all spells or rituals out carefully and learn how to do them correctly and ethically, because with every ritual or spell we do, we aren't just affecting ourselves; we could be affecting many others as well.

Though we may not always know what has been done by something we have worked for, at least we can have the satisfaction of knowing that we tried to harm no one in the process. Some shadows can't be seen. That's the scary part.

—*Cerelia*

Is it possible to disturb Nature by doing something wrong with a spell?

I believe that it is. This isn't to mean that one Witch's spell can affect the entire Universe. What it means, to me, is that I shouldn't bother the Goddess or use magic unless it is for a very important reason. This kind of mindfulness helps keep us from casting petty spells, or spells we wind up regretting.

—*Eileen*

How many spells can you cast in one day?

You don't need to work a spell a day, or a spell a month, unless they are just general protection spells. Choose your rituals or spells wisely. They should only be used for the most important aspects of our lives.

—*Cerelia*

There are no rules about things like this, but since a lot of planning and energy often goes into a spell, it's unusual to cast a lot of them close together. I think of a spell as a stone that I have tossed into the cosmic pond, so I like to sit back and watch how far its ripples extend before I do any other magical work.

Everything is connected, so a spell that you cast for one aspect of your life will often surprise you by having a positive effect on other areas. This is just my take on it, and I tend to be something of a minimalist when it comes to magic. As always, you should go with what feels right for you.

—Eileen

Is it possible to cast too many spells?

You can overdo it with magic, just as with everything else. The spell-a-day crowd will learn this lesson the hard way. Part of respecting magic, for me, is using it wisely by saving it for the big stuff. Magic should not be used for the ordinary day-to-day issues that we all face. I don't even cast five spells, many years. For everyday things I just use symbolic acts, my magical attention, burn candles or incense with specific intent, and so on.

—Eileen

Can I do spells for myself?

Here are a few thoughts that I have on your question: of course Witches can work with spells and rituals for themselves. Being Witches means taking responsibility for ourselves and our lives, so working with spells and such to make ourselves spiritually stronger, and attract all that is good, is more than alright. It is what we do.

When you do any kind of spell, most of the time you are really working on yourself, internally, psychologically. You are also working to attract the energies that help you accomplish whatever you want to do. So of course, you can do spells for yourself, whether you want to attract, money, love, protection, or whatever.

—Cerelia

Why am I hesitant to cast spells for myself, especially financial spells?

This is how it should be. Spells are for need. They should be used sparingly, and wisely. You shouldn't be so afraid of financial spells, though, especially since you sound like you would only use them when truly needed.

—Cerelia

Are words really important in spells?

It is very important to think out what spells or rituals we are creating. This is why words become so important; exact words. We can't just say, "The Goddess knows what I mean." We aren't dealing with a godhead that decides whether we've been good enough or not. Witches don't assume that the Universe will try to decide what they really mean. That is our responsibility.

We are dealing with the energies of every living thing in the Universe. This is quite a responsibility, and one that shouldn't be taken lightly. Words are very important, and we must also remember to not go against anyone else's will. That means actually saying that your intention is to harm no one.

—Cerelia

Precision is crucial in spellwork. Adding "with harm to none" is a necessity.

—Eileen

I have learned (the hard way) to be very careful about how I word my spells.

You have indeed learned something important.

—Eileen

How elaborate do my spells have to be?

You can do spells or rituals very simply, or very elaborately. Neither is more powerful than the other. Only your intent is important.

—Cerelia

Is it amateurish to always go with whatever feels right to me for each spell?

Not at all. The things which feel right to us, magically, are usually the ones which achieve the best results.

—Eileen

Can I cast a spell by picturing it in my mind, instead of speaking the words aloud?

Yes, if your intent is clear enough, and your will strong and focused enough.

—Eileen

Do you have some music that you would recommend?

My favorite CD is *Chanting* by Robert Gass. His choral group is absolutely mesmerizing. The beautiful choral chanting is so spellbinding that it gives you shivers. It's wonderful to work your spells and celebrate your rituals with.

—Cerelia

If my spell isn't working, should I cast it again?

If you feel the need to cast a new spell, or recast the old one, go ahead and do it. It was your spell, so you are the best one to judge whether its magic has worn off.

A mistake I often see new Witches make, however, is to become impatient, think a spell hasn't worked, and ruin the working by recasting the spell repeatedly. This muddies the waters, at the magical level. It can cancel the spell out; or worse yet, cause unintended results. When we cast spells we have to know in our bones they will work, and wait patiently but expectantly for manifestation.

Spells sometimes do not work for our own good. If you cast a spell twice and it still doesn't work, I would assume it isn't in accord with the Universe, or that the Goddess was protecting me in some way. In any case, I'd forget about it and move on to something else.

—Eileen

What if I'm worried that I bungled the spell?

Magic surprises you sometimes, by working even though you thought you made a sloppy job of it.

—Eileen

What's the spell for changing your eye color?

Here we go again, sigh. There is no such spell. It's Hollywood, not magic. Weight loss can be about health, but trying to change your eye color is just a waste of time and magic. You need color contact lenses for that.

—Eileen

But my eyes seem to change color all the time.

I have eyes like that, gray eyes that look green when I wear green, or blue when I wear blue. They were blue until I was about twelve, then they turned gray, with some brown spots. This is genetics, not magic.

—Eileen

Is there a spell for raising the dead?

Magic is natural, subject to the laws of physics, so raising the dead isn't possible. Even if it were . . . shudder, what a creepy thing to do. You can raise the dead in a symbolic way, though: raise a dead issue, revive a dead plan, bring a dead relationship back to life, and so on.

—Eileen

ETHICS

What are the ethics of Witchcraft?

A basic rule of Witchcraft, for me as a Wiccan, is that I cast spells for people and not on them. Unless there are very special circumstances, I never cast spells for anyone without their permission. Interfering with someone else's karma affects your karma, too. This might be something you have to straighten out with that person in your next lifetime.

—Eileen

Who or what's responsible for all the evil in this world?

There is no blaming anyone but ourselves when we do something evil. I tell my son that good people do good things, and bad people do bad things. That's a simplistic explanation, but it is also a true one. We each have free will, are each personally responsible for our actions and inactions. There are Christians who may try to claim "the devil made me do it" as an excuse, or New-Agers who blame the planets, but Wiccans know that we are each responsible for ourselves and accountable for our actions.

—Eileen

Are there different kinds of evil?

Deliberately hurting another is active evil. Passive evil is driving right past an accident, not calling the authorities when you know a child is being abused, or not going for help when you see someone drowning, and so on.

—Eileen

How does a Witch know when he or she is trying to help someone else, or if it is really for self-gratification?

We all struggle with our intentions with every spell. Your own conscience will usually let you know if there are selfish reasons for your spells. I don't see this as a major problem for Witches with good hearts.

—Cerelia

How do you tell if you want to help people, or if you want to help yourself by helping others?

That question never even comes up, for me. I help someone because I want to help her or him. I never think about what blessings might flow back to me because of it.

—Eileen

How does a Witch know if the good they are doing is actually good for everyone else?

Sometimes you don't. That is why magic should be taken very seriously, and used sparingly.

—Cerelia.

Is working magic to benefit myself black magic?

Why? Just because you want to attract good energies to yourself, this does not mean that you are sending anyone else bad energies. One misconception about Witchcraft is that trying to help yourself in any way is wrong. We were taught in our former religions, when we believed in a god that served punishments or rewards, that we were not worthy, that we were sinners. We have to get over that idea.

That idea is wrong, to me. You are a child of the Universe, entitled to everything good and wonderful and magical that you can possess through magic and/or hard work. You have every right to want and expect all the wonderful, good things out of life. That does not make you a bad person. You are no less nor more than any creature of the Goddess.

If you were to ask for anything with the intent of harming another in the process, this would be wrong. But directing the subtle energies for yourself, or for anyone else, is part of being a Witch. It's not really confusing. If you always do your spells or rituals for yourself, or for anyone else whom you love and want to help, from your heart and for the good of all, it is all the same. Whether you help yourself or another, it is good magic.

—*Cerelia*

There is nothing wrong with personal gain, so long as it isn't our sole focus, and we don't seek to harm anyone else in our efforts to help ourselves.

—*Eileen*

Are we allowed to charge money for casting spells?

Magic is not for sale. To accept money for casting a spell is to dishonor yourself, and to dishonor the Craft. A greedy Witch is usually a frustrated Witch. It's generally considered ethical to sell things you make, your craft, but never ethical to accept money for casting a spell.

—*Eileen*

Isn't it wrong for a Wiccan to banish someone?

There are situations in which it is very necessary to banish certain people from our lives. You can banish someone without harming him or her.

—*Eileen*

Isn't harm sometimes actually a blessing in disguise?

I hope this isn't what it sounds like—an attempt at an excuse for hexing.

—*Eileen*

Is it okay to work spells for someone without their knowledge?

My belief is that if the person does not know of your offerings or prayers or support, he or she will either feel the effect of it, or if they do not want it, on some level, it will just not work. I don't believe there is any adverse effect to you by offering love and best wishes to others.

Everyone thinks with goodwill toward those we love, especially at times of crisis such as operations, hard times in their lives, and so forth, but if you are consciously working a spell, I would not do it without permission. Sometimes, without knowing it, we are messing around with someone else's life lesson. We don't have the right to try and change that. That's when we run into trouble.

—*Cerelia*

Casting spells on people without their permission falls under the heading of magical meddling. Who are we to decide who is right for whom, or whose personality needs adjusting? Interfering magically may prevent the person from paying a karmic debt, or learning a specific karmic lesson they are here to learn, for all we know.

Questions about interfering magically with other people's lives usually come from Witches who are very young, or very new to the Craft. It's one of those things you wise up to as you progress along your path. Some Witches say that if you cast a spell on someone without permission, even if you do it with the best of intentions, it comes back on you negatively.

—Eileen

Don't you think that doing positive spells for people, even without anyone's knowledge, is only common sense and for their own good?

Many people have life lessons to deal with. Your interference may not be welcomed by them, or it might interfere with a lesson that they may have to learn again, in another life, because of your interference.

It is not your decision. You may be a Witch, but you are definitely not a Wiccan if this is how you think. I am sure there are many Witches who think the way you do. To me it sounds like complete selfishness; doing whatever you want, and anyone else be damned. I am not disrespectful of your opinion, just in total disagreement with it.

—Cerelia

Is it ethical to do a reading for someone without their knowledge, when you're worried about them?

With the person or situation in mind, I would just ask the cards, "Tell me what I need to know." If the meaning of the card or cards I drew was unclear, I'd draw a clarification card. If that still didn't set everything straight in my mind, I'd wait a few days and repeat the process.

—Eileen

If I'm not supposed to manipulate anyone or anything, why bother casting spells?

This is exactly what some people of other faiths and spiritual beliefs think we condone and practice: manipulating others, and causing harm to others. This is not ethical, and not what we do. The purpose of spells and casting is to attract the subtle energies to ourselves, to improve ourselves and to improve our lives. Witches also do this for others.

Witches should not want to change others. A Witch who strongly wants to manipulate others is the one who has the problem. Changing ourselves for the better is hard work. When someone thinks there is nothing wrong with them, that it's everyone else who needs help, that person is the one who has a problem. Manipulating and harming others is fun, to some Witches.

As individuals, we must decide if we want to learn to be better people and let the Law of Three, or karma, take care of those who we think need manipulating. As Witches, we must learn to take responsibility for ourselves, and to leave so called justice to the Goddess . . . to the Universe.

Though some Witches cannot see it, there is great freedom in finally realizing that you really don't want to harm anyone.

You just don't have the time to waste on petty people. You know that justice will be there in this life, or the next. It is really a release, a wonderful feeling. You must practice and believe in this every day, in order to attain this freedom of thought. This is much harder, and makes a much more powerful Witch, than a Witch who uses every excuse to manipulate or harm others. To me, that is very depleting.

—Cerelia

Is it ethical to cast spells for friends, like for success?

Most Witches cast spells like that for friends all the time. I burned amber incense and an orange Success candle all day today, to help a friend who had a court date. (I wasn't meddling, she had requested the help.) Her case was postponed for several weeks, which was a good outcome for her.

—Eileen

What should I do if someone from another religion asks me to cast a spell for them?

I would not cast spells for others of different religions. This is mainly because they really don't understand why or how magic works, or because they think that going outside of their own faith was their only way out of a problem. I would decline; but of course, the choice is yours.

—Cerelia

There is no one answer to this. It depends on the request, on who makes it, on what your relationship is with this person, and on what the circumstances are.

—Eileen

Do we ever use body parts in spells?

Old spells often call for blood, hair, or nail clippings. I think that kind of stuff is creepy, and have never had to use any of them in a spell. A picture of the person, a poppet named for them, or their name written on a candle or piece of paper work just fine.

—Eileen

Is it true that working with your own hair in spells is dangerous?

Once again, it depends on your outlook. As far as being dangerous, in my opinion any spell can be dangerous if you do not take great care. I work with my own hair during some spells. I don't think there is anything more personal than your own hair. It feels very powerful to me, yet Eileen will tell you she doesn't use hair because it feels creepy to her. As always, it is a personal decision.

—Cerelia

How do you feel about working with blood?

We have talked about giving your own menstrual blood back to Mother Earth. There is certainly nothing wrong with this, but pricking and poking for blood is not my thing. I won't do that to myself.

It is definitely wrong to use someone else's blood without their knowledge. Using their own menstrual blood is creepy to some Witches, but I have no problem with that.

This is a Witch's choice, and has nothing to do with black magic. Sacrificing or using someone else's blood without their knowledge or consent, no matter what your intent, is definitely considered unacceptable by ethical Witches.

—Cerelia

One's own menstrual blood (or that freely given to you by your female partner) is the only kind of blood considered ethical by some Witches.

—Eileen

What should you do when you need to cast a spell, but have a question about its ethics?

When this issue concerns you, but you feel there is a need for the spell, add a line to it asking the Goddess to only let the spell work if it is accord with the Universe. Word this in any way that makes sense to you.

—Eileen

Isn't it always wrong to bind someone from speaking their thoughts?

There are situations in which binding someone from spreading false rumors could be necessary.

—Eileen

Are there ethical issues about smoking?

I cheerfully admit to being a total health nazi when it comes to smoking. I loathe the smell of cigarette smoke, and can never understand why so many otherwise intelligent Witches smoke cigarettes, since cigarettes are a direct violation of the rule against harming others, or harming yourself. I imagine that any addiction interferes with Witchcraft, but that's just my opinion.

People who smoke near children, especially babies, make me sick to my stomach. Nicotine is a terrible addiction that millions of humans are unable to break, but there is no excuse for smoking anywhere that will risk another person's exposure to your toxic cloud. People who smoke near other people are unforgivably selfish, in my view. I think smokers should be at the bottom of the list when lungs become available for transplant, and that people who didn't cause their own diseases should be given preference.

Congratulations to everyone who has been able to beat this terrible addiction. Giving up smoking is a great kindness to Mother Earth and all her creatures. Just think about how much pollution one smoker sends into the air each year, and how much toxic trash one smoker throws on the ground in a year. Blessed Be everyone who stops smoking, and everyone who helps their loved ones to stop.

—*Eileen*

Was it okay to pray for someone to hit rock bottom, so she would finally stop drinking?

It's a good thing you were just praying, not casting spells, because rock bottom could have harmed many people. Suppose rock bottom would have been having to deal with the consequences of drinking, driving, and slamming into a school bus full of kids? Or if rock bottom had meant becoming so dissolute that her own children were taken away from her and placed in foster care, where they were abused or molested? Or if . . . well, I can imagine a lot of horrible scenarios.

—*Eileen*

——————THE REDE——————

Why do Wiccans say "with harm to none" when they cast spells?

When you say, "And it harm none," that is exactly what it means in your work. It is important to say this, because you are therefore asking for an outcome that will not harm anyone. If you ask that no one gets harmed in the process, you are stating that your intention must be granted only under these terms. If it is possible that someome may get harmed, then it will not be a fulfilled spell.

With practice, you will get in the habit of saying "harm to none" readily. I think of my family especially, and do not want them to come to any harm because of a spell I might cast. Saying "with harm to none" protects anyone who may get in the path of one of your spells, even your own family members. This is very necessary, to me. This fact alone may make you very careful of always saying it. If you forget, just say it out loud afterward and visualize harm coming to no one.

—Cerelia

What can happen if you forget to say "with harm to none"?

A good example would be casting a prosperity spell, then having a loved one die and leave you money in his or her will. You may or may not have caused the death with your spell, but if you had added "with harm to none" it wouldn't be something you'd have to wonder about.

—Eileen

It's impossible to do no harm.

Wiccan experience proves otherwise.

—Eileen

As long as I follow my conscience, I believe that my instincts are better than anyone else's. I think anyone who can't see this is in the wrong religion!

I hope you find a religion that agrees with your thinking.

—Cerelia

I feel that you can only "do as you will and harm none" until you get pushed too far. Do you agree?

How far is too far? What would have to be done to any of us to justify harming someone else? Is murder justified if someone you love is murdered? Will the law agree with you that you were just pushed too far? I doubt it. I know that I would do just about anything to protect my family or myself from physical harm, or from extreme mental harm. Yes, I would even kill someone if it were in self-defense, but your question relates to magic.

We should always try first to get help from the proper authorities before depending on spells to physically protect us from extreme danger and life-threatening situations. If we truly believe in the Law of Three when it comes to our spells and such, we never ask for someone to be killed. Instead, we ask that they be bound, caught, arrested, and put away for a very long time. We also remember that in asking for someone else to be harmed, it can come back not only on us, but on any member of our family, or on someone we love. If we truly believe in the Law of Three, are we willing to take that risk?

These questions are tough ones that you have to answer for yourself. The Law of Three sounds so simple, but no one ever said it was easy. It's a lot harder to abide by than one may think, especially if you think all your problems can be solved by magically harming someone. Save these kinds of decisions for the big things in life. We shouldn't have too many of these kinds of decisions to make, if we reserve this kind of magic for life and death situations.

—Cerelia

CHILD ABUSE

What do I do if I think a child is being mistreated?

I'd go with legal ethics. If you have knowledge of, or even suspect that a child is being abused, you have the legal obligation to report it.

—Eileen

I know of a child who is being sexually abused. What should I do?

Immediately report the situation to the police and follow through until the perpetrator is locked up and removed from that child's life—even if he or she is your relative. Get the child into therapy, and try to get therapy for the perpetrator as well, so that he or she will be less likely to harm anyone else. These are correct actions, positive ones at the karmic level.

—Eileen

There is a child I am concerned about, but I don't know if it is right for me to intervene.

When a problem concerns someone else, it is usually helpful to remind ourselves that as priests and priestesses of the Goddess our first responsibility is to children, and to others who are unable to help or defend themselves. Examining a situation in that light usually leads straight to the right answer.

The neglect or mistreatment of children seriously bothers me, as a priestess of Isis, and as a mother. I see it as part of my service to Isis to intervene whenever possible on behalf of any child who enters my sphere. One has to be very sensitive about how one goes about this, though.

—*Eileen*

Is there a spell for child abuse?

It would be irresponsible of me to suggest one. Calling the police is better than casting spells when a child it being hurt. If I give a spell, it might prevent or delay someone from reporting the abuse. We have seen misguided Witches unintentionally protect and enable abusive male family members by relying on magic instead of calling the police.

—*Eileen*

What should society do about child molesters?

I would make the mandatory sentence life without the possibility of parole on the first offense for anyone who sexually abuses a child. This is the only way to break the sad cycle of some abused children growing up to be abusers themselves.

—*Eileen*

——————————————EXAMS——————————————

Is it cheating, to cast a spell to pass a test?

No, because no spell will get you a good grade on an exam unless you have done all your reading and studying as well as cast a spell.

—*Eileen*

If I cast a spell for luck with an exam, is this black magic because if I got good results someone else would get worse results?

You also have to take responsibility for yourself by studying for the exam. If you do a spell for good luck but never pick up a book, odds are you will never pass that test. Good luck comes from what you do for yourself. It is by responsible actions that you open yourself up to these energies.

Just because you pass a test doesn't mean you hoped some- one else would flunk theirs. Your intent makes magic white or black. You are entitled to do magic for yourself, as long as you wish no one else harm in the process.

—*Cerelia*

Why would your good score cause someone else to have a bad score? Take away the word luck, and it might be clearer. Try a spell for focus, or concentration, or a good result instead. Such spells are unlikely to cause harm to anyone, but you can ensure this by adding a phrase such as "with harm to none" to the spell itself.

—*Eileen*

————JUSTICE————

Is there anything wrong with doing a spell to bring someone to justice?

There is nothing wrong with that, so long as you leave it up to the Goddess to determine what is just. I think that it is always ethical to ask the Goddess for justice. Ma'at is very active in the world now, and she is an excellent deity to invoke for justice in any situation. If the person has been falsely accused, justice means they go free.

—*Eileen*

——————LOVE AND SEX——————

What do you think of love spells?

To me, love spells are very frivolous and dangerous. Love is magical in itself. I don't believe you can go out and harness it, or try and catch it and control it. Love is the most powerful magic of all, and yet so many Witches want to control it and make it do what they wish.

Many people can't love themselves, so they search desperately for someone else to make them feel loved. I understand that some people have been dealt some pretty rough childhoods. The thought that they are worthy of love and respect is totally impossible for them to understand, but that is the first lesson all Witches must learn: self-respect and love. Without it, how can we expect anyone else to be attracted to us? That is step number one, in love spells.

Witches must work on themselves, internally, to find the magic and love within themselves. Then it will show itself to others, and they will never have a need to cast a love spell.

—*Cerelia*

What kind of love spells are okay to cast?

I believe that attracting love or making yourself more open to it is fine, if you are not using exact names and remembering to harm none. When you are trying to force a particular person's will, that is when the question of ethics sets in.

—*Cerelia*

Most Witches would agree that spells that invite love into your life are okay: spells that invite love into your life in a general way, rather than focusing on a specific person. Casting a spell that invites love or lust is a way of informing the Universe that you are open to an encounter, or a relationship. Such spells don't manipulate anyone, they just broadcast your desire.

—*Eileen*

When you do an ethical love spell, you are asking that someone be attracted to you, but not anyone specific. You must be extra careful when you do this. Do you just want anyone? It is important to be exact with your intention and words, as to what or whom you want to be attracted to you. This is important in any spell, important as to what the outcome can be.

Sometimes the shadows in our spells are hard to see. When spells cause problems, we possibly hadn't thought everything completely out, and we weren't very careful with our words.

Even when we think we did everything perfectly, we can still have unforeseen things occur. That is why working with magic is very serious, and should be thought out as much as possible.

A lot of the time, the magic is in waiting for an outcome to occur naturally, instead of doing a spell for everything. It is always a possibility that something may not turn out exactly as we wanted. That too may be a lesson in itself. Sometimes, especially with love spells, we need to wait for the Goddess to bestow her magic.

—*Cerelia*

Is it okay to cast a spell that tells someone the way to my heart is open to them?

The R.S.V.P. approach is ethical, in my opinion. If something is meant to be, it will be.

—*Eileen*

What kind of spell should I cast to bless the marriage of two friends?

Have they asked for this? Would they welcome it? Witches would, but your friends may have different belief systems.

If your friends are open to a spell or ritual, love, happiness, health, fidelity, fertility, and prosperity are the kinds of blessings usually invoked for new couples. You could create (or help them create) a spell, charm, or ritual that attracts such blessings. Aphrodite has dominion over the sanctity of marriage, so she is the goddess I always think of for weddings and handfastings.

The Blessing of Union[19] in *The Wicca Handbook* has been used by many couples. It has also often been adapted for a priest/ess to cast for a couple. Here is part of the spell:

> Aphrodite rising
> From the wine-dark sea,
> Grant us health and fertility,
> Fidelity and trust,
> Grant us wealth and virility,
> Honesty and lust.
>
> . . .
>
> Aphrodite,
> Bless this union,
> And smile upon our Love.

—Eileen

How can I get someone to love me back?

Remember the old saying that you can lead a horse to water, but you can't make it drink. You're asking for advice to force the horse to drink. That's manipulative magic, psychic rape.

—Eileen

If I cast a love spell for someone else, will it work?

Probably, but think of what you'd be letting yourself in for if you manipulated someone's feelings on behalf of someone else. Think of all the possible consequences and remember that if the spell causes harm, that negativity will be returned to you as well as to the one who asked for the spell. Witches don't generally cast love spells for people. That's more in the line of the sort of practitioners who accept money for casting spells.

I think this is the kind of magic you have to do for yourself. I wouldn't cast a spell that meddled in someone else's relationship, and casting a love spell for someone else is almost never a great idea. If you do something to break up any relationship, chances are that it will rebound badly on a relationship of yours. This is a good way to ensure problems in your own relationship(s), present and future.

The best advice I can give you is this: never get involved, magically or otherwise, in the love lives of other people. You're only getting one side of the story, and second hand at that.

—Eileen

LUCK

If I try to bring others good luck, the outcome would come back to me threefold. So would this be white magic?

The doing of a ritual for good luck for others or yourself is white magic, because your intent is not to harm. Whether it is for friends or yourself, there is nothing wrong with working with the Goddess and her energies for yourself, or for your family and friends. Having a better life is something we all want. We want love, happiness, and financial security. There is nothing wrong with that, unless you get greedy.

—Cerelia

I'd consider it white magic.

—Eileen

---PROTECTION---

What do we do if someone attacks us, magically or otherwise?

We can protect ourselves, of course. There are many protection spells and rituals. In very dangerous situations, don't forget the world we live in: the police, mental health agencies, or any other agencies that may be of help.

—*Cerelia*

I hope no one thinks that biding the Rede means we have to passively accept whatever crap people around us are dishing out. We absolutely do stand up for ourselves, it's just that we do it in lawful ways.

Bounce evil or negativity back to whoever sent it, and they get it back three times; whereas simply attacking them leaves you open for a threefold backlash from your working. We also make use of the police, the courts, the media, and so forth.

We never need to harm anyone. Reversing whatever they're sending, or casting protection around yourself that's strong enough to bounce things back, basically causes them to self-destruct. Those who aren't up to visualizing mirrors sometimes put actual mirrors in their window sills, for the same purpose.

—*Eileen*

Are Witches justified in casting reflecting spells, even when they are not sure who the negativity came from?

I do protection spells on a regular basis, as do most practicing Witches, as I believe we should. If you have absolute proof that a particular person is causing you harm, you can reflect the negativity back.

Keep in mind that some Witches believe that it goes against the Law of Three, because you are sending back negativity and harm to the person who has sent it. They believe that when you do this, anyone can get in the way, and harm can be caused to someone innocent. Instead, some Witches just use a mirror to reflect it into the Universe, so the energy will harm no one. Also keep in mind that it can become very dangerous when two or more Witches start sending these types of spells back and forth.

—*Cerelia*

Some Witches say that it's best to deflect the negativity out into space, where it will harm no one. Other Witches would debate that, saying that the negativity will cause harm somewhere, somehow. Another approach is to craft a spell that directs the negativity back to its source, but with a safeguard worked in that makes the spell null and void if no one was responsible for it.

We can drive ourselves insane if we aren't balanced enough to deal with paranoia. If your house is destroyed in an earthquake or a wildfire, were you hexed? No, your house just happened to be in a place where Mother Nature was doing her thing. If you came down with the flu on the same day you were terminated from your job, were you hexed? Not likely. It's far more plausible that flu germs and a sinking economy caught up with you. If your car is stolen, is it because you were cursed? Again, not likely.

The human mind is very powerful. If someone believes that he or she has been hexed or cursed, he or she can actually create, empower, and perpetuate the "curse." If your life is in a negative cycle, do something to reverse it, such as a clearing ritual.

—*Eileen*

Do we only depend on magic when it comes to physical or mental threats?

Absolutely not. No Witch has to put up with physical or verbal threats. We must always go through the proper channels when physical threats of any kind are made. We live in this reality, and when we need the police, mental health institutions, hospitals, and so on, we access them. That is the very first thing we do, then we work with our magic behind the scenes. Just because someone is spiritual, it does not make them anyone else's door mat, punching bag, or any other kind of victim.

—Cerelia

How do I deal with harassment by a black magic Coven?

If it's possible to do this where you live, report them to the police for harassment. If you can't do that, try laughing at them. Black magicians usually take themselves extremely seriously, so laughter and ridicule are potent weapons against them. Why else would the Druids have performed satires upon the kings who wronged them?

Remember that your fear and distress are empowering these people, and instead laugh at how pathetic they are. Get together with others who are being harassed by them, and laugh until the tears run down your faces and you can hardly breathe.

—Eileen

Stand strong. Do not give them the tiniest idea that you are worried about them. You really shouldn't be worried. They have no power over you unless you give it to them, by showing weakness and fear. Do some protective spells within your own Coven.

—Cerelia

What can I do about an abusive husband?

First, I have to say that because abuse issues vary from country to country, my suggestions may not really apply where you are. But do whatever you can do to get this man out of your life.

If the law enforcement can help you, take him to court. Do this right now. Get documentation, and restraining orders against him, one for every person he has threatened to harm. Get something in writing from anyone who personally knows what he is doing to all of you. See what a big man he is when he is in court, with restraining orders against him for his physical threats of violence. The court will think very little of him.

Of course, as I said, this depends on how your legal system works where you are. I know it is hard, but try to be very strong. Don't let him know how afraid of him you really are. These kind of people feed on the fear of others.

Get any kind of protection from law enforcement you can. This will make you feel stronger, and safer. Don't be afraid to call him on his threats. Go to the courts before he seriously hurts someone. I wish you and your family well.

—Cerelia

Can I cast a spell on my abusive mate?

This is not advisable. Getting out and calling the police are the best options. As with child abuse, reliance on magic may keep someone in an abusive situation longer. Please, please, please safeguard yourself by getting out—especially if children are involved.

—Eileen

Am I allowed to use magic if I am being stalked?

Biding the Rede does not mean we give up our right to self-defense. Of course, we use words before magic, but when someone's obsession prevents her or him from hearing or seeing the truth, it's time to consider magic. Try a banishing spell.

Depending on the seriousness of the threat this person poses to you, also consider reporting what is happening to the police, and taking out an order of protection that will get this person arrested if he or she comes near you.

—*Eileen*

Real Estate

If I use magic to obtain an apartment, am I going against someone else who also wants it?

Someone has to get it, and if it is meant to be, you will. You should not feel guilty. If you are brand new to this path, start reading some simple books, and learn just how easy it is to cast your own spells and rituals.

—*Cerelia*

Revenge

What about revenge spells?

Revenge becomes very dangerous, not just to those you want to manipulate, but also to yourself as a Witch. You are just feeding fuel into the flames, and making situations much more dangerous than they probably ever started out being. Both parties end up getting burned with revenge spells, one way or another.

—*Cerelia*

I'm a teen looking for a spell to get back at the man who abused me.

Someone who has been abused is justifiably angry about it, but this is the wrong frame of mind in which to cast a spell. You may want revenge, but justice is what you need. The Universe rights all wrongs and balances all imbalances, in time. If you have it in you to be patient, you will see the Universe right the wrong that was done to you. If faster action would help your healing process, access the legal system on your own.

Contact child advocacy groups and ask them to help you find a legal representative to help you get justice. Ask the adults in your life to help you with this: parents, teachers, school counselors, your therapist, etc. (I am assuming that you have a therapist, but if not, please do make your parents or school get you one.)

Child molesters do not stop, they have to be stopped. If you choose, you could make it your sacred mission to stop him from ever hurting another child. This doesn't mean casting spells to harm him, it means seeing that he pays legally for his crime and is put in jail where he cannot hurt children.

—*Eileen*

A hover of hummingbirds ... a clash of bucks ... a murder of crows ... an unkindness of ravens ... a pride of lions ... an exultation of larks.... English can be an exquisitely expressive language, one that contains some beautifully precise words for collective groups of creatures. We once had a discussion about this on the Open Sesame e-list, and naturally the conversation turned to the question of what a group of Witches is properly called, besides a Coven.

I joked that it definitely wouldn't be a "wealth of Witches," and then I did some research. The *Malleus Maleficarum* (a guide written by witch hunters during The Burning Times) spoke of conclaves of witches, as did Sir Walter Scott, so this seems to have been a traditional term. I gave it a lot of thought, and finally came to the conclusion that the most precise term for a group of Witches would be a "wisdom of Witches."

You are (or perhaps will become) whatever type of Witch you are meant to be. As you progress along your path, even if you are a solitary, remember how much insight and information there is to be gleaned from other Witches. We must be careful in choosing our mentors, companions, and advisors, though, and be sure to only align ourselves with Witches whose ethics are the same as our own. We have to guard against being so needy for the company of other Witches that we wind up associating with negative people. That said, there is much to be learned, and many a mistake to be avoided, by having concourse with other Witches, be this in person, on the Web, or through books.

Walk always in the light, and you will never go astray upon your path.

Blessed Be,

Eileen Holland

You as a Witch have the real power to change your life, with every word you utter, every thought you visualize, and every action you partake in. Our lessons in life are gifts, not punishments. Gifts that we grow from as spiritual beings. As hard and painful as these seem at times.

You can make the choice to live your life in the light, or be dragged down by hatred, jealousy, and revenge. Deciding to walk in the light isn't as easy as it sounds. In fact it is very hard. It takes heart, intelligence, and a very, very strong will. And when someone tries to tell you that being kind is a weakness, laugh at their ignorance. You know you are never anyone's spiritual doormat.

Integrating the light and the dark within ourselves is where the power lies, not denial of either. Laughter and Love are the most powerful magic of all. No matter how sappy it sounds to those who use hate and intimidation.

The Craft is Power.

The Power is within.

FIND IT.

It's worth the journey.

Blessings of Love and Laughter,

Cerelia

1. Eileen Holland, *The Wicca Handbook* (York Beach, ME: Weiser Books, 2000), p. 7.

2. Starhawk, *The Spiral Dance* (San Francisco: HarperSan-Francisco, 1989), p. 91.

3. Starhawk, *The Spiral Dance,* p. 113.

4. Doreen Valiente, *Witchcraft For Tomorrow* (Blaine, WA: Phoenix Publishing, 1978), p. 30.

5. Doreen Valiente, "The Charge of the Goddess" in Stewart and Janet Farrar, *A Witches' Bible: The Complete Witches' Handbook* (Custer, WA: Phoenix Publishing, 1996), pp. 297–98.

6. Scott Cunningham, *Wicca: A Guide for the Solitary Practitioner* (St. Paul, MN: Llewellyn Publications, 1990), p. 53.

7. Doreen Valiente, "The Search for Old Dorothy" in Stewart and Janet Farrar, *A Witches' Bible: The Complete Witches' Handbook*, p. 284.

8. Friedrich Nietzsche, "The Skirmishes of an Untimely Man" in George Seldes, compiler, *The Great Thoughts* (New York: Ballantine Books, 1985), p. 112.

9. *Holy Qur'an* (Elmhurst, NY: Tahrike Tarsile Qur'an, 1985), p. 422.

10. Dion Fortune, *Psychic Self-Defense* (York Beach, ME: Samuel Weiser, 1992), p. 82.

11. Scott Cunningham, *Wicca for the Solitary Practitioner,* p. 20.

12. Nancy Garen, *Tarot Made Easy* (New York: Fireside Books, 1989), p. 57.

13. Robert Graves, *The White Goddess* (New York: Farrar, Strauss and Giroux, 1948), p. 166.

14. Witches' skills which weren't discussed on the e-list, and which are therefore not included in this book, include numerology, and other forms of divination such as runes and palmistry.

15. Cerridwen Iris Shea, "Integrating Work and Magical Life," *Llewellyn's 1999 Magical Almanac* (St Paul, MN: Llewellyn Publications, 1999), p. 284.

16. Raymond Buckland, *Practical Candleburning Rituals* (St. Paul, MN: Llwellyn Publications, 1970), p. 11.

17. Silver Ravenwolf, *To Ride a Silver Broomstick* (St. Paul, MN: Llewellyn Publications, 1993).

18. Starhawk, *The Spiral Dance*, p. 124.

19. Eileen Holland, *The Wicca Handbook*, pp. 110–11.

Adler, Margot. *Drawing Down the Moon*. New York: Viking Press, 1979.

Buckland, Raymond. *Practical Candleburning Rituals*. St. Paul, MN: Llewellyn Publications, 1970.

———. *Witchcraft from the Inside*. St. Paul, MN: Llewellyn Publications, 1995.

Budapest, Zsuzsanna. *Grandmother Moon Lunar Magic in Our Lives*. San Francisco: HarperSanFrancisco, 1991.

Budge, Sir E.A. Wallis. *Egyptian Book of the Dead: The Papyrus of Ani*. New York: Dover Publications, 1967.

———. *Egyptian Magic*. New York: Dover Publications, 1971.

———. *Egyptian Religion*. New York: Gramercy Books, 1959.

———. *Gods of the Egyptians*. New York: Dover Publications, 1969.

Bulfinch, Thomas. *Bulfinch's Mythology*. New York: Modern Library, 1988.

Campbell, Joseph. *The Masks of God* (4 volumes). New York: Viking Press, 1975.

Castaneda, Carlos. *The Fire From Within*. New York: Washington Square Press, 1991.

———. *The Power of Silence*. New York: Washington Square Press, 1987.

———. *Tales of Power*. New York: Simon and Schuster, 1974.

———. *The Teachings of Don Juan*. Berkeley: University of California Press, 1968.

———. *A Separate Reality*. New York: Simon and Schuster, 1971.

Chodron, Pema. *The Wisdom of No Escape: And the Path of Loving-Kindness*. Boston: Shambhala Publications, 2001.

Cunningham, Scott. *Earth Power: Techniques of Natural Magic*. St. Paul, MN: Llewellyn Publications, 1999.

———. *Wicca: A Guide for the Solitary Practitioner.* St. Paul, MN: Llewellyn Publications, 1990.

Drury, Nevill. *The History of Magic in the Modern Age: A Quest for Personal Transformation.* New York: Carrol and Graf, 2000.

Eliade, Mircea. *Archaic Techniques of Ecstasy.* Princeton, NJ: Princeton University Press, 1964.

Farrar, Janet and Stewart. *A Witches' Bible: The Complete Witches' Handbook.* Custer, WA: Phoenix Publishing, 1996.

Ferguson, Anne-Marie. *A Keeper of Words: Legend, The Authurian Tarot.* St. Paul, MN: Llewellyn Publications, 1995.

Fischer-Schreiber, Ingrid; Franz-Karl Erhard; Kurt Friedrichs; Michael S. Diener. *The Encyclopedia of Eastern Philosophy and Religion.* Boston: Shambhala, 1994.

Fortune, Dion. *Applied Magic.* York Beach, ME: Weiser Books, 2000.

———. *The Esoteric Philosophy of Love and Marriage.* York Beach, ME: Weiser Books, 2000.

———. *Psychic Self-Defense.* York Beach, ME: Weiser Books, 1992.

Frawley, Dr. David and Dr. Vasant Lad. *The Yoga of Herbs: An Ayurvedic Guide to Herbal Medicine.* Twin Lakes, WI: Lotus Press, 1986.

Frazer, Sir James G. *The Golden Bough: A Study in Magic and Religion.* New York: The MacMillan Company, 1953.

Garen, Nancy. *Tarot Made Easy.* New York: Fireside Books, 1989.

Gimbutas, Marija. *The Goddesses and Gods of Old Europe: Myths and Cult Images, 6500–3500 B.C.* Berkeley, Los Angeles: University of California Press, 1982.

———. *The Living Goddesses.* Berkeley, Los Angeles: University of California Press, 2001.

Graves, Robert. *The Greek Myths,* Volumes I and II. Baltimore: Penguin Books, 1955.

———. *The White Goddess.* New York: Farrar, Strauss and Giroux, 1948.

Grimassi, Raven. *The Ways of The Strega.* St. Paul, MN: Llewellyn Publications, 1991.

———. *The Wiccan Mysteries, Ancient Origins and Teachings.* St. Paul, MN: Llewellyn Publications, 1997.

Holland, Eileen. *The Wicca Handbook.* York Beach, ME: Weiser Books, 2000.

Jacobsen, Thorkild. *The Treasures of Darkness: A History of Mesopotamian Religion.* New Haven and London: Yale University Press, 1976.

Leland, Charles. *The Gospel of the Witches.* London: University Books, 1963.

Lewi, Grant. *Heaven Knows What.* St. Paul, MN: Llewellyn Publications, 1985.

MacLennan, Bruce. Biblioteca Arcana. *www.cs.utk.edu/~mclennan/BA/*

Monaghan, Patricia. *The Book of Goddesses and Heroines.* New York: E. P. Dutton, 1981.

Noble, Vicki. *Motherpeace: A Way to the Goddess Through Myth, Art and Tarot.* St. Paul: Llewellyn Publications, 1997.

Selby, John. *Kundalini Awakening: A Gentle Guide Chakra Activation and Spiritual Growth.* New York: Bantam Books, 1992.

Sharman–Burke, Juliet and Liz Green. *The Mythic Tarot: A New Approach to the Tarot Cards.* New York: Fireside, 1986.

Starhawk (Miriam Simos). *The Spiral Dance: A Rebirth of the Ancient Religion of the Great Goddess.* San Francisco: HarperSanFrancisco, 1989.

Valiente, Doreen. *An ABC of Witchcraft.* London: Robert Hale, 1973.

————. *The Rebirth of Witchcraft*. London: Robert Hale, 1989.

————. *Witchcraft for Tomorrow*. Blaine, WA: Phoenix Publishing, 1978.

A

activism, 128–130

adept, 258

altar, 264–271

ankh, 10

anger, 125–127

anointing, 239

astral traveling, 208, 209

astrology, 240–241

atheists, 33

B

Bast, 46

BDSM, 13

black magic, 14, 132, 286–293, 354

Book of Shadows, 261–264

broom closet, coming out of, 104–106, 108

Buddha, 34

Burning Times, 14

C

candle magic, 306–317

Catholicism, 153–154, 156

chaos magic, 292

children, 148–154

Christian fundamentalists, 130

Christians, 108, 127, 132–133, 163–164

clearing, 242–244

consecration, 245–246, 313, 314

Coven, 18–19, 20, 24–26, 98, 99, 111

Craft, 71, 86, 87

names, 64–68

cultures, different, 48

curses (hexes), 293, 294

D

Dali Lama, 34

deities, 43

demons, 181

devil, 12

divination, 211

dreams, 87, 99, 166–174

drugs, 260–261

Druidism, 21

E

Elemental Magic, 299

elementals (entities), 175–180

ethics, 332, 337–340

evocation, 203

evolution, 34

F

fairies, 36, 181

fluffy bunny, 16

G

Gardnerian tradition, 101–102

ghosts, 183

God, 39, 47

Goddess, 34, 35, 36–47, 69

gods, 40, 45, 49
grounding, 246–248

H
hair, 14
Hazrat Inayat Khan, 70
healing, 221–227
holy water, 318–319

I
incense, 301–304
incubi, 182
initiation, 97
intent, 257–258, 273, 282
invocation, 199–202

J/K
Jesus, 34
karma, 29, 121

L
Law of Three, 28–30, 344
left-hand path, 31
Lords of the Watchtower, 296
lucid dreaming, 208, 209

M
magic, 7, 89-90, 255–257,
        277–281, 282, 284–285,
        354
magic circle, 295–298
Maiden, Mother, Crone,
        144–145

meditation, 189–194
men, 20–23, 146
menstruation, 235–238
mirror, 14
mojo bag, 10
Moon,
    Blue, 243
    Dark of the, 233–234
    Full, 231–232
    New, 230
    Waning, 233
    Waxing, 231
    working with the, 228-234
Multiple Sclerosis, 124
myths, 43

N
necromancy, 292
new home, 140–141

O
omens, 207
ouija board, 184–185

P
Pagan/Paganism, 3, 6, 7, 26, 32,
        34, 36
pantheons, 40, 48
parenting, Pagan, 147–152
perfect love, perfect trust, 28
pentacle, 10, 275, 276
pentagram, 276
prayer, 90, 322

protective shield, 158

psi-magic, 320–321

psychism, 204, 205

R

Ra, 46

raising power, 283–284

Rede, 342

Reiki, 224

right-hand path, 31–32

S

Satanism, 12, 136

scrying, 211

Sekhmet, 46

sexual energies, 22

skyclad, 58

smudging, 242, 243, 304

sorcery, 259

soul mates, 159–160

spells, 322–331

   love, 347–351

spirits, 183

sucubi, 182

T

tarot, 212–220

teacher, 96

Thoth, 45

tools, 272–274

traditions, 57

twitch, 77

V

veil, 18

visualization, 195–198, 224

W

warlock, 21

Web, the, 109, 133

white magic, 14

Wicca Handbook, The, 31, 32,
   350

Wiccan, 7, 17, 26–28, 32–33,
   135

Witch(es), 3–7, 100

   appearance of, 8–11

   becoming a, 55

   Christian, 32

   and Christian families, 138

   disagreements, 83

   eclectic, 15, 56, 58

   gay, 118

   hereditary, 16–17, 19

   kitchen, 139

   living like a, 71

   male, 20–21

   misconceptions about,
      11–14

   and organized religion,
      32–34

   and organizational skills, 249

   Satanic, 12

   solitary, 15, 18–19, 60, 61,
     62

title of, 91–92
urban (city), 23–24
or Wiccan, 26–28
the word, 7–8, 131
young, 74
Witchcraft, 73, 253–254

Witch's Box, 272
wizard, 4

Y
Year and a Day Program,
94–95